Colonial ARTIST S. T. Gill

A Window Into Nineteenth-Century Australia Through Colonial Art

Printed in Australia
Cover and internal design by Shawline Publishing Group Pty Ltd
First Printing: September 2023

Shawline Publishing Group Pty Ltd
www.shawlinepublishing.com.au

Paperback ISBN 978-1-9229-9387-8
Ebook ISBN 978-1-9229-9393-9

Distributed by Shawline Distribution and Lightning Source Global

A catalogue record for this work is available from the National Library of Australia

Colonial ARTIST S.T. Gill

A Window Into Nineteenth-Century Australia Through Colonial Art

DOUG LIMBRICK

Other non-fiction books by the author

From the Wars of the Roses to Colonial Victoria

The Stag Diary—Passage to Colonial Adelaide 1850

A Guide to Running Your First Marathon

Running the Marathon with Cancer

A Church With no Walls

Farewell to Old England Forever

Death Ships—the story of life & death on six big emigrant ships

For more details see: www.douglimbrick.com

Comments/enquiries to: info@douglimbrick.com

His extensive graphic work is EARLY AUSTRALIAN HISTORY. - just imagine there being no artist S. T. GILL from 1844 to 1865, the period over which he executed so many pictorial albums and portfolios of the Australian scene. We know, through his work, see the exact rendering of the people, costumes, houses, habits and occupations of those years.

—Rex de C. Nan Kivell[1]

1 Cited in Keith Macrae, Bowden. *Samuel Thomas Gill Artist.* 1971, p.xiii.[self-published] Note that Rex Nan Kivell donated and sold to the National Library of Australia his extensive collection of books, paintings, prints, documents, manuscripts and artefacts relating to the history of Australia, New Zealand and the Pacific.

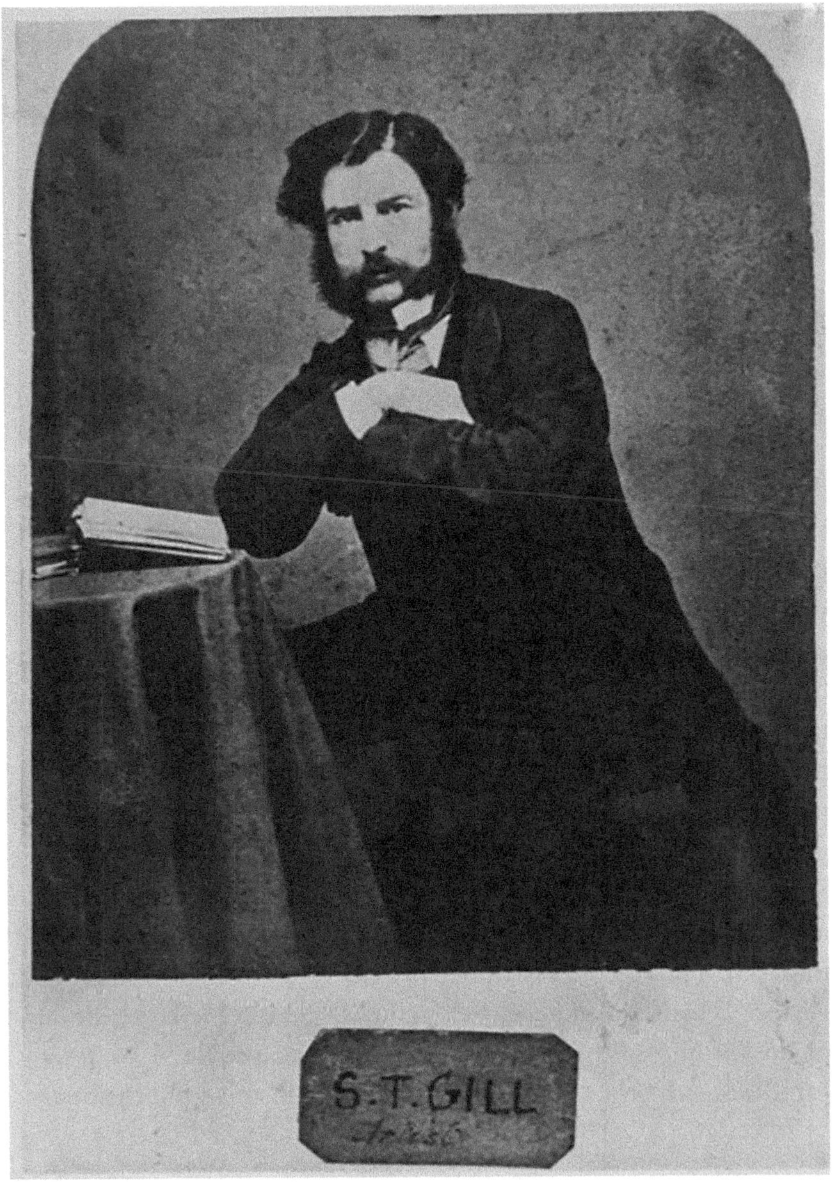

S. T. Gill, artist c.1870 (unknown photographer) (State Library of Victoria)

Acknowledgements

A number of people provided invaluable assistance during the course of my writing this book. I am particularly grateful for the resources available through the vast collection of material at the National Library of Australia (NLA). Original documents and old manuscripts were readily available through the various library reading rooms. My thanks go to the staff of the NLA for their assistance and patience. The Woden Valley Branch of the Libraries ACT has also been of considerable assistance in locating publications for me to borrow while researching this project. I would also like to acknowledge the assistance provided by the State Library of South Australia, the State Library of Victoria and the State Library New South Wales with pictorial and other material. The editing assistance provided by Dr Christina Houen, Perfect Words Editing, was extremely valuable. A large amount of design and graphics assistance has been provided by Jeremy Limbrick, which has considerably enhanced this publication.

Author's Note for readers:

Measures of distance and weight and type of currency have been maintained, as they were in nineteenth-century Britain and the Australian colonies. Hence metric and decimal terms are not used. Thus, to assist readers who may want to convert terms used in this book the following may be of use:

- 1 mile is approximately equivalent to 1.6 kilometres
- 1 yard is approximately equivalent to 0.9 metres
- 1 foot is approximately equivalent to 0.3 metres
- 1 ton is approximately equivalent to 1.02 tonnes
- 1 ounce is approximately equivalent to 28.4 grams
- 1 gallon is approximately equivalent to 4.5 litres
- 70° Fahrenheit is approximately equivalent to 21° Celsius.

Currency used in this book comprises pounds (£), shillings (s) and pence (d).

This book contains many quotations from historic sources, including letters, diaries, pamphlets and newspapers. In using these quotations I have left any misspellings intact and avoided, as much as possible, the use of commonly used terms to identify misspellings (such as the Latin word: *sic*).

Table of Contents

Introduction

The great work of the painter is the narrative
—Leon Battista Alberti, De Pictura (15th century)[2]

This book is a deviation in the subject matter I normally focus on in my writing. My usual writing is about groups of people, places and events in nineteenth-century Australia. So why have I decided to write about a colonial artist? There are many reasons, but most importantly, I believe that our understanding of the story of nineteenth-century Australia has been enormously enhanced by the images left by the artists who were active during the colonial period. It would be a mistake to see those images only as pieces of art and to assess their significance in terms of the quality of the artwork. From a historian's viewpoint, I believe their value and importance as a window into life in the colonies should not be underestimated.

Frequently, events in history, even the important ones, may not seem personal to us as individuals. We may, for example, not feel concerned about a disaster or adverse condition because we are

2 Leon Batista Alberti was an Italian humanist author, architect, poet, priest, linguist, philosopher and cryptographer; he epitomised the Renaissance Man. *De Pictura*, published in 1450, was one of three treatises that formed the Renaissance concept for fine arts, painting, sculpture and architecture.

not emotionally invested in it, most probably because it occurred so many years ago. For most of us, lack of emotional involvement is not about not caring, but often because the information about those events isn't reaching us in a way that evokes an emotional response. Images help us become involved. With images, we can often 'see' the event rather than imagine it through a written description. The images help contribute to the storytelling process that can make history more engaging.

I believe it's important we know our history. This usually happens by learning the dates, people, and places of important events, and sometimes we can even learn why and how they occurred. This process of understanding our history is enhanced by art, which gives us a different insight into our past. It shows us how those events impacted the people living then. Through art, we have the opportunity to learn the joy felt during times of happiness, and we see the pain and despair during times of suffering. It's possible to see the hopes and the dreams, the fears and the regrets of the past.

The earliest of artists probably used art supplies which consisted of ground ochre and charcoal, while the nineteenth-century artists had a greater range of art materials to work with, thanks to the birth of modern science and the Industrial Revolution in eighteenth-century Europe, which led to an unprecedented expansion in the artist's palette. Initially, watercolour artists ground their own colours from natural pigments, or in some instances were able to purchase paint in liquid form. In the last two decades of the eighteenth century, however, artists could purchase small, hard cakes of soluble watercolour. By the turn of the century, the most popular form of art for amateurs and professionals was watercolour. The availability of watercolour in tubes by the late 1840s made it easier to use and possible for nineteenth-century watercolour painters in the Australian colonies to more easily paint on location, including in remote places. The rise of watercolour painting as a serious artistic endeavour progressed hand-in-hand with the improvement and commercial development of its materials. A *Guide to Pictorial Art* (1849) outlined the advantages of watercolour:

> *The advantages of water colours are the purity and lightness in the skies and distances, unattainable by any other material... the process is simple, clean, and inodorous; the work dries rapidly; the materials are very portable; they are admirably adapted for slight sketches, while they are equal to the richest effect, and the most elaborate finish.*[3]

Until the twentieth century, much of Western art was narrative in style and comprised stories from religion, myth and legend, history and literature. Audiences were generally assumed to be familiar with the stories in question. From about the seventeenth century, this type of painting was known as genre, that is, painting that showed scenes and narratives of everyday life. Seventeenth-century Dutch artist, Johannes Vermeer, was noted for his paintings of everyday life, particularly domestic interior scenes of the middle class. In the eighteenth century, the painting of history was regarded by many artists as the highest form of painting, but for them, history was the painting of events from the Bible and classical antiquity. In Victorian England, narrative painting of everyday life subjects became hugely popular and is often considered as a category in itself, referred to as Victorian narrative painting. While the twentieth century saw a move to other art forms such as abstract, there were post nineteenth-century artists who painted large numbers of images of everyday life. One of the most prolific was American artist, illustrator and historian Norman Rockwell. Rockwell was possibly best known for producing the image for the cover of the *Saturday Evening Post* for over 60 years. It has been said these covers provide a story of 'everyday activities which are 'a living, vibrant,

3 H. O'Neill. *Guide to Pictorial Art: How to use the Black Lead Pencil, Chalks, and Water Colours in the Fine Arts.* George Rowney, London, 4th edn, 1849, pp. 32-3.

unvarnished documentation of America[4].'In narrative painting, it's the content that's important and not the style. Regardless of the subject, narrative paintings contain elements of realism, that is, things or objects that are recognisable to the viewer.

Many of the painters who were creating artwork in the nineteenth-century Australian colonies were telling stories about places, people and events. These images were an important form of communication about colonial activities for those living in the colonies and those in the home country. At this time, images were widely used in illustrated newspapers and pamphlets and were useful in directly conveying messages, particularly in a population where illiteracy was significant. It's likely some people made decisions about their future, including the decision to emigrate, as a result of stories and images from the colonies. This is an example of how such images had the ability to grab the attention in a way the printed word was unable to do.

For the Australian historian, these nineteenth-century images are a very important visual reminder of what occurred at the time the painting was made. In some paintings, the artist may have managed to capture the emotions associated with the subject recorded. An important bonus in understanding the significance of the event painted by the artist. Many of the colonial artists were able to convey not only emotion, but mood, narrative, ideas, and messages, all of which were very important elements of storytelling. The paintings that depict everyday life in the nineteenth century are clearly very important, given that photography didn't emerge as a significant method of recording everyday life until late in the century.

My long-time interest in photography has made me very conscious of the importance that photographic images have played in providing a comprehensive record of my history and of events in the twentieth and twenty-first centuries. Capturing an image on film and then seeing it appear in the darkroom was

4 Donald, R. Stoltz, Curator, Forward, *Norman Rockwell and The Saturday Evening Post*, Norman Rockwell Museum, Philadelphia, Four Productions Inc., 1976.

like magic to me when I was a young boy, starting to explore photography. The magic of those images has remained with me, although photography has become much more sophisticated and instant. With the expansion of technology that allows people from all walks of life to create and share photographs with a few clicks, our world seems to value visual media more than ever before. For many, photography is an experience that engages our curiosity as much as artwork does.

We are fortunate that many of the colonial artists were prolific in creating large numbers of narrative style paintings. We thus have many images of life in the colonies during the nineteenth century.

In writing about nineteenth-century Australia, I have tried to transport readers to that period, so they can have a sense of what it was like to live in such times and what it felt like to experience the life-changing events occurring for those who emigrated to the colonies. Clearly, the description of those events is extremely important in achieving that goal. I have found the words of people from the nineteenth century provide a powerful opening to that period. Hence, locating letters, diaries, journals and newspaper stories has been an integral part of my research work and writing and often very time consuming. The value they add is enormous.

This process is further enhanced by the inclusion of images. I have spent a considerable amount of time searching for suitable illustrations to support and enhance the text. They grab the attention of the reader; they tell a story (often more clearly than words) and they convey a message quickly. I have often spent hours searching through databases from around the world, trying to find suitable illustrations to accompany the story. This can be a frustrating process, but at times when I had just about given up the search, a gem of an illustration was uncovered. Those finds have always been very rewarding.

Early colonial art in Australia was generally scientific in nature, designed to explain a strange distant land to Europeans.

Most artwork around that time is of Australia's distinctive flora and fauna. The very first professional European artists to work in Australia did not come by choice, but as convicts transported from England, usually for crimes of forgery, since an artist's skill could easily be utilised to design a forged banknote. The first to arrive was probably Thomas Watling in 1792, then John Eyre in 1801, followed by Joseph Lycett in 1814. These three returned to England at the completion of their sentences. Their work has some value, illustrating the appearance of the colony of New South Wales and showing the progress made in the early years of colonisation.

A number of the naval and military officers in the colony were able to draw competently. This included Governor Phillip King, whose drawings were copied in London as engravings to illustrate a book about Port Jackson and Norfolk Island. The convicts and amateurs provided a body of images which form a visual record of early colonial days. Their work was chiefly for an English audience and made available through London publishers. It's also clear that many of the first artistic representations of Australia by European artists were natural history illustrations.

Many artists followed these early arrivals, including more convict artists. Most stayed, and many began to paint the real Australian landscape, its flora and fauna, and the Indigenous people.

Artists like Conrad Martens left paintings that provided carefully composed, picturesque panoramas of places and scenes like Sydney Harbour. After a scientific expedition with Charles Darwin, he arrived in Sydney in 1835. Martens, possibly the most significant artist of his time, painted mostly in watercolour. Like many people, he was in love with Sydney Harbour in all its moods, and between the bread-and-butter commissions for his patrons, he returned to paint it. John Glover, already a successful artist in England before emigrating to Van Diemen's Land (VDL), set himself up as a country gentleman and a painter with a town house. He was a sympathetic and conscientious painter, becoming one of the best landscape artists in nineteenth-century Australia. Also from Van Diemen's Land, artist, Thomas Griffiths Wainewright, a forger, became well known for his pencil drawings of the daughters of VDL society. Louis Buvelot, who didn't arrive until 1865, became a key figure in landscape painting, remaining in Melbourne until his death in 1888. He was one of the artists able to express the strange beauty of the Australian landscape and was dubbed the 'father of landscape painting in Australia' by some. It's likely his work inspired the next generation of Melbourne painters like Tom Roberts, Arthur Streeton, Charles Condor and Fred McCubbin.

We live in an age where millions of photographs are taken every day, most often using a mobile phone. This should mean that writers in the future will have available to them many images to illustrate the events of the twenty-first century. For much of the nineteenth century, illustrations were only available in the form of sketches, drawings and paintings. Some of this work was transformed by skilled engravers for wider circulation, often through illustrated newspapers, pamphlets and books. We are fortunate that we had a number of artists in the Australian colonies who were prolific in their output. The images they left are precious and a wonderful resource in telling stories about nineteenth-century colonial Australia.

Many of the paintings produced during the nineteenth century were idealised representations of life in the colonies. However, there were some artists such as Augustus Earle and S. T. Gill, who were interested in making social statements through their art and in presenting a snapshot of life in the raw, as it was at that time.

The professional artists of the colonial period, unless they were men of means, like Glover, were generally poor. There was no mass art-buying public as such. Wealthy people commissioned portrait paintings of their daughters or their homesteads for sentimental purposes or to flatter their vanity. Hence, in part, the life of the colonial artist was generally one of poverty. They 'sang' for their supper and it was usually inadequate. It followed that most colonial artists painted or drew whatever provided some income.

To assist the reader with an overview of the range of artists operating in the colonies, Appendix IV provides a list of some of the better-known names, including a brief history and some comments about their artistic activities. Some focused on portrait work, possibly as a means of making a living, while some others, such as Adam Buvelot, came to recognise the beauty of the Australian landscape and mainly concentrated on painting scenery. A small number focused on documenting and painting slices of colonial life, much as the camera was able to capture at a later date. S. T. Gill was possibly the best example of this type of artist.

We have been left with a wide variety of pictures from the nineteenth century by European painters; these are to be seen, not only as works of art or craft, but as chapters in a story, which began at Sydney Cove on 28th January 1788, when Captain Phillip read his commission establishing British sovereignty over the whole of the eastern part of the Australian continent and Van Diemen's Land to the people of the First Fleet. This was, of course, the start of a very different story for the Aboriginal people.

Australia's art scene began well before the Europeans arrived on the continent's shores in 1788. Australia's Aboriginal peoples had been painting long before this time. In fact, their art scene dates as the oldest continuing tradition of art in the world. Sadly, despite the very long traditions of Australian Aboriginal art, it seems that nineteenth-century colonial artists had virtually no contact with the art of the Aborigines. Traditional Aboriginal art was often regarded as inauthentic and this attitude, no doubt reflected the prevailing nineteenth-century attitude towards

Aboriginal Australians more generally. From my research, writing about Aboriginal art in the context of Australian art is still controversial for some art historians. Andrew Sayers' book *Aboriginal Artists of the Nineteenth Century*, published in 1994, appears to have had a significant impact on this discussion by drawing attention to the existence of work by a number of nineteenth-century Aboriginal artists and to the cross-cultural encounters that occurred with some European artists. According to Sayers, there were indigenous artists using European materials to record colonial events and activities. There is a considerable amount written about Aboriginal art in the context of Australian art by those who have made this their area of study and expertise. It's not appropriate that I make any further comments about this matter, but it is important to recognise the long history of Aboriginal art in the context of my examination of how colonial art contributed to our understanding of the Australian colonies in the nineteenth century.

In this book, I focus on the stories told by S. T. Gill. I believe there were no others with Gill's zest for the rough-and-tumble of the times–or at least, none able to express it like he did.

Gill's sketches of everyday, rustic and active life, circulated widely, thanks to lithography, are among the best examples of Australian colonial genre painting. As rendered, they are often earthy, with a real vigour, contrasted to the more genteel nature of his very early sketches in South Australia, which no doubt reflected his training in England and his understanding of European painting styles.

Writer and journalist, W.H. Newnham, saw Gill and his work as follows:

'His skill as a draughtsman and illustrator can be appreciated if a magnifying glass is used to study the extraordinary details he managed to include.'[5]

5 W. H. Newnham. Introduction & Notes. *Victoria Illustrated 1857 & 1862. Engravings from the Original Editions by S. T. Gill & N. Chevalier.* Lansdowne Press, 1971, p.16.

It's particularly this ability to capture and include details in his artwork that makes Gill's work so special and such a valuable record of nineteenth-century Australia. He was present during the formative years of development in the colonies of South Australia, Victoria and New South Wales, and this makes his work very important. Literary historian, Geoffrey Dutton, comments on his approach in these early colonial years:

With an unmatched honesty, sympathy, and energy, Gill had recorded that shaping process... None of the other artists of his period lived their way into the country as he did.[6]

Ansel Adams (1902-84), famous American landscape photographer and environmentalist, commented that, 'A photograph is usually looked at—seldom looked into'[7]. Adams' advice was that we should linger and explore the layered understandings that each photograph contains. This may reveal the deeper meaning and possibly the occasional mystery contained in the image. In examining Gill's work, I have found many layers, sometimes revealed in the incredible detail he included, sometimes in the unexpected inclusions or activity in the background that raises the viewer's curiosity. There are frequently multiple stories in his paintings or drawings if we pause and take time to look into them and particularly to view them multiple times. Sometimes his messages are subtle, while at other times, very clear. He has left us with an interesting and revealing window into his nineteenth-century Australian colonial world.

I have long admired Gill's style of recording events and scenes. In many instances he provided a window, almost like a photograph, into an event or activity. His work has been criticised by some art critics from an artistic or technical viewpoint, but from a historian's perspective, I believe he provided an extremely valuable and very large collection of images of colonial Australia. His images are extremely important to our appreciation and understanding of nineteenth-century people, places and events.

---

6 Geoffrey Dutton. *Paintings of S. T. Gill.* Rigby, Adelaide, 1962, p.10.
7 Richard Wigley. *Ansel Adams, Images of the American West.* Bison Books Ltd., 1992, p. 6.

For this book, I have selected many images of Gill's artwork (but only a small subset) to illustrate his contribution to our understanding of people, places and events in the colonies of South Australia, Victoria and New South Wales. I have also tried to select different types of his artwork, including watercolours, pencil drawings, sepia washes and lithographs. Fortunately, a substantial amount of his artwork is readily available from a number of Australian libraries and galleries; this has been marvellous, but a little overwhelming, as I spent many hours viewing the images electronically. At first, I selected far too many images and was then faced with the very difficult task of discarding many wonderful pieces of his artwork. I have still included over 130 images, and hope that my selection will enable readers to appreciate Gill's contribution to our understanding of nineteenth-century Australia (see Appendix II for the list). For readers who are unfamiliar with S. T. Gill's artwork, let me encourage you to further explore the many images available electronically on the websites of Australian libraries, museums and galleries. I hope you enjoy the story of S. T. Gill and his recordings of Australian colonial people, places, and events.

Doug Limbrick

Chapter 1—The Gill Family, Adelaide and the Port

The city is a large place and not yet one quarter built upon. Building plots are for sale in all directions except in the main streets. The majority of the houses at present are built for persons of small means–mainly constructed of nine inch brick work—the roofing generally being shingles from Van Diemen's Land.

—Adelaide Times, June 7, 1851

Samuel Thomas Gill was born on 21 May 1818 in the small village of Perriton in Somerset, England, the first born in a family of five to parents Reverend Samuel Gill and Winifred Gill (nee Oke). In 1825, the Gill family was living in Plymouth. By the time Samuel Thomas Gill was sixteen, he was advanced enough to paint a self-portrait in oils, one of the few pictures he is known to have created in that medium[8] (apparently later destroyed by fire). He had been exposed to the work of many great artists during a three-year period in London. There is incomplete information of his education and training. He was apparently apprenticed as a

8 I found only one of his work in Australia in that medium, which is held by the Dixon Library, State Library of New South Wales. Its title is *The Shepherd,* 22 cm. square canvas, in a circular frame, S. T.G. at the lower left. It's normally on display at the library.

carver and gilder[9] in Plymouth before joining the Hubard Profile Gallery in The Strand. The Gallery was a major establishment which specialised in silhouette art. Gill later announced he had worked as a '*draftsman and watercolour painter to the Hubard Gallery*'.[10] His three years in London were probably very important in shaping Gill's artistic future and it is likely he was introduced to lithography when working as a carver and gilder.

During the 1830s, the British community of Baptists, of which Samuel Gill senior was a member, had become increasingly interested in the possibility of establishing a new, more Christian way of life in a new country–Australia. A strong advocate of this policy was George Fife Angas, a wealthy shipowner and coach builder and native of Newcastle-on-Tyne. He moved to Devon in 1832 and, two years later, became a commissioner for the new colony of South Australia.

Angas was greatly concerned at the persecution of the Lutherans of South Prussia, and in 1838, assisted three hundred dissenters to migrate to South Australia in his ships *Bungalee* and *Prince George*. A further 350 were carried in other Angas ships, *Zebra* and *Catherine*. By this time, he was chairman of the Torrens District Commission in South Australia and was entrusted with the responsibility of distributing land around Adelaide to sellers.

In 1839, Samuel Gill senior made the momentous decision to support the enterprise by migrating to South Australia. While the main reason may have been to achieve religious freedom, it's also possible this was prompted by the death of two younger sons in 1833. The family departed from Plymouth in the 450-ton Angas ship, *Carolyne*, and arrived in South Australia on December 17, 1839. S. T. Gill arrived with, in addition to his parents, a brother and sister, a servant and two carpenters. The Gill family travelled intermediate class and the servant and carpenters travelled steerage.

9 A carver and gilder carved decorative details on fine furniture, picture & mirror frames, architectural details for buildings, and other wooden objects and applied gold leaf to the objects.
10 *South Australian Register*, March 7, 1840.

The Gills apparently found Adelaide a charming rural village-town nestling in flat, partly cleared country; it was extremely fertile, surrounded by hills and enhanced by the presence of the Torrens River.

The development of the colony of South Australia was undertaken in a more planned manner than the other Australian colonies. It took shape from a widespread critique of other colonising ventures by people from liberal circles in Britain in the 1820s and thirties. A prominent spokesperson was Edward Gibbon Wakefield, whose *Letter from Sydney*, actually penned while he was confined in Newgate Prison in 1829, outlined many of the principles of 'systematic colonisation' that were to guide the creation of South Australia. Foremost among these were a commitment to free settlement, the belief land should be bought not granted, and bought at a sufficient price both to ensure an adequate supply of labour by preventing potential labourers from acquiring land too quickly, and to provide the funds for assisted emigration. There was also a preference for young, fit families as assisted emigrants to ensure a balance of the sexes. A South Australian Association, formed in December 1833, actively promoted the creation of such a colony. Its members included many who were active adherents of various dissenting sects and were influenced by prevailing radical and utilitarian ideas.

South Australia was also created initially as a commercial and administrative partnership between the British Government (represented by the office of the Governor) and the South Australian Colonisation Commission. The precise distribution of administrative powers between these two groups was never adequately defined and constant conflict between them marked the early years of settlement. To further complicate matters, in 1835, some members of the Colonisation Commission had formed a joint stock company, the South Australian Company, to raise sufficient funds in land sales to satisfy the British Government that the new settlement was viable. The South Australian Company became, in effect, the financial basis of the new settlement, building much of the early infrastructure and providing banking and other financial services. It was founded by George Fife Angas and other wealthy British merchants. Its immediate purpose was to encourage the purchase, in advance, of land in the planned colony.

While Colonel Light, Surveyor General for the colony, and his team searched for an actual site for the city, the immigrants from the first seven ships camped in the sand dunes at Holdfast Bay, the site of Glenelg. From January-March 1837, migrants set up in tents and wooden huts in two camps named after two of the first migrant ships, *Buffalo* and *Coromandel.*

Under the Angas land allocation scheme, Gill senior acquired seven acres in the Coromandel Valley. Tragedy hit the family in 1840 when their daughter died of typhoid fever, to be followed in a short time by the death of Mrs Gill. Gill senior remarried two years later.

The colony of South Australia had only been settled for a little over three years when the Gills arrived. S. T. Gill made his first sketches of Adelaide and the immediate surrounding area very soon after his arrival and sent them to relatives in England by the first available mail.

Within a few months of his arrival, aged just twenty-one, he announced in the *South Australian Register*, 7 March 1840, his availability as an artist and his willingness to tackle any subject on commission. His advertisement reads:

S. T. Gill, Artist, &c., late Draftsman and Water Colour Painter to the Hubard Profile Gallery, London, begs to announce to his friends and the public generally of Adelaide and its vicinity, that he has opened rooms in Gawler Place where for the present he solicits the attendance of such individuals as are desirous of obtaining correct likenesses of themselves, families or friends. Parties preferring attendance at their residences may be accommodated without additional charge. Correct resemblances of horses, dogs, etc., with local scenery etc., executed to order. Residences sketched and transferred to paper suited for home conveyance. Orders executed in rotation. Open daily from eleven to dusk.

Gill soon became a compulsive recorder on paper of people, animals, architecture, landscape, and all manner of activities and incidents. Art critic, Alan McCulloch, describes the development of Gill's style and method of painting as follows:

He had evolved a swift, cursive style of work, using broad, pale washes of colour for the masses, while treating the edges of his subjects as linear contours breaking into short, robust brushstrokes, depending on the textures he wished to convey. It was the ideal field artist's technique, providing scope for the production of large numbers of works painted spontaneously and at high speed.[11]

Gill spent his first twelve years in Australia, from the end of 1839 to the beginning of 1852, living in South Australia and during that time, painted all the subjects specified in his advertisement in the *South Australian Register.*

When the Gill family arrived in Adelaide the estimated population was 14,600, and there were over 1600 buildings. European settlement after 1836 soon put pressure on the tenure of the land of the Aboriginal people, and once the original inhabitants of the Adelaide Plains were displaced, Adelaide grew in stages. Migration to Adelaide occurred in waves, usually due to world events such as wars, famines and religious persecution. The waves of migration during S. T. Gill's time in South Australia included the 1840s Irish immigration (particularly women), and the 1850s mining boom together with religious refugees. When he left South Australia in 1852, the population had increased to an estimated number of almost 69,000.[12]

11 Alan McCulloch. *Artists of the Australian Gold Rush,* Lansdowne, 1977, pp. 65-6.
12 Douglas Pike. *Paradise of Dissent: South Australia 1829-1857,* 2nd edition, Melbourne University Press, 1967, p. 517.

Colonel William Light, as Surveyor General for the new colony, was instructed by the British Government to find a site which had a number of attributes: a harbour; fresh water and effective drainage; ready internal and external communications and easily obtained building materials. When the site of the new city was chosen, places such as Port Lincoln, Kangaroo Island and the Murray Mouth region were rejected because of limited water supplies, inaccessibility, restricted hinterlands and poor soil and vegetation for agriculture. In the case of the Murray mouth area, while there was ample water, the narrow, shallow and exposed southerly facing mouth of the Murray River made it inaccessible for shipping.

Light had no instructions for a grid town except: '... to make the streets of ample width, arranging them with reference to convenience, beauty and salubrity; and making the necessary reserves, for squares, public walks and quays.'[13]

The site chosen was considered the best available for drainage and fresh water, and within a reasonable distance from the harbour. Colonel William Light was clearly a surveyor with considerable vision. The area south of the River Torrens was surveyed and divided into 700 one-acre lots, while North Adelaide was divided into 342 such lots. The streets were arranged with a number running north-south, crossed at right angles by a larger number running east-west. Light provided for a number of town squares to be placed strategically throughout the city, and it was surrounded by parkland. He and Governor Hindmarsh clashed, as Hindmarsh disagreed with his choice of site for Adelaide. Hindmarsh went so far as to ask Lord Glenelg, Secretary of State for the Colonies, for authority to move the settlement. However, Light prevailed, but did not see his dream come true, for he died three years after his arrival in the colony.

During Gill's twelve years in the colony he witnessed the development and became very familiar with the streets, squares

13 J. Stephens. *The Land of Promise*, Smith Elder, London 1839, p. 97.

and parks of Adelaide, painting and drawing many streetscapes, such as the two examples below, which are full of activity (in the left foreground of the North Terrace image, members of the British Regiment then stationed in Adelaide appear).

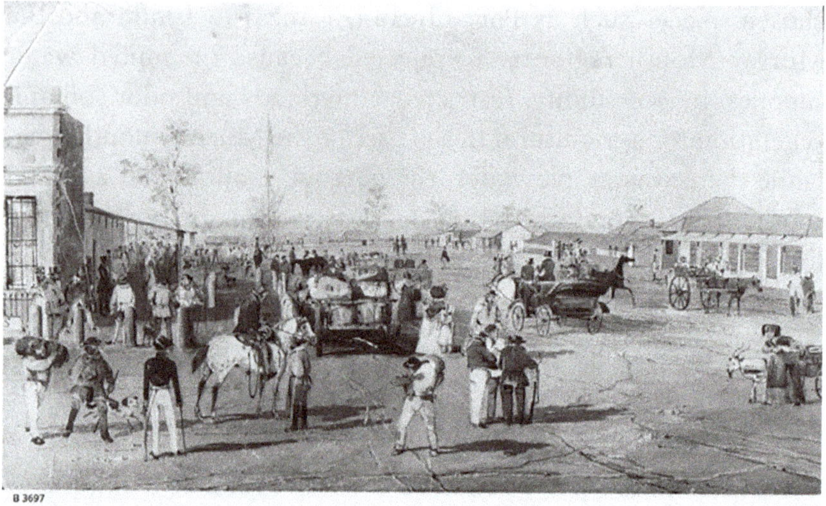

King William Street, looking north 1845 (State Library of South Australia, B3697)

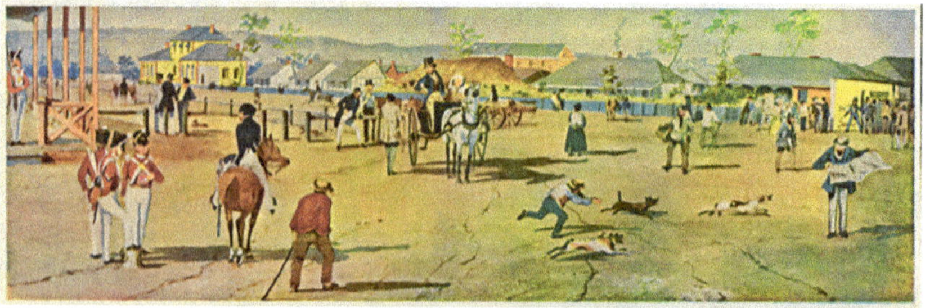

North Terrace, Adelaide 1845(State Library of South Australia, B7170)

When Light completed surveying the city, the town acres not purchased before settlement were auctioned in one-acre lots, and the temporary campers who could afford to buy quickly claimed their new town lands. The first building material was wood from lands around the River Torrens. The original inhabitants of the area, the Kaurna people, earned some income from selling timber.

Apart from tents, the earliest buildings constructed in Adelaide were prefabricated wooden buildings from Britain, or pisé construction (rammed earth) using clay mud from the river banks. But limestone lying close to the surface and the river's extensive clay deposits meant that brick and stone soon replaced mud and timber for more substantial buildings. By the 1850s the Adelaide City Council had banned timber construction, and bluestone quarried from Glen Osmond had become a popular building material. This went on to become a distinctive feature of the Adelaide built environment. Public buildings were constructed in the parklands reserve along the northern side of North Terrace, including Government House.

Limestone also became a popular building material. In most cases, it was easy to obtain, as much of the Adelaide area sits on a bed of nodular limestone (calcrete) less than two feet below the surface. Several early public buildings, including the Mounted Police Barracks, Government House, Adelaide Gaol, the Treasury Buildings and Parliament House, were built of limestone from the several quarries along the River Torrens. The Holy Trinity Church on the western end of North Terrace was constructed in limestone in 1838, as was Christ Church in Palmer Place, North Adelaide, in 1848. The Catholic Bishop's House on the corner of West Terrace and Grote Street was also built of limestone in 1846. Early private dwellings, erected using limestone found on site, were often built with semi or full basements to create bedrooms or a retreat to escape the summer heat. King William Street, the city's major thoroughfare, contained many financial and commercial institutions, while the narrower cross streets remained the centre of retail focus, with small shops and hotels. Much of the activity occurred in Hindley and Rundle Streets.

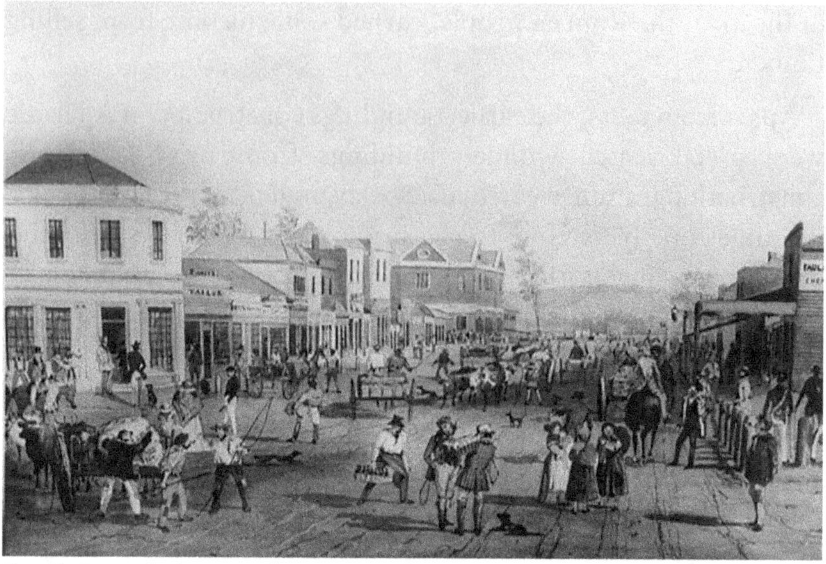

Rundle Street, looking east from King William Street c. 1845 (State Library of South Australia, B3703)

Gill's paintings of Adelaide streets in the 1840s provide wonderful images of mid-nineteenth-century Adelaide. They include paintings of Government House (North Terrace), North Terrace looking south-east, Hindley Street looking west, Hindley Street looking east, Rundle Street, Rundle Street looking west, and Hindley Street from King William Street. In each case, there are a range of people, animals, and activities depicted in each painting. Gill arranged people and animals in each of his street scenes to create a carefully orchestrated and interesting composition. The selection of colour for costumes and clothing added to the impact of the paintings. His set of paintings and drawings of Adelaide streets and architecture provided a comprehensive record of customs, dress, accoutrements, architecture, and modes of transport of colonial Adelaide in the 1840s.

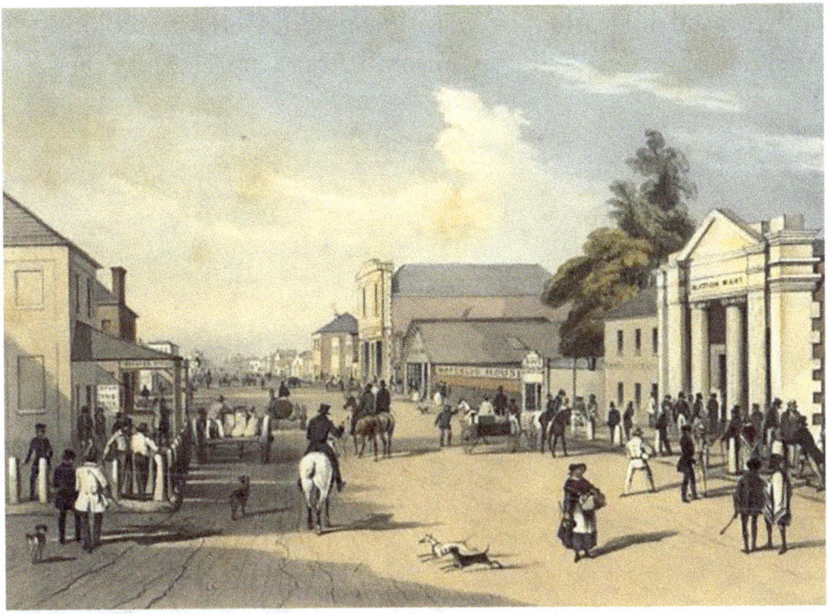

Hindley Street from the corner of King William Street c. 1847 (National Library of Australia, nla.obj-135639117)

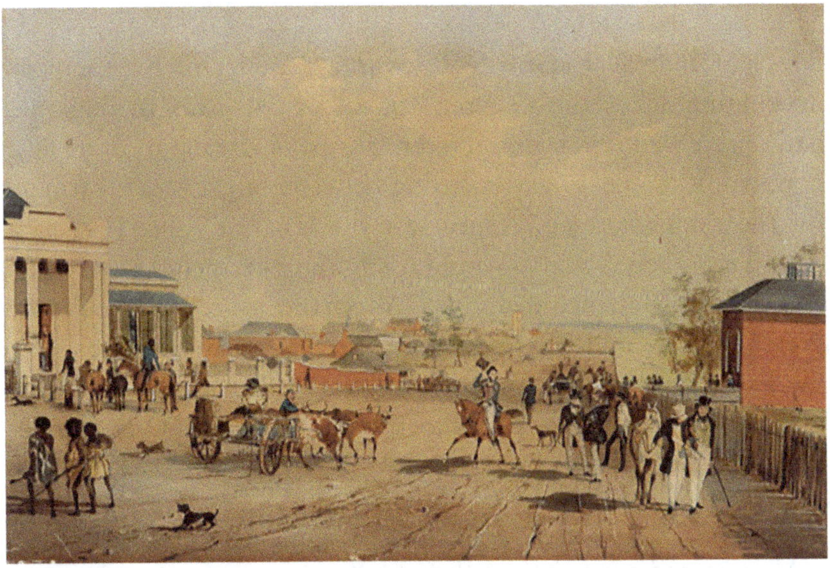

Bank of South Australia and Legislative Council Room, North Terrace, Adelaide (National Library of Australia, nla.obj-134361613)

Gill pleased his father by painting a series of watercolours of Adelaide churches: Trinity Church, Christ Church and others.

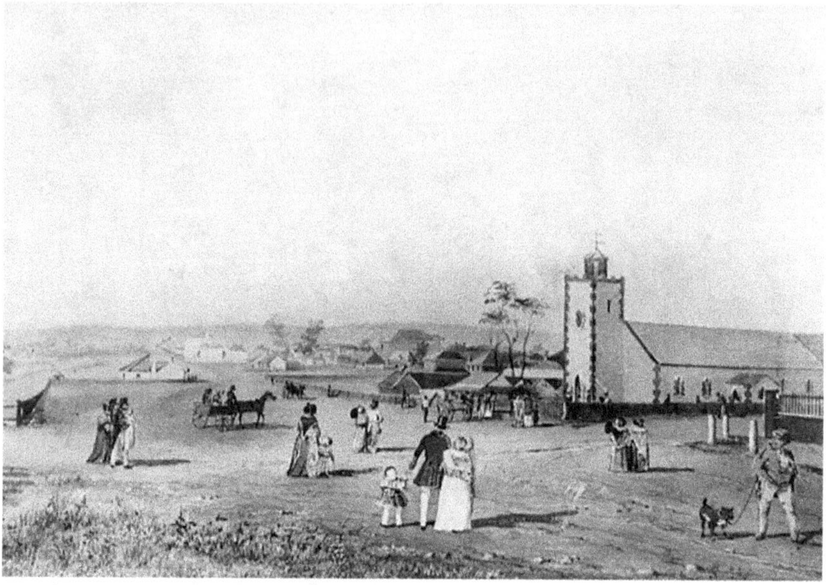

North Terrace, showing Trinity Church (State Library of South Australia, B6821)

It's clear that S. T. Gill (STG) was a product of his religious upbringing. The family, being critical of the order in England, had emigrated to seek greater religious freedom and new opportunities. There was a strong belief in fairness of treatment for the disadvantaged, respect for the law and adherence to a strong moral code which would no doubt have included sobriety. The Rev. Gill had included some verse in the last part of the shared sketchbook he and STG produced in England (see next chapter for more details). The verse below taken from the sketchbook was clearly meant to be an exhortation to S. T. Gill to remember and uphold the family values.

Well if with all their misspent leisure,

Men valued peace before their pleasure,

And while they other good pursue,

Sought God and his Salvation too,
Be this my boy thy chief concern,
For this thy soul with ardour burn,
Some others may be needful too,
But this most needful keep in view.[14]

As the eldest child in the family and having a close relationship with his father, STG was most likely troubled by his failings, probably felt guilty for not being able to live up to the standard expected by his father, and was most likely troubled by this dilemma for all of his life.

Before the 1860s, when manufacturing in the city was more like a cottage industry and when residents lived alongside, it was often difficult to differentiate between residential, industrial and retail areas. Self-employed citizens who followed such occupations as blacksmith, saddler, butcher and carpenter often had workshops attached to their homes which they expanded into something other than a cottage industry. A street which looked residential because it was lined with homes would often have a front room extended to become a small shop, providing the local grocer, butcher, or hardware merchant.

The permanent site for Port Adelaide was not chosen until 1839. The South Australian Company paid £12,000 for the construction of a two-mile road and had a wharf and warehouse buildings constructed. The government had a Customs House and a number of sheds constructed. Gill was asked to record these developments and produced several watercolours between 1845 and 1848. His work showed that by about the mid nineteenth century, a number of essential and basic buildings and facilities were in place at the port. His paintings are typical Gill 'snapshots', incorporating people, animals, nets, fish baskets, anchors, and ship masts.

14 Ron Appleyard, Barbara Fargher, Ron Radford, *S. T. Gill. The South Australian Years 1839-1852*, Art Gallery of South Australia, 1986, p. 45.

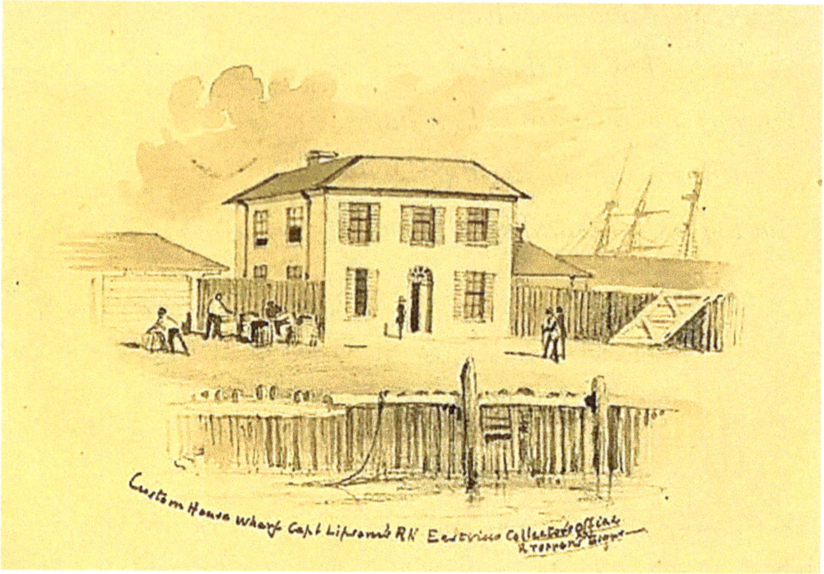

Custom House Wharf, Collectors Office, East View, Port Adelaide 184? (National Library of Australia, nla.obj-134362254)

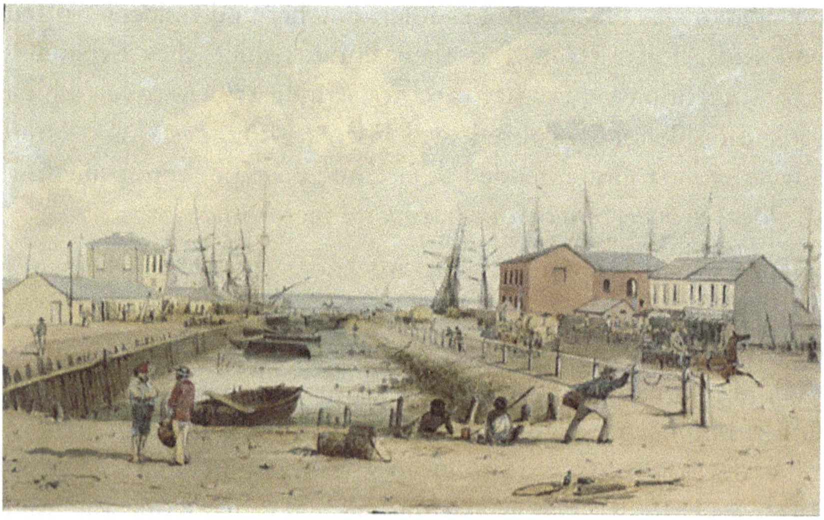

Port Adelaide (National Library of Australia, nla.obj-134655619)

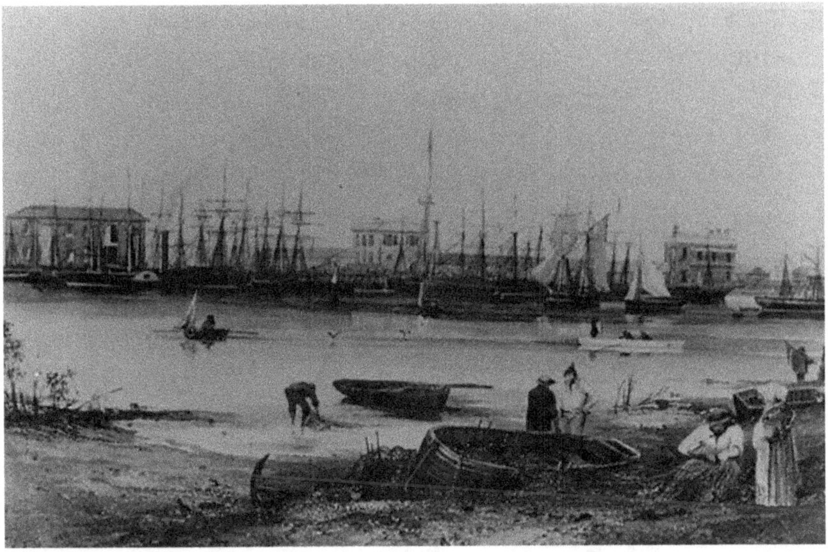

Port Adelaide 1848 (Note: Steamship Juno far left was the first vessel to steam up the Port River in 1847) (State Library of South Australia, B3701)

Some of Gill's early work of Adelaide and Port Adelaide were part of a commission undertaken in 1845 for James Allen. Allen was former proprietor and editor of the *South Australian Register* and sailed for England in December 1845, where he gave a series of illustrated lectures during 1846-47. Gill not only painted a group of watercolours for Allen's lecture tour, but assisted in preparing transparencies. It appears Allen may have had official backing for his venture to promote the colony, as he had meetings with the Registrar General for the Colony, Bartley, and involved Gill in at least one of these meetings. The meetings with Bartley are recorded in Allen's diary. For example, an entry for 23 October 1845 reads, 'meet Mr Gill at Mr Bartley's for tea.'[15].

During the voyage to England, Allen gave a lecture on South Australia in Cape Town on February 25, 1846, where the paintings were displayed. The *South Australian Register* reported Cape Town news on Wednesday, June 10, 1846, including a lecture by James Allen:

15 R. Grandison, *Art & Enterprise –Images in the Barossa Valley in mid 1840s*, unpublished paper, 1991, p. 4, State Library of South Australia, 994.2302G753b.

A lecture was given last evening by Mr James Allen, in the Commercial Exchange Rooms, on the 'Pastoral Commercial and Mining Progress of South Australia,' which a six years' residence at Adelaide, as Editor of one of the principal Journals (the South Australian Register) had enabled him to gather, and to ornament with fluency and intelligence. A kangaroo, brought from that district, added charm and a curiosity to his mission, particularly as it had been announced, that the animal "was to speak for himself"" But it merely danced the new Polka. Twenty-two faithful and spirited views of the City of Adelaide, in water colours, painted by Mr Gill, were exhibited, which afforded palpable and striking proofs of the sudden rise and prosperity of the colony.

On arrival in England, his proposal for a series of three lectures was supported and advertised by the South Australian Company. In an advertisement in the *South Australian News*, London, June 1, 1846, it was stated that:

Mr. Allen has brought with him a large number of Drawings, executed by a Colonial Artist... and is encouraged to exhibit them as a Series of Dissolving Views.

A further lecture was given on the subject of the mines of South Australia, followed by four more lectures in other parts of London and in eight other cities. It's understood the watercolours remained in England, probably with the South Australian Company.

It wasn't long after the establishment of Adelaide the people organised sporting activities to add pleasure to their lives and to recreate English social life in South Australia. Horse racing and hunting were popular with the early settlers of Adelaide. Gill's work included a hunt meet *(Hunt Meet at Dry Creek near Adelaide)* and an Adelaide race meeting *(A Race Meeting at*

Adelaide). Both painted in 1845. Hunting became a theme Gill returned to many times almost to the end of his life.

In keeping with his 1840 advertisement claiming he could draw animals, he was apparently commissioned to paint a number of horses, including *Fuz-Buz* (1849), *Cydnus* (1851), *Fidget* (1851), *Merry Monarch* (1851), and *Death of Boomer* (1853).

The early development of the Agricultural and Horticultural Society of South Australia led to the conduct of an annual agricultural and horticultural exhibition. The fourth of these exhibitions took place in Adelaide in 1845 and was recorded in two paintings by Gill (*Agricultural and Horticultural Exhibition Parklands 1845*). He also produced sketches and two watercolours on the same theme, each containing lots of people and activity. These events were an important celebration for the settlers; they were able to showcase the variety of fruit, vegetables and grains they produced for local consumption and for export. Gill would have enjoyed recording these events as he excelled at capturing the bustle and life of crowd scenes.

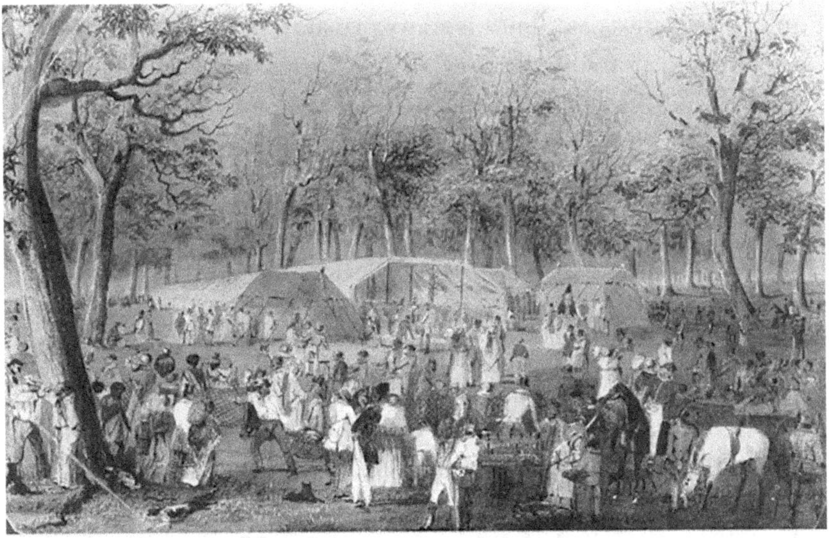

Agricultural and Horticultural Show 1845 (State Library of South Australia, B16066, photograph of sketch)

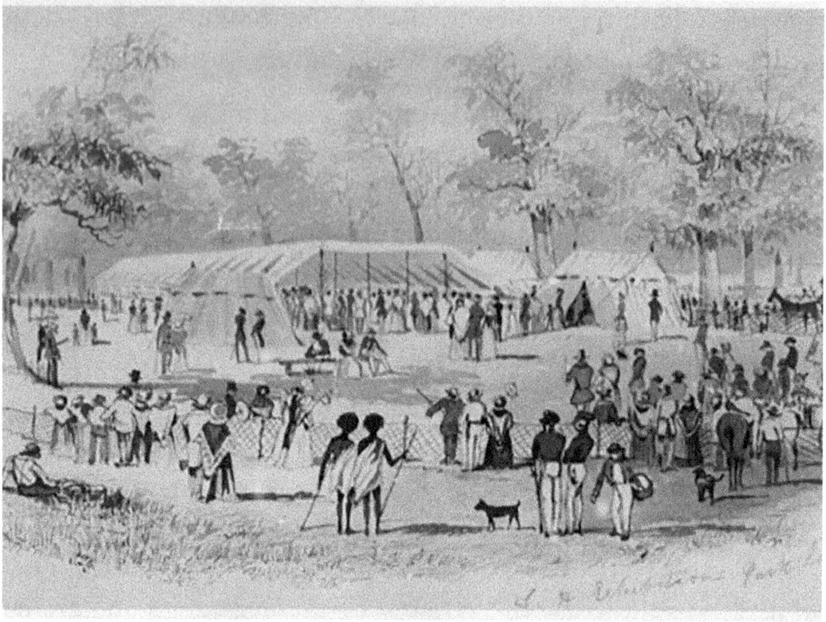

Agricultural and Horticultural Show, Adelaide (State Library of South Australia, B3695)

Gill's announcement that he was available to paint individuals, families and friends did not lead to a rush of requests for portraits to be created. Possibly, his style of painting in watercolours and his fairly small sized paintings were not regarded by the wealthy folk of Adelaide as being grand enough for them. They probably preferred more formal portraits in oil. This may have also suited Gill, as he clearly enjoyed painting groups of people and recording the atmosphere of the event rather than painting portraits. He did make one small watercolour portrait in 1850 (*R.F. Macgeorge*, who was a timber merchant and was drowned in the wreck of the *Royal Charter* 1859). Possibly the only other portrait painted by Gill is contained in a private collection belonging to the M. J. M. Carter; it is a watercolour, entitled *Thomas Harding of Kapunda* (1850). This collection contains a private view of Australian colonial art compiled by Max Carter. The Thomas Harding in Gill's portrait was the great-great-grandfather of Max Carter, and like S. T. Gill, had emigrated to Adelaide in 1839. A builder by trade, he helped build Government House before settling in Kapunda.

While in South Australia, Gill produced his first lithographs, a medium which became an ongoing part of his practice. He may have learnt this skill while apprenticed as a carver and gilder in Plymouth. In May 1848, with Penman Galbraith and Co., he published a series of 12 lithographic portraits of Adelaide citizens, called *Heads of People*. The South Australian *Gazette* on May 31, 1849, reported:

...twelve lithographic sketches of colonists—all pretty well known—have been published during the week under the title 'Heads of People'. They are from the pencil of Mr Gill and show that the ability of this artist is not confined to landscape drawings but that it extends to a branch of art hitherto unexplored by him. These sketches are for the most part well done, one or two of them inimitable; and there is just that spice of quiet humour, bordering upon caricature, which redeems them from the dull monotony of staring portraits, without the slightest offence to the individuals introduced.

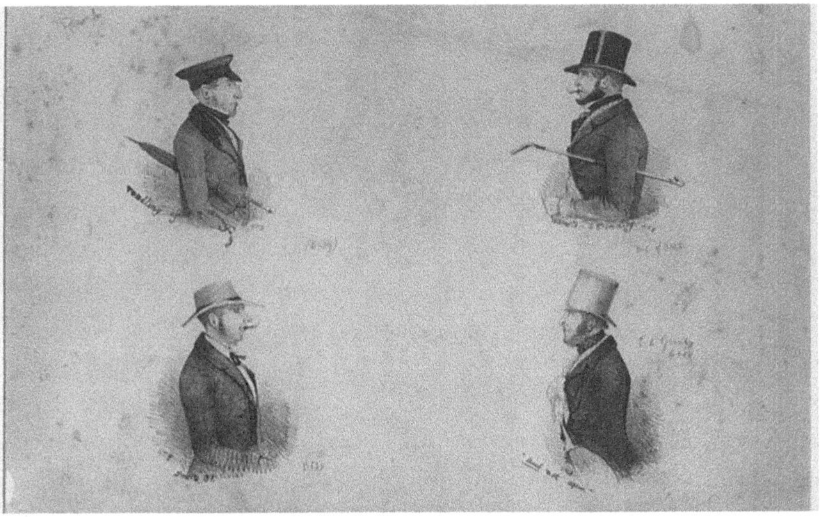

Heads of People (Sheet 3) (State Library of South Australia, B71555)

These were followed in July and September by two more sheets of five heads each, 22 in total. The subjects were all male. They were entirely set up with no names and only a caption underneath to give a clue to the identity of the subject. It seems they were easily recognisable; each portrait had strong features and most likely represented politely satirical likenesses of leading Adelaide identities. Comments in the press indicated those individuals who were drawn regarded their selection as a signal of their importance. These lithographs apparently enhanced Gill's reputation in Adelaide and demonstrated his versatility.

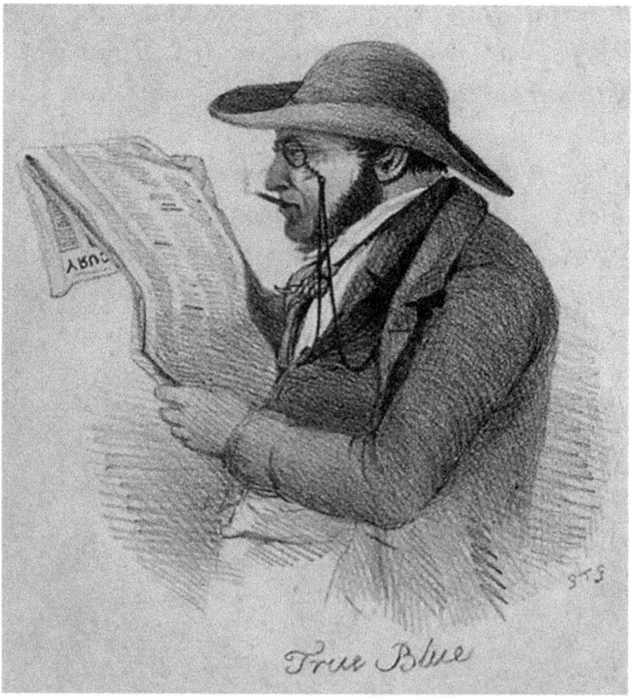

Captain John Finnis, True Blue (from heads of people)
(State Library of South Australia, B343)

This was possibly the start of Gill's creation of slightly humorous, caricature-style drawings, which he continued, developed and sometimes used in a comic and amusing manner to make a point. It was clear these lithographs of heads of well-known

Adelaide people caused lots of interest and some amusement and entertainment for the people of Adelaide. This is evident from the following extract taken from a letter by William Matthews:

> *Dear Mr Adams; I believe you want me to give you the history of the Lithographs called the "Heads of the People" that you sent to me yesterday. Well they were sketched direct from nature and then drawn upon stone by the late S. T. Gill...immediately he had done his part they were printed by your humble servant; myself and then published. The first sight of them caused a flutter of excitement to pass through the City, where the parties whom S.T.G. had sketched were seen daily and the fidelity of his sketches to the original was at once seen and commented on; especially by the Crowd who daily assembled before the Exchange Hotel in Hindley St. then kept by George Coppin (one of the Heads) ...whom S.T.Gs pencil had at that time made famous. Now in regard to the mottos attached to the Heads ... Each Motto refers to some peculiarity or characteristic of the party represented as for instance Kingston's Shabby Hat and the dismal appearance of Old Bouch as he responds to the toast of sweethearts and Wives, ...I remain yours Sincerely; William G. Matthews.*[16]

In advertising his availability to paint, Gill had also made it known he was available to paint houses. He was a very proficient horseman and often rode into the countryside to record landscape scenes that sometimes contained buildings. By the middle of the nineteenth century, larger and grander houses were being built in South Australia. Gill was commissioned to paint two of these houses (Vale Farm and Prospect House) and clearly was asked to prepare several views. Vale Farm was built near the River Torrens, in what is now the suburb of Vale Park. Gill painted two scenes at Vale Park (*Vale Park* and *From the Verandah of Vale*

16 R. Grandison, *Art & Enterprise –Images in the Barossa Valley in mid 1840s*, unpublished paper, 1991, p. 4, State Library of South Austr

Park). Prospect House is a far more pretentious dwelling, looking somewhat like a castle from a distance, with a formal garden. It was the first gothic revival mansion in the Adelaide area with thirty rooms. This commission involved four paintings (two entitled *Prospect House, The Seat of J.B.Graham, Esqr., near Adelaide, South Australia,* and two of the garden: *View from the Leads of Prospect House, Looking towards Hindmarsh* and *View from the Leads of Prospect House, Showing west-north-west portion of Garden Grounds).* The watercolour paintings of these two houses were made around 1850 and were some of the last paintings Gill created before leaving South Australia.

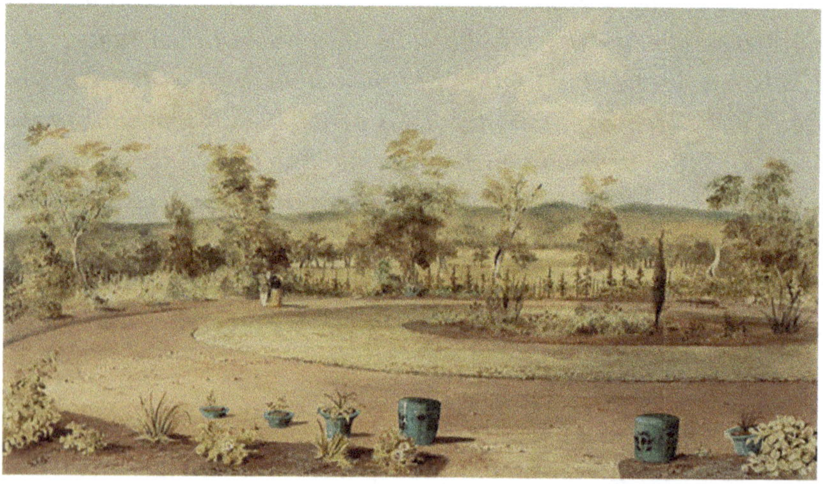

From Verandah of Vale Farm (National Library of Australia, nla.obj-134366454)

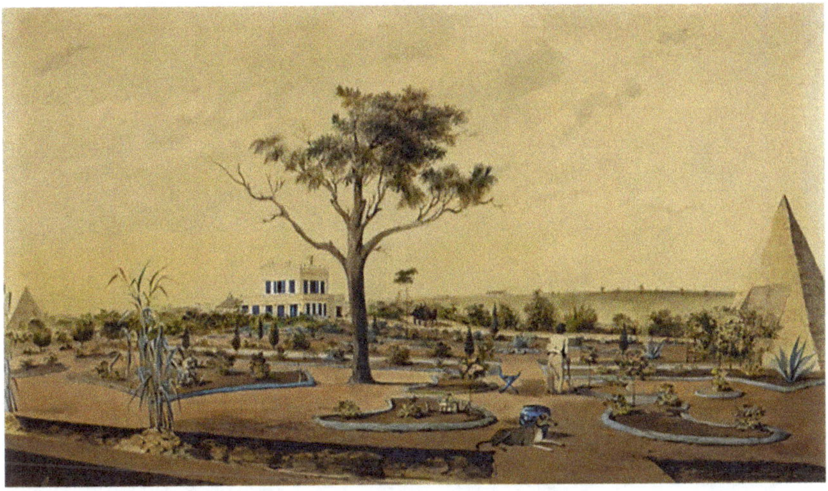

Prospect House, the seat of J.B.Graham, Esqr., near Adelaide, South Australia (National Library of Australia, nla.obj-137297103)

After he produced the series of lithographic portraits of people, Gill was engaged to undertake a more difficult project involving the preparation of a large lithograph in 1851; the subject was the attendance of some 600 colonists at the Old Colonists' Festival dinner. It was held in a canvas-covered pavilion, located at the rear of the City-Bridge Hotel, Morphett Street. The event took place on Thursday, March 27, 1851, in commemoration of the first sale of town land on March 27 1837. The diners were entertained with music and song by the Adelaide Amateur Band, while two emus, a kangaroo and a wallaby, were allowed to move around at will. This would have been a challenging assignment for Gill. The lithograph contains an incredible amount of detail of the event and is framed by a number of scenes, a coat of arms and the words 'Advance Australia' at the top. The whole scene was produced with a slightly humorous touch, which the report on page 3 of the *South Australian Register* on April 19, 1851, suggests was appreciated:

The artist has - bestowed immense pains on his task, and the execution is most credible. Judging from the attitude of some of the figures, we should say it pictures the scene as it appeared rather late in the evening or towards 'early dawn'.

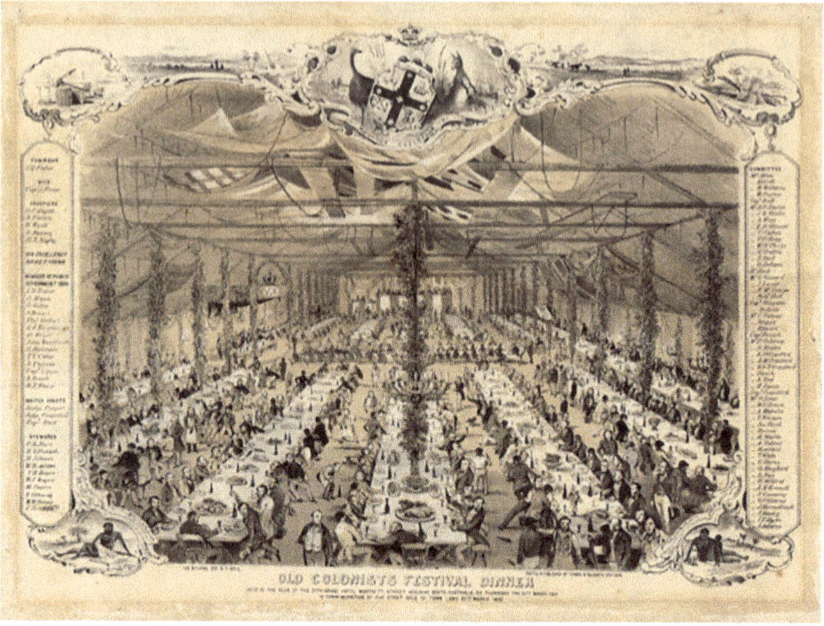

Old Colonists' Festival Dinner (State Library of South Australia, B21360)

While the *South Australian Register* reporter may have appreciated Gill's rendition of the dinner, it seems that some of those involved were displeased with his honest depiction of the drunken antics at the dinner.

Gill was involved in a humiliating court appearance as the result of an Aboriginal woman alleging that Gill's dog had attacked her. Although the case was dismissed in May 1849, it probably contributed to a period of depression for Gill. He would have been very conscious that litigation and lawlessness were equated with disgrace in his father's eyes. His lifestyle and drinking were also clearly not what was expected of members of the Gill family. Matters deteriorated even further when he declared himself insolvent in September 1851.

Gill prepared two further lithograph portraits in 1852, entitled *The Chair* and *The Vice*. They had a satirical and even sarcastic touch about them. The subjects are not named and the location is unknown, although quite likely they were of people present at the Festival dinner who had their names recorded by Gill in the left side of the lithograph (Chairman: J. H. Fisher, Vice-Captain J. Finiss). Gill may have produced these two lithographs after he arrived in Victoria in 1852, and he may have been displeased, even angry, about the hypocrisy of some who voiced their displeasure at his image of that event.

S. T. Gill was present in Adelaide almost from the start of the new colony for a period of twelve years, during which, despite significant economic problems, there was substantial development of the city. The population had more than quadrupled and many wonderful buildings had been constructed. Gill's many streetscapes record this development and provide wonderful views of broad streets populated with colourful people engaged in a range of activities. He also left some revealing images of the development that took place at the Port. Robert Campbell, a former director of the State Gallery of South Australia, summarised Gill's contribution to our understanding of the early history of Adelaide as follows:

The draftsmanship is excellent and the animated groups of figures could scarcely be bettered. The keen observation of gesture and costume, the traffic in the streets, the lively drawing of the animals, particularly of dogs - Gill was quite obviously interested in dogs, for there are few of his pictures without them busily chasing somebody or something - and the fact that the shops carry the names of the owners in the 'forties and the public buildings are so carefully rendered that I believe they even satisfy my friend the Archivist, adds considerably to their historical interest.[17]

17 Robert Campbell, *Early South Australian Artists*, lecture (undated), pp. 11-12, State Library of South Australia, Call No. 759.99423C189.

Chapter 2—Gill's *Seasons* and *Months*

Winter is an etching,
Spring a watercolour,
Summer an oil painting,
Autumn a mosaic of them all.
—Stanley Horowitz

Before leaving England, Gill had prepared a small leather-bound sketchbook containing 70 pen and ink sketches, one pencil drawing, and seven watercolours (the sketchbook is in the possession of the Art Gallery of South Australia). It also contained four pen and ink drawings by his father, the Reverend Samuel Gill, together with 57 of his poems. The sketchbook shows S. T. Gill and his father were very close and that Gill senior believed in his son's talents as an artist. The scenes contained in the sketchbook are of everyday subjects, including seascapes, village life, and country lanes. Towards the end of the sketchbook, a verse by Samuel senior shows something of the depth of affection he had for his son and hints at the type of subjects that would be fit for S.T.G to record:

This book dear boy shall be
A fond remembrance of thee,
Whose virtues fair our souls approve
By our first dear pledge of mutual love.
Nor shall it merely bring to mind
Thy industry and labours kind,
It shall a true recorder be
Of others dearly loved as thee.
A Brother, who may here afford
Some filial tribute of regard.
A Sister, who upon some page
May copy from a bygone sage
Ambitious that their name should stand
As written by each other's hand
But chiefly boy its page shall be
A strong remembrance of thee.
Here shall thy vivid pencil trace
The landscape green and dreary waste.
The figure stout, and tall, and high,
The beasts that roam, the birds that fly.[18]

One of Gill's earliest works in South Australia was a series entitled *Seasons* and *Months*. It's highly likely that the subject matter chosen for these paintings would have pleased S.T.G's father. The scenes in the series are reminiscent of those contained in the English sketchbook. The seasons and months were often subjects that appeared in English and European art. Clearly, Gill

18 Robert Raftopoulos, *Famous Australian Art: S. T. Gill's Rural Australia*. Oz Publishing Co., 1987, p. 6.

would have been aware of this thematic work. He would have also been familiar with the popular British illustrated calendars which featured these subjects. However, while painting scenes that would have been familiar to British viewers, adopting the familiar themes, and using an English framed style, he nevertheless painted each one as an authentic Australian scene, adopting a vignette style. This is probably a unique series of early Australian paintings. We don't know why Gill undertook this project so early in his time in South Australia. It's possible that, based on the work he had produced in his English sketchbook, he had always planned to do something similar as soon as the opportunity arose in his new home. Gill had been influenced by his mother and he may have felt paintings of the seasons and months, depicting change and renewal, might have comforted his mother following his sister's death from typhoid fever in April 1840.

It is also possible that Gill was asked or encouraged to paint the scenes contained in the *Seasons* and *Months* series. The South Australian farmer, like most colonists, had to gain a foothold in this strange place in order to provide shelter and food. Unlike some pioneers, the South Australians were encouraged in this task by the inspiration provided through the utopian ideals of the colony's founders, incorporating notions of civil liberty, social opportunity and equality for all religions. The task was to conquer nature and create a new and improved landscape. The early settlers in South Australia were clear they were involved in colonising, civilising and christianising, and lest they forget this, they were constantly reminded by the founders in London. Unfortunately for the Aboriginal people, they were part of the wilderness that had to be civilised and domesticated. Hence, the Aboriginal people, like the land, had to be saved and subdued. S. T. Gill's *Seasons* and *Months* scenes clearly demonstrate that this was successfully taking place. They showed order, success (fences, cultivation, produce) and 'nice' peaceful looking Aboriginal people.

The exact locations and dates of painting of this series is not known. However, expert eyes have carefully examined the subject matter and determined they were painted around 1840-42. These paintings are clearly important in depicting early South Australian scenes, activities and practices. They are presented in an album-like arrangement showing typical occupations and the results of the successful settlement of the land. They provide an insight into the state of development that had taken place only four to six years after the colony was established. It's clear, for example, that much of the work is labour intensive, with very little machinery being used.

Spring is a watercolour depicting two men planting trees, with a large group in the background washing sheep.

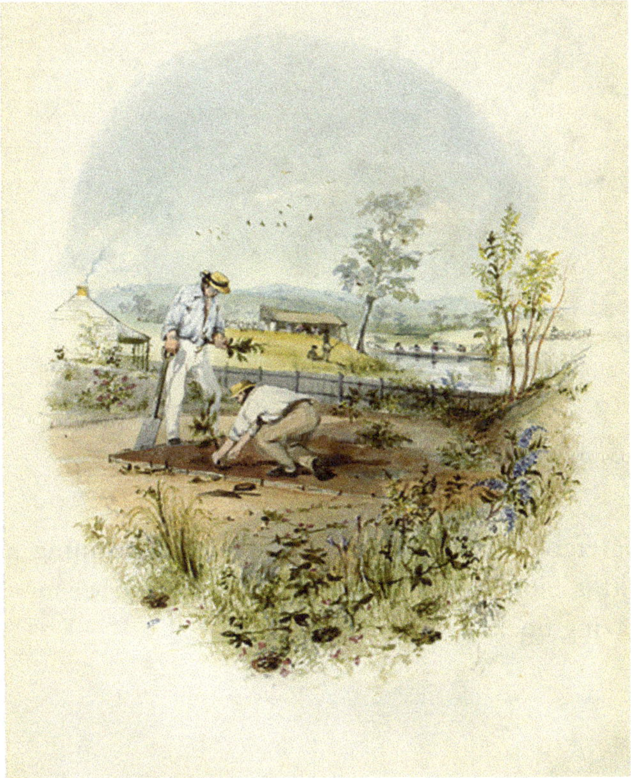

Spring (National Library of Australia. nla.obj.-134359133)

Summer depicts harvest time with men reaping, stooping, carting and threshing (smoke is rising in the background).

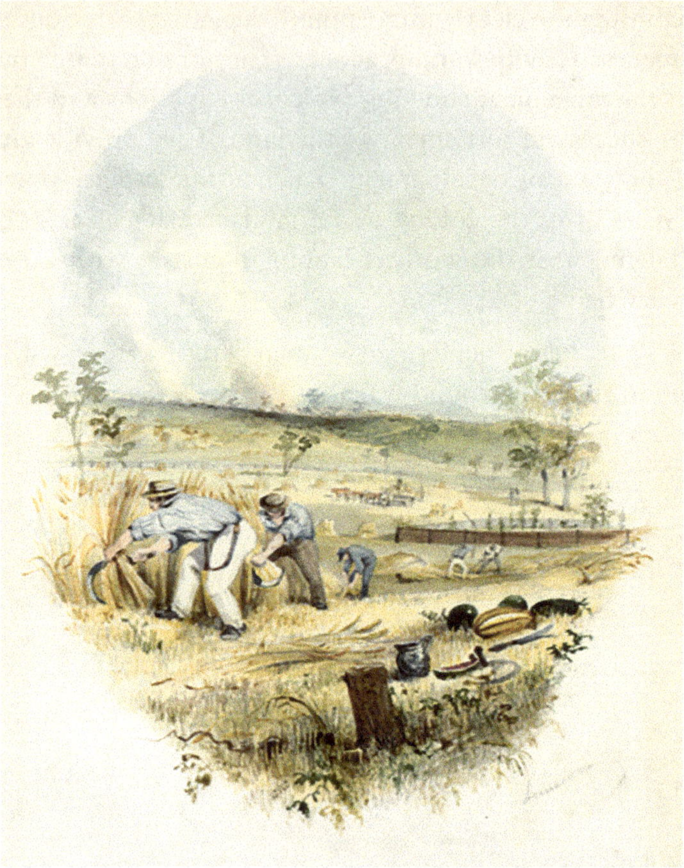

Summer (National Library of Australia, nla.obj.-134359859)

The *Autumn* watercolour is a mixed farm scene, containing a bullock team with a ploughman tilling the soil and another man casting seed (grazing flocks are in the distance).

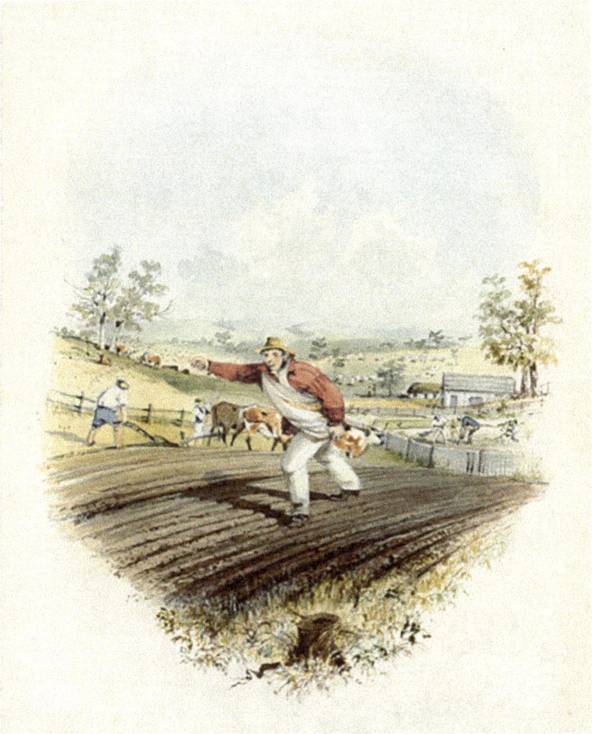

Autumn (National Library of Australia, nla.obj.-134359296)

The *Winter* scene features a hunter in a pink coat with duck shooters and riders in the background (Gill also included an Aboriginal group with a campfire). It's as though the English hunt has been transported to an Australian location. The hunting meets were held in winter as a leisure activity in colonial South Australia. Hunting became a popular theme in Gill's work, one which he painted many times (the dress of the hunters in Gill's paintings soon changed to that of bushmen and the type of dogs also changed). The scene includes an Aboriginal group around a small shelter. This may have been a way of showing that Aboriginal people were harmless and a normal part of life in the colony (which was the notion that was being promoted by the South Australian Company).

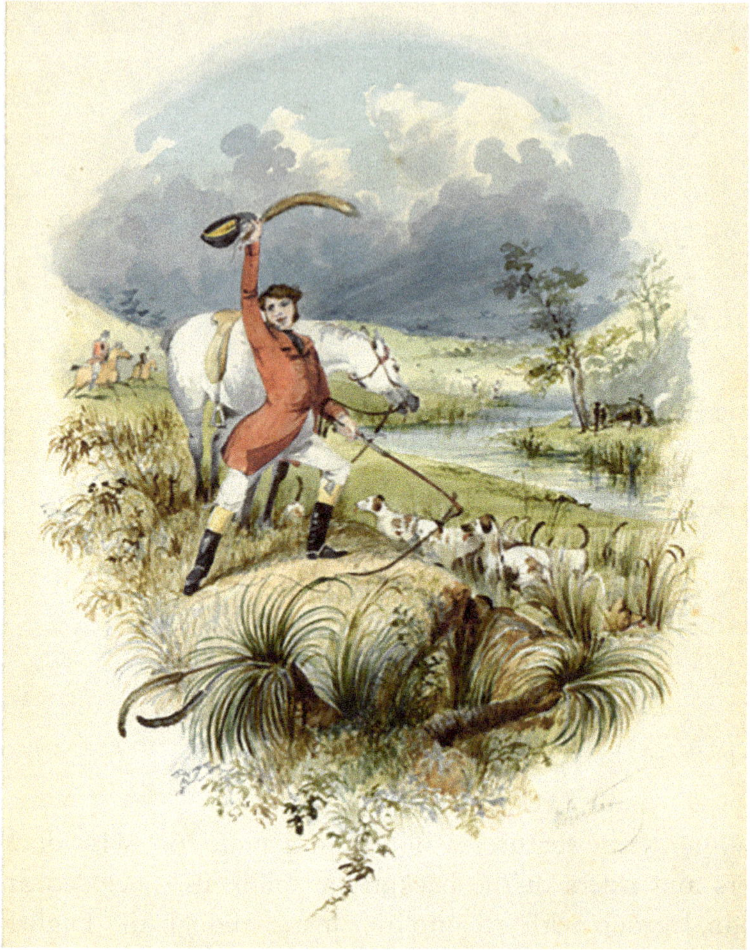

Winter (National Library of Australia, nla.obj.-134359656)

In the *Months* series there are eleven watercolours (July is missing). It's interesting that the subjects in this series correspond closely with the monthly agricultural and farming activities that James Horton recommended the people should be pursuing in the advice he gave, following his time in South Australia. Horton's guide is possibly the first gardening and agricultural guide in Australia. I have included some of his comments with each of the descriptions of Gills paintings. The subjects in Gill's series are as follows:

January—a farmer picking a melon with his wife, both located in a vegetable garden; farm hands in the background are carting and stacking hay.

This is the hottest month of the year, thermometer frequently standing at 90 degrees in the house. The wheat harvest finishes, watermelon and cucumbers very plentiful...[19]

February—a late summer garden scene with grapes being harvested by a man and woman, possibly for wine making; the garden is fenced with a path leading to a slate-roofed cottage where smoke is coming from a chimney.

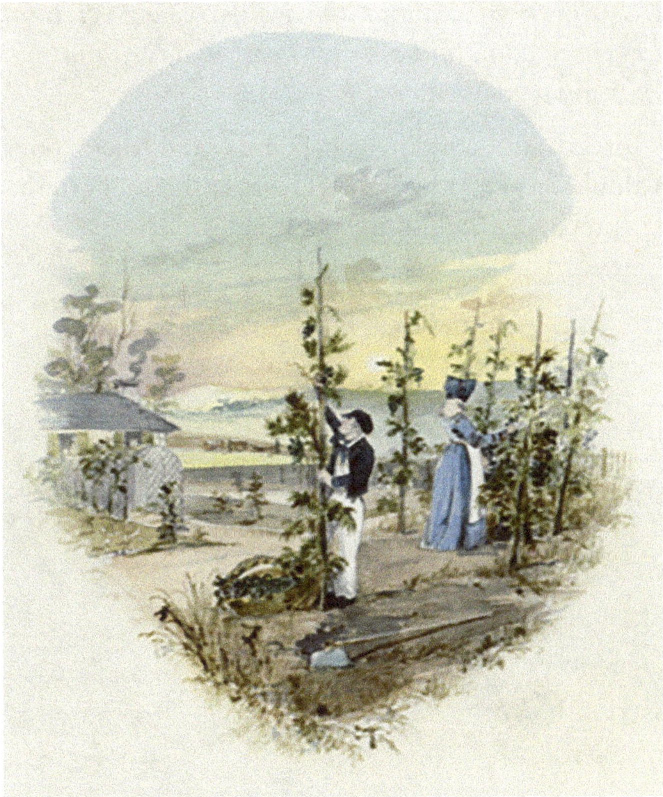

February (National Library of Australia, nla.obj.-134354667)

19 James T. Horton, *James's South Australia, Port Phillip and Australia Felix 1839*, J. Cross, London. 1839, p. 210.

Still very hot, thermometer frequently at 90 in the shade. Wooden houses are not adapted to the country; nothing like stone, brick, to pise, for what keeps out the heat, keeps out the cold... The settlers, this month, ought to have plenty of fruit, such as grapes, pears, figs, apricots, peaches, mulberries and apples.[20]

March—a domestic scene in front of a typical colonial cottage (slate roof and striped verandah) with a group of women and a baby and in the middle ground and a gardener leaning on a spade; roses are blooming, there is an exotic tree contrasting with gum trees in the background.

Latter end of the month, about the Equinox, expect rain. Morning and evening cool, and average heat, in day, about 69. After Equinox begin wheat sowing.[21]

April—the foreground contains shepherds and their dogs grazing sheep along the grassy bank of a creek; in the background a ploughman is preparing the soil for planting.

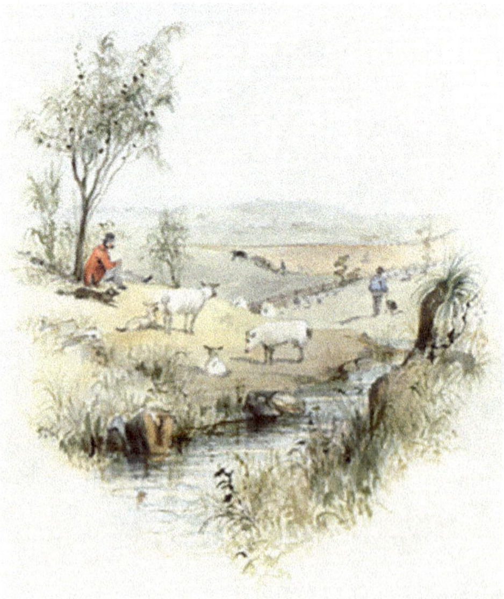

April (National Library of Australia, nla.obj.-134358298)

20 Ibid, p. 211.
21 Ibid, p. 213.

Expect heavy rains. Fires morning and evening very comfortable... Busy time for the plough and spade.[22]

May—a well-dressed farmer and his wife survey cattle and sheep being overseen by herdsmen; depicts a well-grassed and watered property with rolling hills typical of country close to Adelaide.

May and October are the finest months of the year, and the best months for the half-yearly agricultural meetings, ploughing matches, etc... Plough for barley and oats and sow for a general crop.[23]

June —winter is a time to relax and so there is a hunt scene (same subject featured in the *Seasons*) with hunters jumping a creek, followed by hounds; there are two Aboriginal hunters on the skyline. Gill was possibly contrasting hunting for leisure with hunting for food.

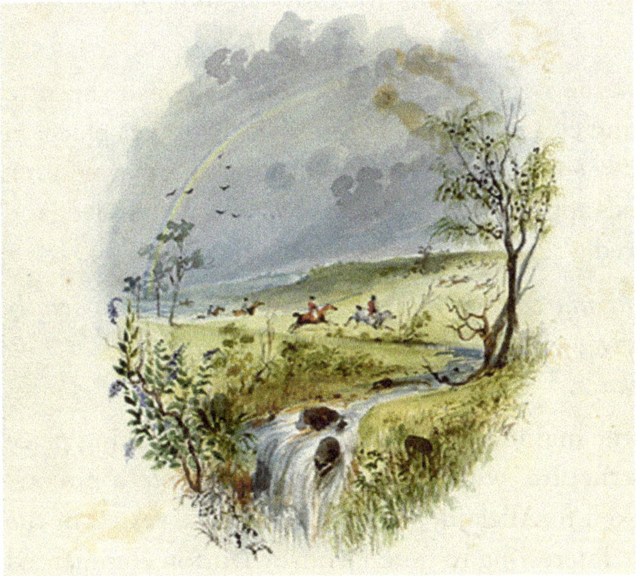

June (National Library of Australia, nla.obj.-134365651)

22 Ibid, p. 216.
23 Ibid, p. 216.

June, July and August are the salting months; pork and beef will not keep long except salted in this quarter. Wheat sowing is now done everywhere.[24]

August—a late winter scene with clear sky, featuring a humble thatched-roof cottage, two men loading a bullock dray, another chopping wood, and a group at the door watching.

...The patch-blossoms aught to be peeping out over all the low plains; nothing can be more beautiful, and no fruit is more easily raised in this fine climate. Expect heavy rains...[25]

September—clearly the first month of spring, with a group shooting ducks along a river bank, watched by two men, possibly farmers, and a dog inspecting wheat (the wheat in the painting is fully grown and ready to harvest).

The country looks beautiful... Rain and wind may be reckoned upon at the end of the month... Plough for maize on low flats of rich land... Dig beds... For planting melons and pumpkins in October. [26]

October—a scene with lots of activity as men wash sheep to remove grease and clean the wool before shearing takes place; in the background men are haymaking. Washing sheep was often a cold task, and apparently the wool washers demanded and probably deserved a few glasses of rum each day.

Begin to plant maize... Finest month in the year, especially before breakfast. Mosquitoes make their appearance on low grounds near water. [27]

November—the main focus is the sheep shearing taking place in a primitive structure, with bales being loaded onto a bullock wagon to be taken to Adelaide; wheat is being harvested in the background. It's interesting to note Geoffrey Dutton commented that this is 'probably the earliest painting of a shearing scene in

24 Ibid, p. 217.
25 Ibid, p. 221.
26 Ibid, p. 233.
27 Ibid, p. 225.

Australia'.[28] Many more were to be painted by other artists in years to come, the most famous possibly being Tom Roberts's work, *Shearing the Rams* (1890).

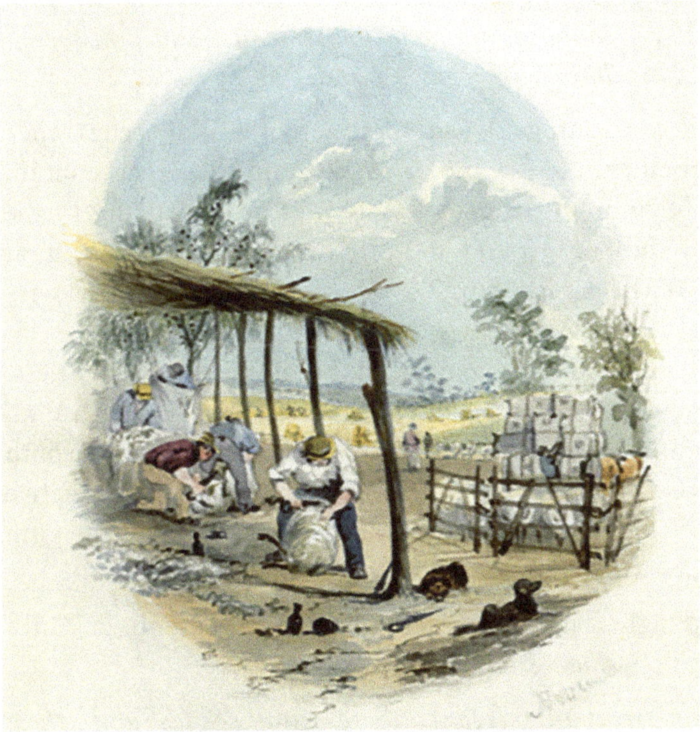

November (National Library of Australia, nla.obj.-134365973)

Go on planting maize. This is the busiest month in the year—Wheat harvest, sheep shearing, maize planting, and hay making. Put on more hands, especially take care to have a stack of hay for winter.[29]

December—the main focus of the painting is the threshing by two farmhands, with harvesting still taking place in the background.

---

28 G. Dutton, *Paintings of S. T. Gill, Adelaide*. Rigby, 1962, plate xi.
29 James T. Horton. *James's South Australia, Port Phillip and Australia* Felix, J. Cross, London, 1839, p. 226.

North-west winds occasionally from the head of the gulfs, but followed by southerly winds, which will bring you arrivals from Van Diemen's Land and Sydney. No fruit this month. Thunder and lightening (sic) now and then... Keep sowing turnips, carrots, celery, cabbage, spinach, peas, beans, and potatoes... Keep the caterpillars from your tobacco...[30]

While these paintings depict rural activities and scenes, they are of particular interest and value because they each contain an incredible amount of detail. Activities are occurring in the foreground and background and often in the mid ground. In at least three of the paintings in *The Seasons* series, the settlers are being observed by Aborigines, and as indicated above, they fit easily into the landscape and are not a bother to the settlers. The paintings in the *Seasons* and *Months* series depict Australian vegetation, including gum trees. After only a short time in South Australia, Gill was able to overcome the European perspective and see the characteristics and beauty of the trunks of the gum trees. He saw and painted each tree as an individual.

Robert Hughes made the following comment about Gill's *Months* and *Seasons* series:

Delicate, Arcadian, elegant, these rural scenes with their swelling pastures, waving grasses and jolly farmers are quite unlike his raucous goldfields work... Gill already had a strong grasp of rhythmic movement.[31]

It's highly likely these scenes, all of which show a reasonably high level of prosperity, were intended for a British audience. Around the time these paintings were created there were clearly efforts being made to advertise the advantages and opportunities available in the colony of South Australia. While the South Australian Company undertook promotional work in Britain, there were also many examples of individuals writing letters of encouragement, urging friends and relatives to consider

30 Ibid, p. 227-8.
31 Robert Hughes, *The Art of Australia*, Penguin Books Ltd., 1966, pp. 20-21.

emigrating. Some of these letters found their way into newspapers and pamphlets in Britain. An example is a letter by colonist Joseph Gould:

> *It is not the lazy gentleman farmer that is wanted here; but if many of the diligent hard-working farmers of England, who can make nothing with all their hard labour, were situated as many others are with myself as tenants of the South Australian Company here, it would be a blessing both to themselves and their families.*[32]

These two sets of paintings were purchased by the National Library of Australia in London in 1933.

Gill's *Seasons* and *Months* contrast markedly with his paintings of later rural scenes in South Australia and other colonies, where his work is much less formal and orderly in its depiction of the real Australian landscape. This is even more apparent in the work he produced during the Horrocks expedition (see Chapter 7), where he shows the ruggedness, the colours, and the vastness of the landscape. A major benefit in these images of the *Seasons* and *Months* is they provide a window into very early rural South Australia. While they show achievement and a level of prosperity, they also show that rural activities were undertaken by manual means or at least using very basic equipment. At the same time, Britain was undergoing an industrial revolution, which was possibly why some of the South Australians in Gill's images had emigrated. If the paintings were made in the 1840-42 period, then they show a remarkable degree of progress in only a few years, realistically presenting a range of rural activity including fences, sheds, houses, grapes, wheat harvesting, shearing, bales of wool, livestock, and afterwards, there is time to dress and go hunting for pleasure. Aboriginal people are included to demonstrate their presence, possibly to add some local colour,

32 Joseph Gould, *South Australia in 1842, by One Who Lived There Nearly Four Years*, J.C. Hailes, London, 1843, p.10.

but they are a small part of the scene indicating they are harmless, inoffensive, and possibly useful to the farmer.

R. Grandison says of Gill's early work in South Australia:

it appears that he did not take much licence with his scenes, especially his landforms... His paintings are rich in human activity and interest, carefully showing the quiet retreat of the indigenous giving away to new cultural impact.[33]

In order to demonstrate that Gill's paintings accurately recorded the scenes, Grandison spent time in the 1990s identifying the location of the scenes painted by Gill in the mid-1840s. He concluded that, using Gill's paintings, he was able to identify the locations of many of the subjects—the landforms, some very old trees and even some man-made structures (fence lines) as recorded by Gill. This is further evidence that, even though his early works were more formal in structure than later, he recorded what he saw, including the different Australian landscapes, particularly the trees.

33 R. Grandison, *Art and Enterprise: images in the Barossa Valley in the mid-1840*s by S.T. Gill, research paper, 1991, p. 6, State Library of South Australia Call No. 994.2302G753b.

Chapter 3—Rural South Australia

For the most part we passed through green valleys with rich and luxuriant pasturage. The hills adjoining the valley were grassy, and lightly wooded on the slopes facing the valley; towards the summits they became scrubby, and beyond, the scrub almost invariably made its appearance.

—Edward John Eyre, 1845[34](commenting on S.A.)

In 1836, the South Australian Company imported pure merinos from the German region of Saxony. Cows and goats were also shipped over. Sheep and other livestock were brought in from Van Diemen's Land, and later New South Wales. The wool industry was the basis of South Australia's economy for the first few years, with the first wool auction held in Adelaide in 1840. Vast tracts of land were leased by 'squatters' until required for agriculture. Once the land was surveyed, it was put up for sale and the squatters had to buy their runs or move on.

Most bought their land when it came up for sale, disadvantaging farmers who had a hard time finding good and unoccupied land. Farms took longer to establish than sheep runs and were also

34 Edward John Eyre, *Journals of Expeditions of Discovery into Central Australia and Overland from Adelaide to King George's Sound, 1845, Vol. 1*, p.156.

expensive to establish. A major cost was fencing, at £60 to £70 to fence about 80 acres with a three-rail wood fence.[35] Despite this, by 1860 wheat farms extended from Encounter Bay in the south to Clare in the north. In the early years, South Australia had problems attracting a sufficient number of farm labourers. This was partly solved by James Ridley's development of a machine capable of stripping grain and threshing it to separate the grain from the ears. The machine was suitable for the hot dry conditions in South Australia, requiring a minimum of labour and capable of keeping the grain dry. Ridley was awarded £10.10s by the South Australian Agricultural and Horticultural Society in February 1844.

As discussed in the previous chapter, it was the colonists desire and duty to conquer nature, subdue the wilderness and create a new and improved landscape. In fact, E. G. Wakefield, who was so influential in the establishment of the colony, believed that this was inevitable:

The goodness of God and the progressive nature of man are unquestionable.[36]

S. T. Gill started making sketches of the Adelaide environment soon after arriving with his parents. He spent much time walking around the Glenelg area where he lived with his parents and in the area between Glenelg and the city. Gill was a competent horseman and was able to move more widely within the colony. The range of his subjects demonstrates that he travelled extensively in order to explore the colony and seek out new subject matter to paint. However, he also painted and drew many subjects near Adelaide in the Adelaide Hills.

35 M. Williams, *The Making of the South Australian Landscape*, Academic Press, London, 1974, p. 130.
36 E. G. Wakefield, *Letter to Colonisation Commissioners, 1835*. British Parliamentary Paper, Second Report of Colonisation Commissioners, 1841, App.35.

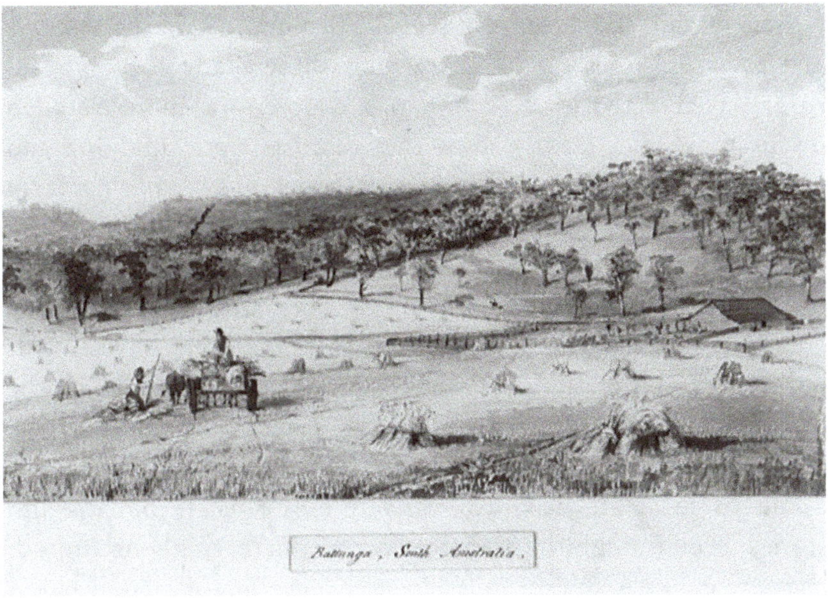

'Battunga', Echunga, South Australia (State Library of South Australia, B12247)

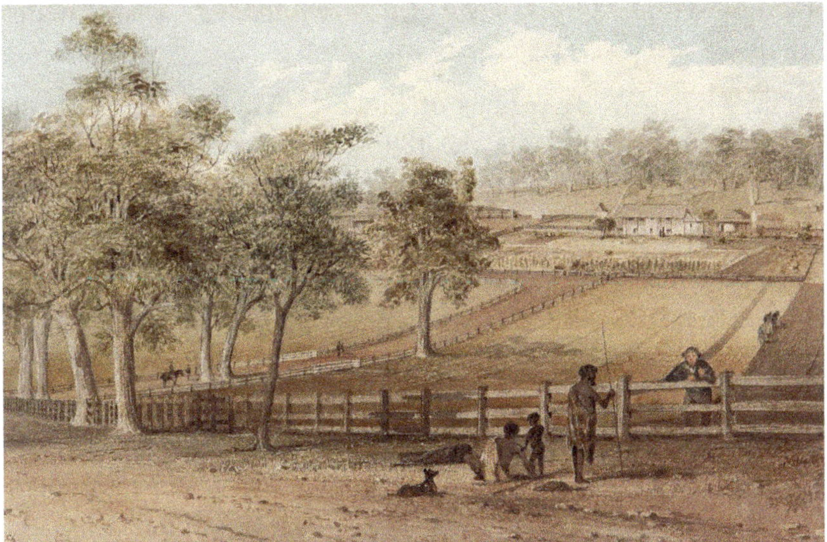

Captain Davidson's House, 'Blakiston', near Mount Barker (National Library of Australia, nla.obj-134362737)

Some of Gill's earliest rural scenes are contained in the *Seasons* and *Months* series (1840-42), which show many farming and rural based activities (see previous chapter for more detailed discussion). They clearly show the colonists were subduing and domesticating the land and creating order. It's clear that farm sections had been laid out, cleared, fenced, and cultivated, and plants and animals introduced. Some early pioneers commented on the regular echoing sound of the axe and through it, the creation of civilisation. Even though the real growth (investment, building and population) was taking place in Adelaide, the ultimate in achieving civilisation was seen as occurring in the rural areas. This was later glorified as a love of the country, and a cult of rural life was progressively enshrined in ballads and stories, even though the colonies became increasingly urbanised.

After the death of his sister and mother, S. T. Gill increased his roaming about the South Australian countryside on horseback, possibly to escape the family sorrows. He covered wide expanses and painted many watercolours, including *Near Port Broughton, Adelaide Plains from Sleeps Hill, Tanunda Creek* and many others.

The wine growing regions of McLaren Vale and the Barossa Valley were established in the 1840s. The Barossa development was accelerated in the 1850s with the arrival in South Australia of over 5,000 German settlers. Port Pirie was founded in 1845.

In his studies of the Gawler River in the Barossa, Gill was coming to grips with the Australian landscape, incorporating the large river gums and the radiance created by the summer heat.

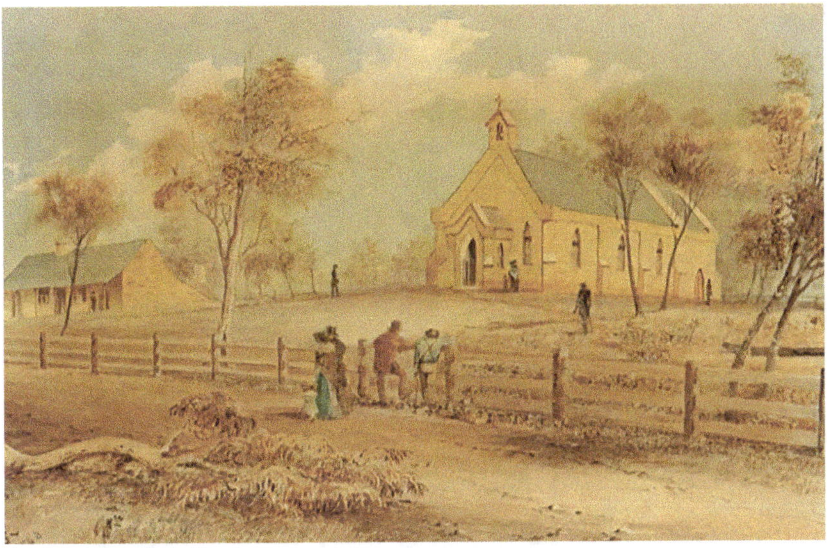

St. James' Anglican Church, Blakiston 1848
(National Library of Australia, nla.obj-134363374)

By 1850, Gill was painting Mount Gambier and the surrounding area. This was one of the most fertile areas in the colony, and although some 300 miles from Adelaide, the distance did not deter a good horseman like Gill from undertaking the journey. His paintings around Mount Gambier included the landscapes and life of Mount Schanck and Rivoli Bay.

One of his Mount Gambier drawings entitled *An Outback District Police Station, Mount Gambier* depicts the interior of the first police station in the district. Other features in the area that attracted his attention were *The Devil's Punch Bowl, Mount Muirhead* found between Mount Gambier and Rivoli Bay and Rivoli Bay itself (the subject of several seascapes).

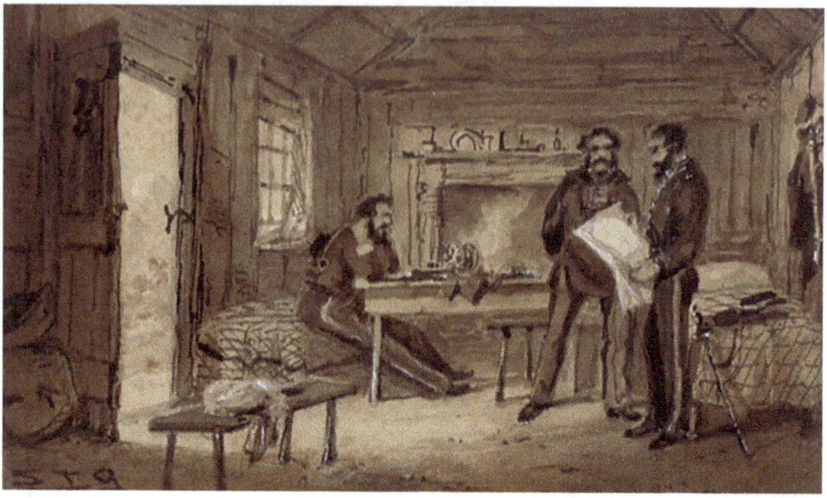

An Outback District Police Station, Mount Gambier
(Dixon Library, State Library of New South Wales, FL8802933)

Gill's urban and rural paintings and drawings become popular in the home country and clearly did much to promote the colony as thriving and prosperous. At around the same time, the first poet of the Australian outback, Adam Lindsay Gordon, became well known in England. Gordon's verse described frontier life in glowing terms, creating wonderful images in words. For example, the way he suggestively 'sketched' a colonial sunrise in verse:

On skies still and starlit
White lustres take hold
And grey flashes scarlet,
And red flashes gold.[37]

Soon after arrival in Adelaide, Gordon joined the South Australian mounted police force and was posted to Mount Gambier. I have no evidence to indicate Gill and Gordon met in South Australia. However, their paths crossed later in Melbourne, where they

37 *A Basket of Flowers, The Poetical Works of Adam Lindsay Gordon*, Butler & Tanner, London, p.199.

were part of a group of Melbourne literary and artistic people who met to drink and talk.

S. T. Gill's rural scenes and landscapes depict the impact made on the landscape by the colonists and show the large range of rural activities they introduced to South Australia. The subject matter in his watercolour paintings and pencil sketches includes a number of water and river scenes, cattle stations, stockmen moving cattle, mountain views and even scenes of bushrangers being chased by mounted police.

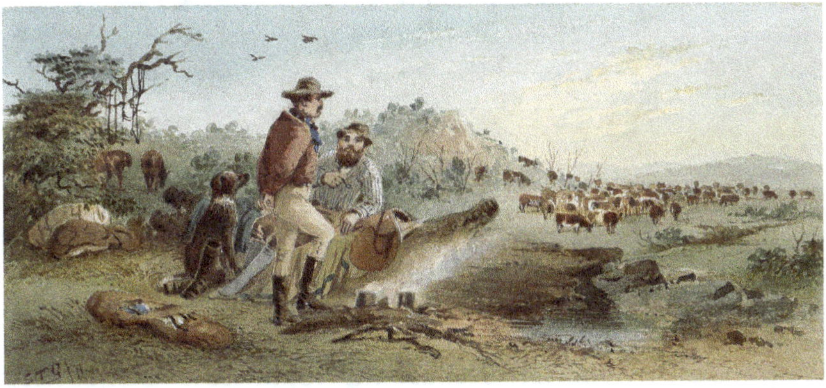

Stockmen in the Morning (State Library of Victoria)

During his meanderings about South Australia, Gill had lots of magnificent subjects to work with. He responded with the character that marked his works. He understood the shape of Australian trees, the light and the landscape. His treatment of foliage showed it as ragged and untidy, in direct contrast to the feathery foliage of earlier artists, who were thinking of the deciduous forests of the home country. Gill often included Aboriginal people in his rural scenes, such as portrayed in the image below of a gorge with a waterfall being viewed by a number of Aboriginal people.

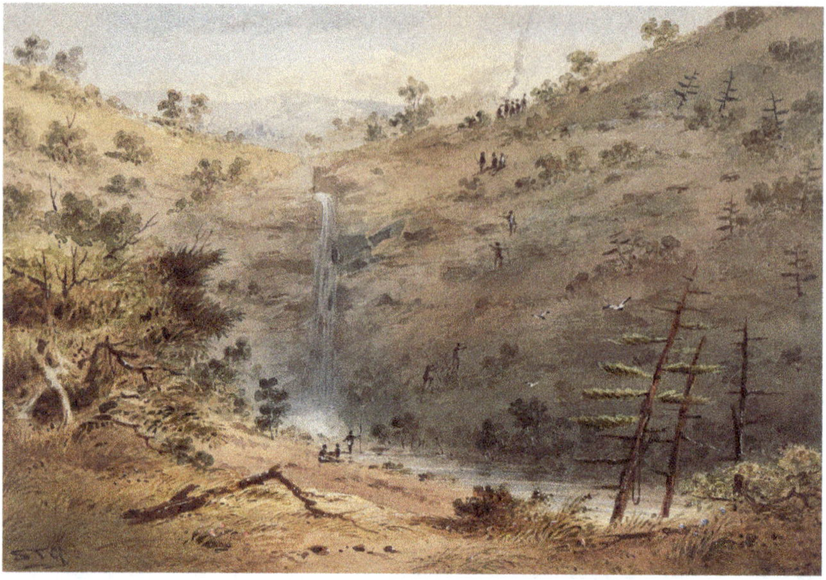

The Gorge, Flinders Ranges, South Australia
(Dixon Library, State Library of New South Wales, FL8803226)

Gill had, at times, struggled for recognition in the South Australian environment, because the South Australian society clung tenaciously to its English origins. He wasn't a good businessman or a socialite, and it was probably the hard drinkers rather than the gentry who took him to their hearts. However, his work was often recognised as capturing the essence of the colony and was the subject of praise, particularly when compared with other colonial artists. An example of this is a letter by F. R. Nixon (assistant surveyor to Colonel Light) published in the *South Australian* on June 17, 1845:

Another artist of less celebrity but real talent - who resides in the colony in comparative obscurity—I allude to Mr. Gill. Anyone who can comprehend the nature of landscape drawings, and who has once seen any of his works, would undoubtedly give him the palm, and ask to see others. For colouring, truth and 'general effect', he undoubtedly stands preeminent.

In his last years in Melbourne, Gill painted a number of large watercolour landscapes of South Australia. They were apparently based on sketches he had made in the 1840s while living in South Australia.

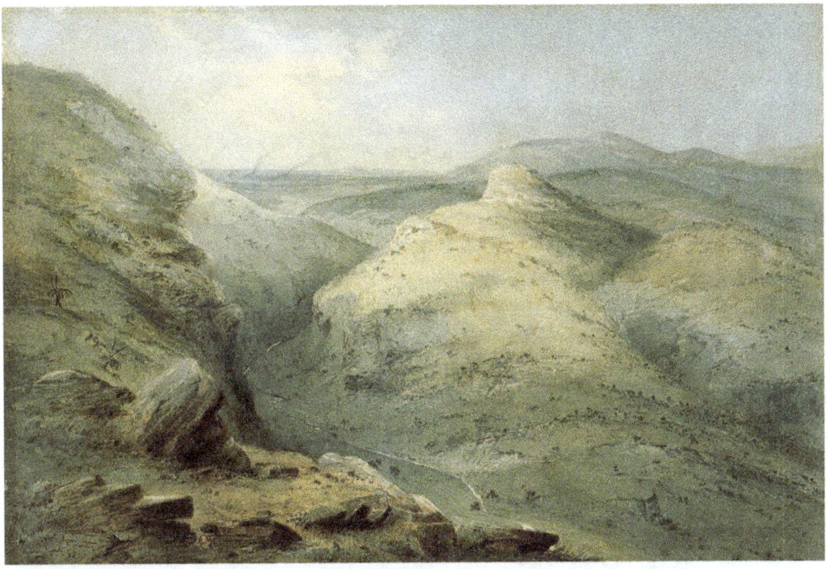

Flinders Ranges North of Mount Brown
(Dixon Library, State Library of New South Wales, FL8803326)

During his twelve years in South Australia, Gill's extensive travels on horseback around the colony made a valuable historical contribution. He clearly made a valuable historical contribution to that state by leaving a significant record of its early years in the form of at least 250 pieces of art. One commentator on Gill's work in rural South Australia remarked:

As a visual reporter he seems to have rejected no minor detail. An accomplished horseman, he travelled alone on horseback throughout the settled areas of South Australia and the watercolours from his travels show a real acceptance of the colours and forms of the Australian bush.[38]

38 Joan Kerr, ed., *The Dictionary of Australian Artists: Painters, Sketchers, Photographers and Engravers to1870*, Oxford University Press, 1992, p.296.

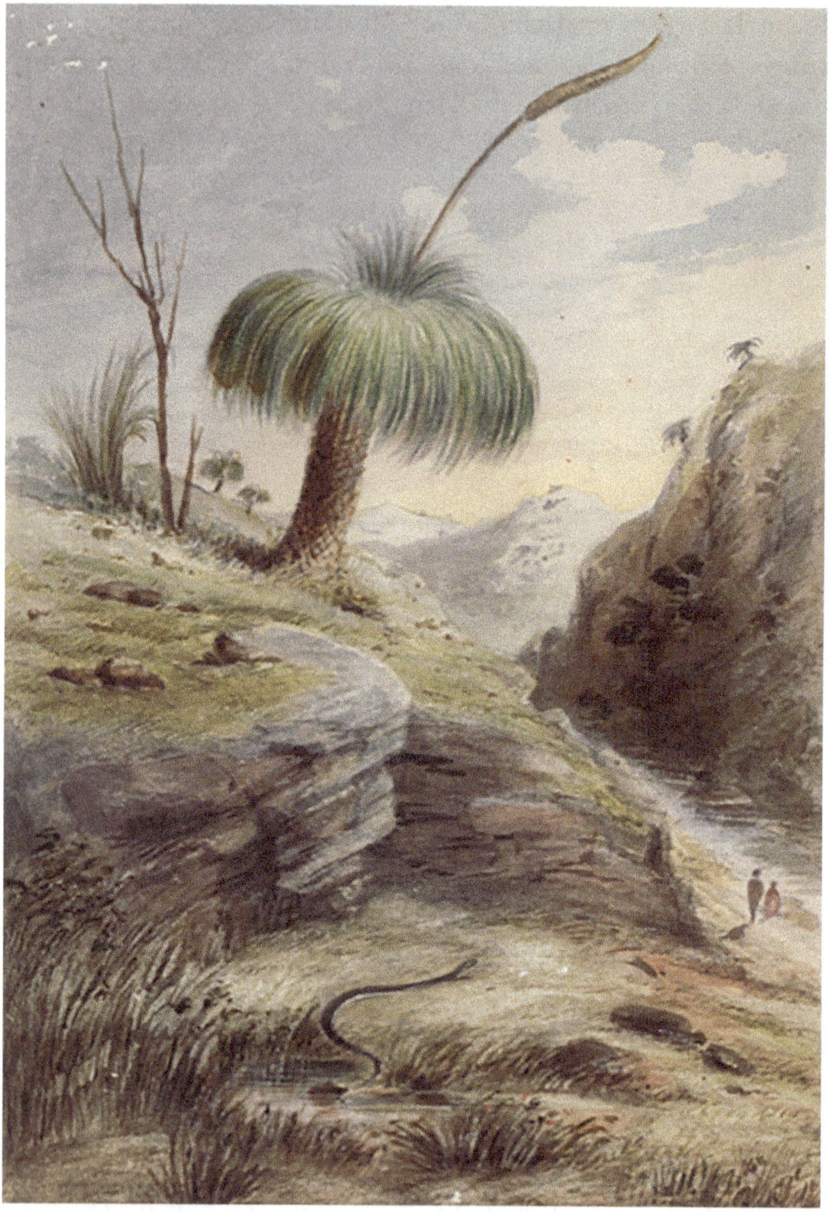

Grass Tree, South Australia, a view (Dixon Library, State Library of New South Wales, FL8803066)

Chapter 4—Native Australians

Another very great advantage on the part of the natives is the intimate knowledge they have of every nook and corner of the country they inhabit; does a shower of rain fall, they know the very rock where a little water is most likely to be collected, the very hole where it is longest retained...

—Edward John Eyre, 1845[39]

The first South Australians in the Adelaide region were the Kaurna (pronounced *Garna*) people. The area was known to them as Tandanya - the place of the red kangaroo. Part of the Kaurna people's spiritual connection to the country is Tjilbruke, an ancestral warrior, the keeper of fire and peace, who journeyed through the landscape in the Dreamtime leaving his mark where he rested. His tears became springs.

Evidence of human activity in South Australia dates back more than 65,000 years, with ceremonial sites and rock art in the Flinders Ranges, and flint mining activity and rock art in the Koonalda Cave on the Nullarbor Plain. Immediately prior to the British settlement of Australia, there were a large number of distinct societies and language groups in what is now South Australia.[40]

39 Edward John Eyre, *Journals of Expeditions of Discovery into Central Australia and Overland from Adelaide to King George's Sound, 1845*, Vol. 2, p.247, Adelaide, 1964.
40 Ben Marwick, Peter Hiscock, Marjorie Sullivan, Phillip Hughes, (July 2017), '*Landform boundary effects on Holocene forager landscape use in arid South Australia*', *Journal of Archaeological Science: Reports*, 19: 864–874.

The South Australia Act of 1834 proclaimed the state as follows:

> *Whereas that part of Australia which lies between the meridians of the one hundred and thirty-second and one hundred and forty-first degrees of east longitude and between the southern ocean and twenty-six degrees of south latitude together with the Islands adjacent thereto* **consists of waste and unoccupied lands** [41]*which are supposed to be fit for the purposes of colonization...*[42]

Despite this statement about unoccupied lands, the Letters Patent, which used the enabling provisions of the South Australia Act 1834 to fix the boundaries of the Province of South Australia, provided that:

> *nothing in those our Letters Patent shall affect or be construed to affect the rights of any Aboriginal Natives of the said Province to the actual occupation and enjoyment in their own Persons or in the Persons of their Descendants of any Lands therein now actually occupied or enjoyed by such Natives.*[43]

Although the patent guaranteed land rights under force of law for the Aboriginal inhabitants, it was ignored by the South Australian Company authorities and squatters. Despite strong reference to the rights of the native population in the initial proclamation by the governor, there were many conflicts in South Australia. Design writer Anne-Marie Willis believes this was inevitable:

> *Ethnocentrism leading to ethnocide infuses every circumstance of colonisation, including the colonisation of Australia by the British. The continent was claimed according to the doctrine of*

41 Bolding added by author to emphasise.
42 South Australia Act, or Foundation Act of 1834 (UK), p. 2.
43 Douglas Pike, *Paradise of Dissent: South Australia 1829–1857*, 2nd ed., Melbourne University Press, Melbourne, 1967.

'terra nullius' meaning the British had the right to claim any unoccupied territory...[44]

However, in the establishment of South Australia, Captain John Hindmarsh proclaimed Aboriginal people should have the same protection as the rest of 'His Majesty's Subjects'. This culminated in the employment of a 'Protector' of Aboriginal people, the first public service appointment in South Australia. In 1839, Matthew Moorhouse was appointed first full-time Protector, to promote understanding between settlers and Aboriginal people, to teach Aboriginal people 'civilised' living skills (reading, building houses, making clothes), and to preach Christianity. Missionaries began to school Aboriginal people. Ration stations were set up across the state, issuing small amounts of what was often poor quality flour, biscuits, tobacco and blankets to Aboriginal people. As early as 1838, a view was expressed by James Horton saying the Aboriginal people would be useful to the colonists, such as at harvest time:

... the blacks will be very useful, and for a cob of maize daily, you may engage a dozen of them to assist in pulling.[45]

By the time S. T. Gill arrived in 1839, the term *Terra Australia Nullius* prevailed, indicating there was land, virtually uninhabited, which could be distributed as the Crown pleased to settlers. Thus, settlers purchased land from the state, which was offered, regardless of Aboriginal occupation. Land was cleared for grazing and cattle herding, resulting in a decrease in native plant and animal-based food. Grazing animals contaminated waterholes which had provided invaluable fresh water. From the 1840s, many Aboriginal people were employed in labour and farming as porters and store assistants. Many of

44 Anne-Marie Willis, *Illusions of Identity, the Art of Nations, Hale & Ironmonger, 1993*, p.95.
45 James T. Horton, *Six Months in South Australia: with Some Account of Port Phillip and Portland Bay, in Australia* Felix, London, J. Cross, 1838, p.216 (NLA NK4126).

these people, however, were paid in rations, board, or promised wages (which were often never received). In Adelaide, they were allocated sections of the surrounding parklands and were forbidden to enter the city naked. In the far north of the state, it is well documented that the pastoral industry relied heavily on Aboriginal labour and would have had difficulty surviving without their contribution, yet reports document Aboriginal employees had very poor working and living conditions.

As stated previously, when S. T. Gill arrived, the local Aboriginal people in the immediate area were already depleted. Gill's early work in painting the *Seasons* includes Aboriginal people in the *Spring* and *Winter* paintings. In the former, there are two Aboriginal people by the river bank watching, and in the latter, he includes an Aboriginal group at a campfire in front of a wurley (traditional shelter). In the *Months* series of paintings, Gill includes two Aboriginal hunters on the skyline in the *June* watercolour. In these early paintings, the Aboriginal people appear as a record of their presence, much like the local flora and fauna. However, it's possible that in one of the images, Gill was contrasting hunting for food with hunting as a form of recreation (see image in Chapter 2). The Aboriginal people in this series look compliant, of no threat to the settlers, and possibly curious about what the white people are doing. These early paintings were a celebration of how the transplanted settler had been successful in taming the land and making it economically useful. This was in line with the prevailing view that the Aboriginal occupants of Australia had a lesser right to the land because they had failed to make it productive. The settlers were not capable of comprehending the Aboriginal notion of custodianship of land and the maintenance of its natural resources.

Gill had made contact with Edward John Eyre at Moorundie on the River Murray in 1841. Eyre was an English explorer for whom Lake Eyre and the Eyre Peninsula in South Australia are named. Emigrating from England for reasons of health, Eyre reached Australia in March 1833. As a sheep farmer, he became a pioneer 'overlander', driving stock from Sydney to Adelaide. He explored the desert northwest of Adelaide and, in the period June 1840–July 1841, made an extremely hazardous journey around the Great Australian Bight. On his return to Adelaide, Eyre wrote to Governor Sir George Gipps offering to lead an expedition from Moreton Bay to Port Essington; but instead, in October 1841, he accepted an appointment as resident magistrate and protector of Aborigines, with a salary of £300, at Moorundie, on the River Murray. There, he had notable success in developing a relationship with the Aboriginal people.

Eyre played an important role in successfully mediating between overlanders and local tribes in his district. For several years, he served as a magistrate and protector of Aborigines, whose language and customs he learned. The knowledge Eyre accumulated formed the basis of the *Account of the Manners and Customs of the Aborigines and the State of their Relations with Europeans*, which he published in his *Journals of Expeditions of Discovery into Central Australia and Overland from Adelaide to King George's Sound in the Years 1840-41* (London, 1845). In December 1844, Eyre was given leave and sailed for England, taking with him two Aboriginal boys to be educated in England at his expense. On the voyage, he prepared his journals for publication.

Gill's meeting with Eyre had an impact on his approach to the portrayal of Aboriginal people in his paintings. He frequently depicted them in a more sympathetic way in their natural state. His work includes paintings of inter-tribal warfare, corroborees, fishing, and burial and there is a watercolour incorporating Aboriginal people in an avenue of trees near Eyre's station at Moorundie.

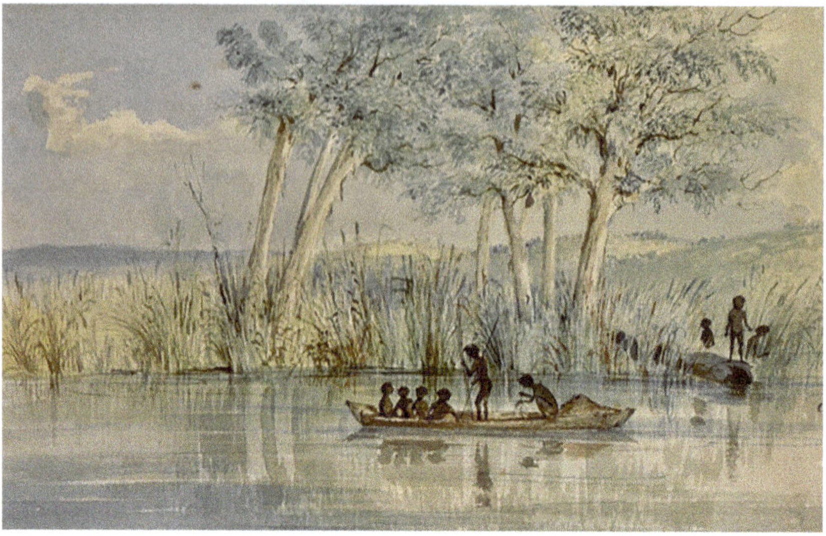

Australian Aborigines, spear and net fishing from a canoe and the riverbank, 1848 (Mitchell Library, State Library of New south Wales, FL3310977)

In 1846, Gill was part of an expedition to find new agricultural land in the remote area of South Australia, north-west of the Flinders Ranges. This was known as the Horrocks expedition (see Chapter 7). Gill's record of the expedition included several images of Aboriginal people, including their life style and aggression shown towards the explorers. In the latter encounters, it was clear the strangers were regarded as trespassers in territory that belonged to the Aboriginal inhabitants. According to Gill's diary, he and Horrocks felt threatened by the aggression shown towards them (see Appendix III).

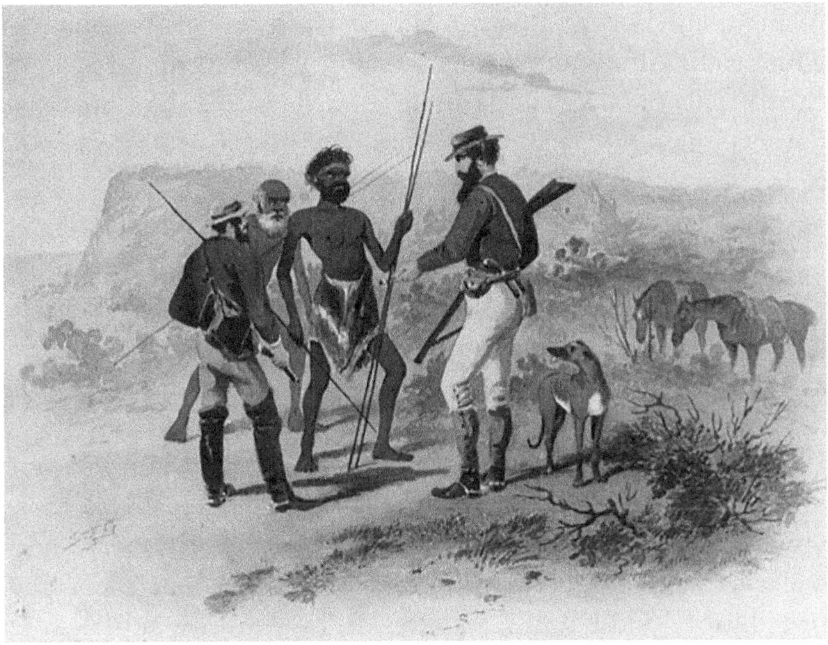

Encounter between Gill & Horrocks and two Aboriginal Men, 1846 (State Library of South Australia, B34382)

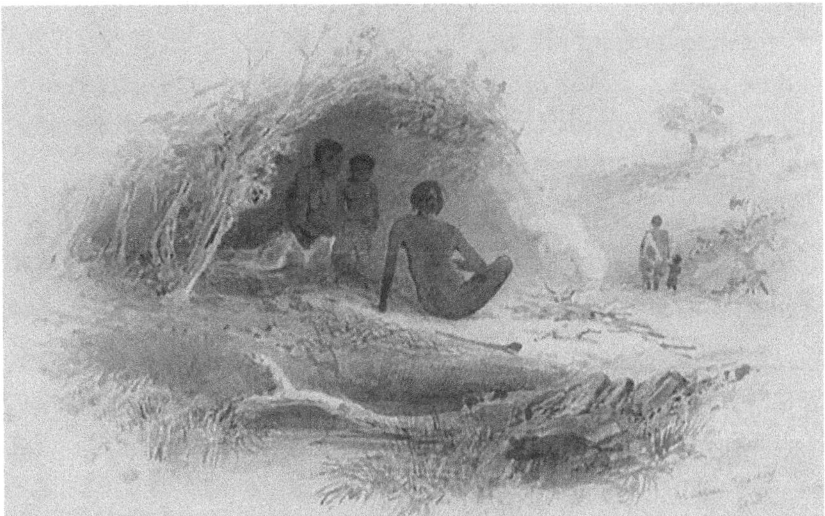

A Native Worley, 1846 (State Library of South Australia, B72816)

Humanities writer, Roslynn Haynes, believes Gill's encounters with hostile Aborigines during the Horrocks Expedition in 1846 changed his opinion and attitude towards them. She states that the encounters:

... changed Gill's earlier attitude towards Aborigines. Formerly he had supported the official line that they were harmless, well intentioned towards white settlers and even under some circumstances employable - afterwards, his depiction of Aborigines are decreasingly sympathetic.[46]

Looking at his work after the Horrocks Expedition, I have come to a different conclusion to that reached by Hynes. I believe he saw, for the first time, examples of a strong and proud people, and this caused him to think more deeply about them and their history and culture. As a result, his sensitive approach to painting Aboriginal people intensified in his work, not only in South Australia, but later in Victoria and New South Wales. As time went by, Gill saw them as the original Australians who had been dispossessed and relegated as outcasts in their own country. It's likely that for Gill, the occupation of the land of Australia had become a moral problem. This view may have been shared by people Gill spent time with, detected by an English visitor who observed:

...the right to Australia was a sore subject with many of the British settlers and they strive to satisfy their conscience in various ways.[47]

While showing that the relationship with the white people was not always harmonious, Gill also depicted the Aboriginal people as important to survival in rural Australia. Examples of this are

46 Roslynn D. Haynes, *Seeking the Centre: The Australian Desert in Literature, Art and Film*, Cambridge University Press, 1998, p 96.
47 Charles Griffith, *The Present State and Prospects of the Port Phillip District, Dublin, 1845*, p.170.

in the *Bush Mailman* and the *Squatter's Tiger.* In the former, it's clear the native 'assistant' is in fact the guide, and in the latter, the native horseman is demonstrating his prowess, skills and ability. These two watercolours appeared in *The Australian Sketchbook* in 1864 (see below and in Chapter 11).

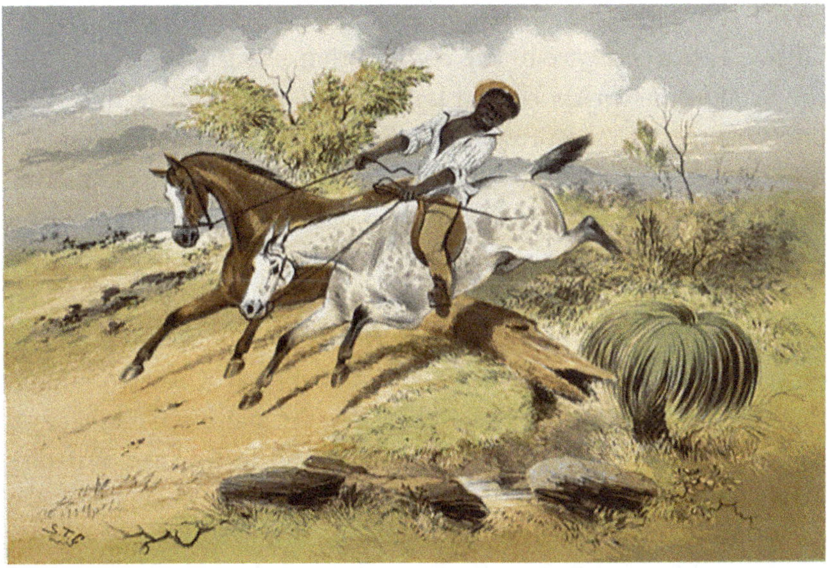

Squatter's Tiger (National Library of Australia, nla.obj-139535865)

Edward Wilson, after travelling to a number of the colonies, concluded the Aboriginal people had made a significant contribution to the maintenance and viability of farming and the cattle industry. He found their skills were often superior and as depicted in Gill's paintings, concluded that the station owners often depended on them for survival:

> *...fetching up horses, carrying messages, chopping wood, occasionally breaking in a colt, riding after cattle, and even sheepherding and shearing... some of the settlers speak in grateful terms of the assistance rendered to them from this quarter when the temptations of gold discovery carried off all other labour, and reduced stockowners to the brink of despair. At one station,*

> *sheep shearing was in progress, and there were more blacks than white men at work in the wool shed. The settler assured me that of the two the natives were the best workmen, being more careful in their shearing, and requiring less watching than the European shearers.*[48]

Gill was clearly aware of the conflict that occurred as a result of the occupation of Aboriginal land by the European settlers, and painting scenes to represent this may have been a problem for him. However, there are some dramatic Gill paintings depicting conflict. The most notable image comprised several similar scenes showing Aboriginal people sitting around a fire and being stalked by armed white men, which Gill called *The Avengers*. The first version of *The Avengers* was drawn in the late 1850s (a pencil on scraper board held by the National Library of Australia) and there is an early watercolour (held by the National Gallery of Victoria). A tinted lithograph can be found in Edward Wilson's *Rambles at the Antipodes* (1859). There was also a version in *Dr. Doyle's Sketches in Australia (1862-63)* and another created for Sydney publisher J.R. Clarke for the cover of a novel (1859).

All known versions show two or three white colonist settlers about to surprise and, according to the title of the image, take revenge upon a group of Aboriginal people gathered peacefully around a campfire. In practically all versions, the avengers are in the left foreground with the Aboriginal people around their campfire in the middle distance. The avengers have their guns ready, while the Aboriginal part of the scene is one of peace and tranquility. Gill used several forms of illumination to encircle the participants and create a sense of drama in an unfolding tragedy. The muted moonlight falling on the trees and shrubs conceals the hunters, who are stealthily advancing. The peaceful group of Aborigines sitting around the campfire becomes the focal point

48 Wilson, Edward. *Rambles at the Antipodes: A Series of Sketches of Moreton Bay, New Zealand, the Murray River and South Australia, and the Overland Route.* W.H. Smith & Son, London, 1859, pp.38-9.

of the drama. The version created for Clarke as a book cover is a vertical view to fit the cover and is the only version to include an Aboriginal mother nursing a baby. Although we do not know if violence occurred, the title implies Gill depicts the moment before vengeance is taken. He conveys the vulnerability of the Aboriginal people through these images.

Gill also painted two images that show Aboriginal people about to attack or following an attack on white people. In the first painting, entitled *Poor Harmless Natives* (Gill may have decided the title wasn't entirely appropriate because a later version of this scene is entitled *Attack on Store Dray*), several Aboriginal men are about to spear two unsuspecting merchants camping beside their dray. The second painting, entitled *The Marauders*, depicts Aboriginal people fleeing by night with stolen sheep, leaving a speared shepherd next to his campfire.

It's interesting to speculate on why Gill painted these scenes when his work was notable for depicting good relationships between blacks and whites (and also, sometimes using satire at the expense of the white subjects). Elizabeth Lawson[49] believes Gill was commissioned by publisher J.R. Clarke, while in Sydney, to produce a number of images for a second novel by Louisa Atkinson. The novel was intended to be an illustrated work with Gill providing the images. However, for some reason, Clarke changed his mind and decided to publish it in 1859 without illustrations, changing Gill's commission to only the cover design.

Lawson believes Gill had already painted two images to illustrate the story. These paintings were *The Avengers* and *The Marauders,* neither of which were now required by Clarke for the novel. The two scenes already prepared, while not used in the novel, were available for possible use in other publications. It is likely these scenes or variations on them were subsequently used in Doyle's sketchbook, Wilson's *Rambles at the Antipodes,*

49 Lawson, Elizabeth. *S. T. Gill's 'Avengers' the Gill-Clarke-Mason-Atkinson connection. The Latrobe Journal, No. 57,* Autumn 1996, p.8-11.

and Gill's own sketchbook. *The Attack on Store Dray* painting may have been painted specifically for Doyle's sketchbook, because he was seeking some drama to take to an English or Irish audience as part of his proposed presentations and lectures. Art historian and critic, Sasha Grishin, believes the three subjects (*The Avengers*, *Attack on Store Dray* and *The Marauders*) were produced as a set for Doyle's sketchbook and the subject matter:

> *...may well reflect Doyle's personal preferences and be geared to a British audience with its developed appetite for tales of danger and adventure set in exotic places*[50].

Clearly, property became a source of potential conflict between the settlers and the Aboriginal inhabitants of the continent. Property was used to define classes in Britain and crimes against property were dealt with severely, including by sentence of death. Most of those sent to the colonies as convicts had committed crimes against property. European customs were also regarded as superior, thus those pursued by the Aboriginal people were regarded as inferior. The Aboriginal and European notions of ownership of property were incompatible. On the one hand, there was the Aboriginal notion of communal responsibility for territories and the sharing of material resources among a group or clan; on the other hand, there was the European model of individual ownership of property and an economy based on money, in which land was bought and sold. The taking of livestock by Aboriginal people was interpreted as stealing property by the settlers. However, the Aboriginal people believed that animals could not be owned by an individual and as livestock was in abundance, it was fine to take one. When conflict broke out and Aboriginal people understood the great value white men attached to their livestock, the spearing of sheep and cattle was used as a tactic against the invaders, as well as a source of food to

50 Sasha Grishin, *Dr. Doyle's Sketches in Australia: A Collection of Prints from the Original Watercolours in the Mitchell Library*, Mitchell Library Press, 1993, p. 20.

replace the traditional sources which were displaced by pastoral development.

Starting in South Australia and continuing throughout most of his life in Australia, Gill painted a number of scenes where he was clearly showing the range of traditional activities that contributed to Aboriginal society, including their continuing lore and tribal law. For example, he created several corroboree scenes as a way of showing the importance of this ritual within their culture. Likewise, he painted native burial customs as another window into their cultural practices. One of Gill's most interesting and dramatic landscapes is *A Native Corroboree at Night*. In this painting (c. 1850) he switches roles, depicting the settler observing the ancient practices of the Aboriginal people, whereas in many other paintings he has the Aboriginals watching the settlers undertake some of their strange practices. The corroboree is lit by a full moon and a fire, creating a mysterious effect. The giant gums and vegetation add to the atmosphere in the painting.

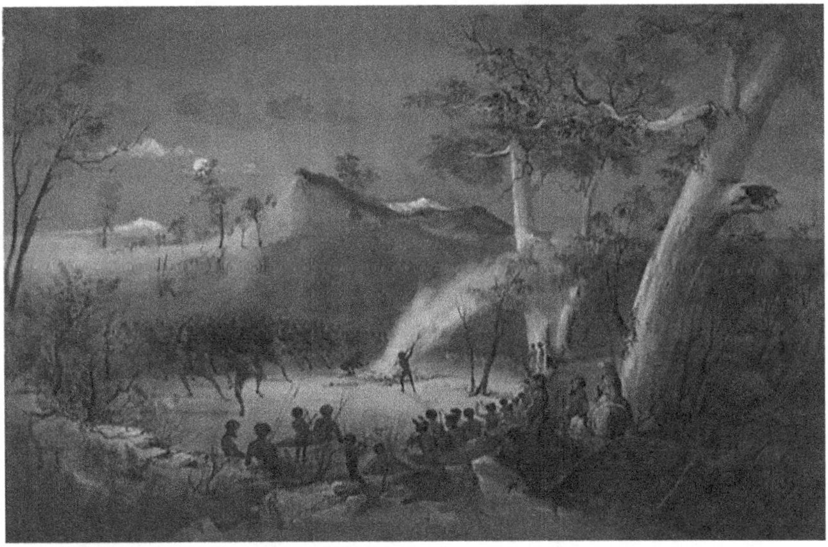

A Native Corroboree at Night (Australian National Library, nla.obj.134781715)

The way Gill captured this scene was similar to a record of a corroboree described by a traveller in 1845:

When I first witnessed one of these corroborees, I was greatly struck with the beauty and wildness of the scene. The mild rays of the moon shining on the dewy grass, the red glare of the fire in part illuminating the stems and foliage of the trees, but rendering the intervals of shadow deeper and more gloomy from the contrast, the painted figures of the natives, now brought into strong relief ...[51]

Corroborees at night were one of S. T. Gill's most popular subjects, which he continued to paint throughout his life. The earliest corroboree scene is dated 1847, but he would have clearly seen and recorded such ceremonies well before this time. Gill's handling of these scenes changed over time, with the focus in the last version (1871) being on the effect of the illumination on the landscape forms at night. Art historian, Caroline Clemente believes that:

Gill's handling of the watercolour medium in this nocturnal piece amounts to a virtuoso performance.[52]

As indicated above, it was not only S. T. Gill that took an interest in the corroboree and its significance to the Aboriginal people; but many colonists and visitors to the colonies mentioned it in their records of Aboriginal customs. Joseph Townsend recorded his impression in 1849 as follows:

During the fine summer nights, the blacks held frequent corroborees, dancing, by the light of the moon...which was accompanied by the clapping together of sticks.

51 Charles Griffith, *The Present State and Prospects of the Port Phillip District of New South Wales, William Curry and Company*, 1845, pp. 158-9.
52 Caroline Clemente, *Australian Watercolours 1802-1926*, National Gallery of Victoria, 1991, p.34.

In these dances they often imitate the motion of animals, the kangaroo for instance.[53]

After returning to Melbourne following his time in Sydney, Gill set to work in early 1864 to produce *The Australian Sketchbook*. By early 1865, the whole sketchbook was on sale. It's interesting that the majority of themes were divided between scenes of Aboriginal life and that of rural outback. Six of the images focused exclusively on incidents in the life of Aboriginal Australians, while a further eight scenes include Aboriginal people. Grishin commented that:

With 14 of the 24 images giving prominence to the Aboriginal presence in rural Australia, Gill appears eager to stress that Australia is a country that has a 'black history' and is far from the 'terra nullius' which once appeared in the English imagination. Although the relationship was not entirely harmonious... rural Australia often depended on Aboriginal people for its survival.[54]

Gill continued to explore race relations between Aboriginal and non-Aboriginal people, including the matter of discrimination, in his work, up until the time of his death. At times he used humour, satire and characterisations to mock the colonists while portraying the Aboriginal people with a sense of dignity. This is clear in his 1860 painting, *Native Dignity,* and in one of his last paintings produced in 1880, about three months before his death, *Grand Locomotive Race*, where he clearly wanted the viewer to be confronted with the issue of discrimination. In *Native Dignity* the Aboriginal couple are wearing their garments with defiance and pride. They are placed against a sign advertising 'Fashion' in an urban area, with a European couple wearing essentially the same ridiculous costume (the man in top hat and jacket and

53 Joseph Townsend, *Rambles and Observations in New South Wales, Chapman & Hill, London*, 1849, p. 98.
54 Sasha Grishin, *S. T. Gill and His Audiences,* National Library of Australia, State Library of Victoria, 2015, p.152.

the woman with hooped dress and parasol). Gill was possibly asking, who is mocking whom?

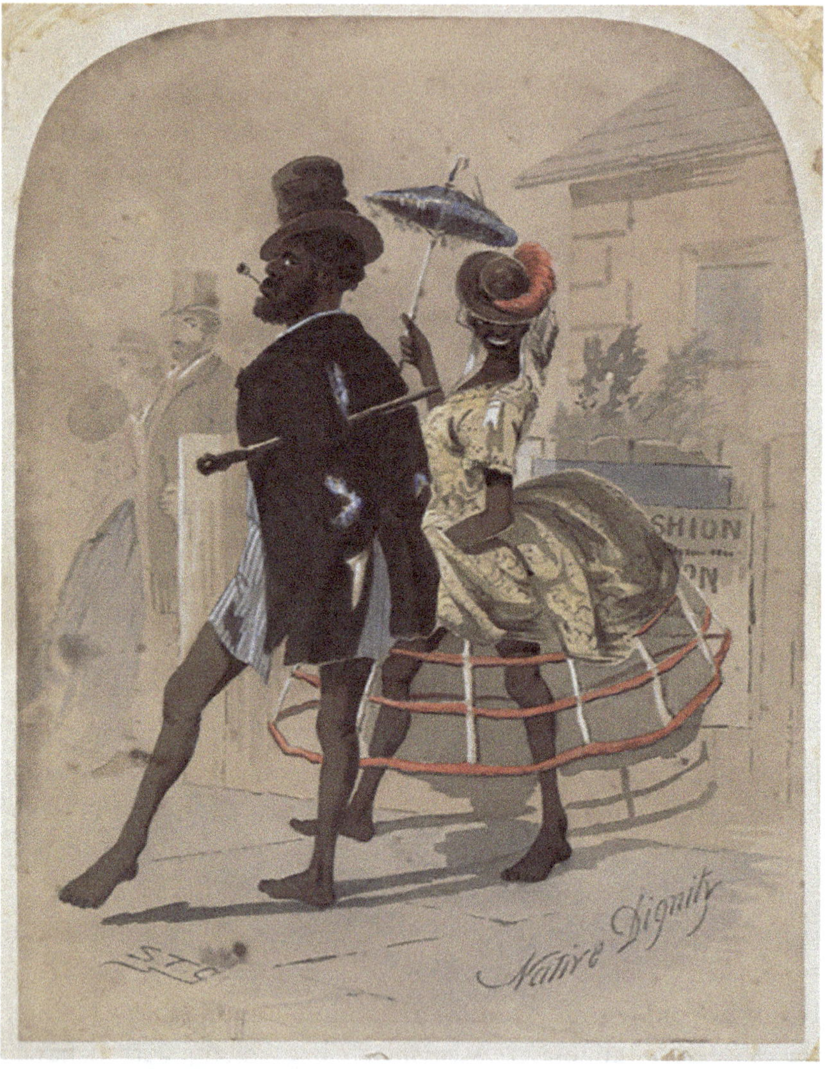

Native Dignity (State Library of New South Wales, FL3258595)

It seems Gill often produced two contrasting images about the same time, designed to be viewed in concert. Henry Skerritt points to two of these contrasting paintings from around 1860,

The Newly Arrived and *The Colonised*. The first of these shows well-dressed settlers being entertained with a dance performed by a smiling Aboriginal man and his son. One of the settlers in the painting appears to have a hand in his pocket, presumably looking for a tip. In the background, a row of neat brick houses suggests a well-established and thriving colony. The second shows a less affluent white pioneer couple in basic clothing (refinements and the neat cottages have disappeared) and an Aboriginal man and his son engaged in heavy lifting, helping them build their shack style home. Skerritt commented:

the life of carefree dancing as exotic amusement is replaced with a heavy burden, as they are roped into the hard labour of empire building.[55]

It's also possible that Gill is pointing to the degradation of the colonial settler resulting from the effects of frontier life. These two images could easily be interpreted as the before and after scenes, contrasting the carefree life of Australia's Aboriginal inhabitants before being colonised with their subjugation under colonisation. It is possible Gill's intention was to produce a portrait of dispossession.

S. T. Gill exhibited eleven paintings in 1866 in the Intercontinental Exhibition held in Melbourne, which were warmly commended in reviews. The *Herald* critic, on October 25, 1866, commented on the eleven works (at least half of which were Aboriginal subjects):

Mr. S. T. Gill's sketches are lively and his landscape picturesque. In…aboriginal subjects he is perhaps without equal in Australia.

The *Illustrated Australian News* on November 17 was also impressed:

55 Henry Skerritt, *Not-so-Marvelous Melbourne: Anxiety on the Urban Frontier in the Art of S. T. Gill*. Blog https://henryfskerritt.com/2015/05/01/not-so-marvellous-melbourne-anxiety-on-the-urban-frontier-in-the-art-of-st-gill/

Mr. S. T. Gill contributes a series of sketches on aboriginal subjects which he treats with unrivalled vivacity.

A more recent assessment by Caroline Clemente agrees that Gill's paintings of scenes of Aboriginal people are among his best work:

...his series of scenes of diggers and diggings have earned him a permanent place in the collective self-image of Australia. Some of the scenes of Aboriginal life, however, are among the most powerful and poignant works he executed.[56]

Gill's record of painting the Aboriginal people sympathetically was in contrast to most of his fellow English artists at that time, who painted with values and prejudices that devalued Aboriginal people. This contrasted with several European artists who came with a different mindset and did not view Aboriginal people as an obstacle to the growth and development of an English colony. They painted the Aboriginal people in a less judgmental manner. A good example is Austrian painter Eugene von Guerard, who demonstrated a general empathy with the Aborigines in his work.

While S. T. Gill continued painting on the subject of Aboriginal discrimination until his death, there were also settlers who attempted to advocate for and assist the Aboriginal people and speak out about the injustices they suffered. Historian Henry Reynolds, has undertaken extensive research and written an enormous amount on this matter and he believes that advocating on behalf of Aboriginal people often came at a price:

Some settlers/colonists stood up for the rights of the Aboriginals and demanded justice. Dissenters who challenged the ways of the frontier were boycotted, bullied and banished.[57]

56 Caroline Clemente, *Australian Watercolours 1802-1926*, National Gallery of Victoria, 1991, p. 4.
57 Henry Reynolds, *This Whispering in Our Hearts*, Allen and Unwin, 1998, p. xvi.

While there seems to be some evidence of encounters and exchanges between some colonial and Aboriginal artists,[58] I haven't found any evidence that Gill had any such cross-cultural art experience.

W.H. Smith, on his travels around some of the colonies, formed a very favourable impression of the Aboriginal people, but he was concerned about their future and hoped that there might be:

...an opportunity... of doing something to arrest the rapid destruction of a very interesting race, whose very good qualities have never been done justice to by the merciless invaders of their territory, and by the cruel neglect of our Colonial Government, will in all time to come remain one of the blackest spots upon the Australian escutcheon.[59]

Gill left us with a range of images of the Aboriginal people he encountered. Influenced at first by the prevailing white European views, he soon concluded that there was much more to the culture and history of these people. He may have struggled with painting the conflicts that occurred between the white settlers and the Aboriginal people, particularly over land. Gill painted images of attacks on white settlers by Aboriginals and attacks on the Aboriginals by people seeking revenge. It's not clear to me if he was trying to be even handed in painting the two opposing images. However, these events occurred in colonial Australia many times, and with Gill's images we sense something of the horror of what took place. As time went by, he saw the Aboriginal people as the original Australians who had been dispossessed and relegated to outcast status in their own country.

58 Andrew Sayers, Aboriginal Artists of the Nineteenth Century, Oxford University Press, 1997.
59 W. H. Smith, *Rambles at the Antipodes: A Series of Sketches of Moreton Bay, New Zealand, the Murray River and South Australia and the Overland Route*, W.H. Smith & Son, London, 1859, p.41.

Chapter 5—
Mining in South Australia 1840-51

Have you not heard of the Monster Mine?
There's never a man to be got to dine,
There's never a clerk who will pen a line,
At my behest or thine,
They are all gone to the houseless North
To gaze on the Monster Mine.[60]

Australia's first metal mines were discovered and developed in the last of the colonies to be settled: South Australia. The first mineral which attracted the attention of the early settlers in South Australia was not copper or gold, but silver. Two Cornishmen discovered a vein of silver-lead at Glen Osmond on the outskirts of Adelaide. The find was reported in the *Southern Australian* on September 29, 1840:

On Saturday last a specimen of lead ore picked up in the Mount Lofty Ranges was brought into our office for inspection, the yield of pure metal from which is, we understand, at the rate of 80%. The portion of silver this ore contains has not yet been

60 J. B. Austin, *The Mines of South Australia, Rigby, Adelaide*, 1863, p. 22 (contemporary verse composed after the Burra Burra discovery).

heard. The parties who made the discovery are practical miners and inform us that the vein from which this is taken is very rich and exceeds one mile in length.

In March 1841, the South Australian Mining Association was formed, the first South Australian mining prospectus was issued and mining at Australia's first mine, the Wheal Gawler, commenced. A second mine, Wheal Watkins, was discovered on the adjacent property in 1841 and was developed in 1843 (wheal is a term traditionally used in Cornwall to denote a mine). The Cornish were among those who emigrated to the colony seeking civil and religious freedom, and they came from the world's centre of metal mining. Hence, they knew minerals and how to work the mines.

It is not surprising South Australia was the first colony to discover and develop mineral deposits so soon after settlement, due to the mineral lodes being so close to the settlement of Adelaide. The foothills of the Mount Lofty Ranges were within walking distance, and the people of Adelaide often explored the area.

Traditional Cornish methods were used in the mines. Tutworkers (men who worked on non-productive but necessary tasks underground, at a fixed price per fathom of ground) sank shafts and drove the levels; they were paid by the amount of ground mined and not by its value. The tributers (skilled sub-contractors who were paid according to the value of ore they extracted and sent to the surface) developed and mined the stopes (large underground rooms created by the excavation of ore). They were the experts who knew minerals and could pick rich ore. The language and culture around South Australian mines was thus emphatically Cornish. Ore was manually broken, bagged and shipped to smelters in Wales as the first mineral export from Australia. Shipping accounted for more than half the costs, and in 1849, Glen Osmond Union Mining Co constructed one of the first smelters in the state. Its closure in 1851 meant that very little ore was actually smelted there.

These discoveries occurred at a time when the economy in South Australia was severely depressed. Development in Adelaide had stopped in its tracks and the worsening situation was not helped when between October 1839 and December 1840, expenditure in the colony was more than four times greater than the revenue.[61]

The discovery of a copper-bearing outcrop at Kapunda in 1842 was economically more important to the relatively new colony than silver. Mining commenced in 1844 and ore was shipped to Wales. Further major discoveries were made at Burra in 1845 in the form of two large outcrops a few miles apart.

The two separate discoveries of copper mineralisation at Burra led to a scramble for land. After government intervention, two mining companies were formed to mine what looked like rich ore at both locations. The northern section, developed by the South Australian Mining Association, proved to be the more profitable mine and became the largest mine in Australia for the first ten years of its life. It supplied five per cent of the world's copper for 15 years, producing a total of 50,000 tons of the metal. It was difficult for South Australia to attract new emigrants when its primary wealth was a cluster of farms and a number of struggling sheep runs. The discovery of copper bred new hope.

The opening of the Burra Burra mine signalled the start of a real copper bonanza. After one year, the mine had one and a half miles of underground galleries. Rich ore was hauled up many shafts by horses. The Burra Burra mine was known throughout the colonies as the Monster Mine. All ore from Burra Burra had to be carted 90 miles to Adelaide and shipped across the world to Welsh smelters. The South Australian Mining Association was a stern but benevolent employer; they established a mining community with some of the characteristics of a small welfare

61 G. H. Pitt, *The Crisis of 1841: Its Causes and Consequences, South Australiana,, Vol XI no.* 2, 1972.

state. The company built rows of cottages with stone walls and earthen floors for its men and imposed compulsory social insurance at sixpence a week to cover a health scheme. The main objective of the company's benevolence was to serve the interests of the company rather than the workforce. The main company town was Kooringa.

The Aboriginal people from that area were from the Ngadjuri tribe. They generally kept their distance from the mining activity and the settlements. The name of the main town, Kooringa, came from an Aboriginal word which meant 'place of the she-oaks'.

The South Australian copper 'rushes' were mainly to purchase mineral land and mining shares rather than rushes to new mineral fields. Copper and lead required mining companies and capital to develop them and smelting works to turn the mineral into saleable metal. They also needed people with experience and expertise to mine them. There was a 'rush' of Cornish miners to the South Australian copper fields.

In 1845, Gill painted a watercolour of each of the three mines: Glen Osmond, Kapunda and Burra Burra. Each of the paintings show surface operations, including a number of workers. It appears these three paintings were commissioned by James Allen to illustrate the mining boom in South Australia for his lecture tour of Great Britain.

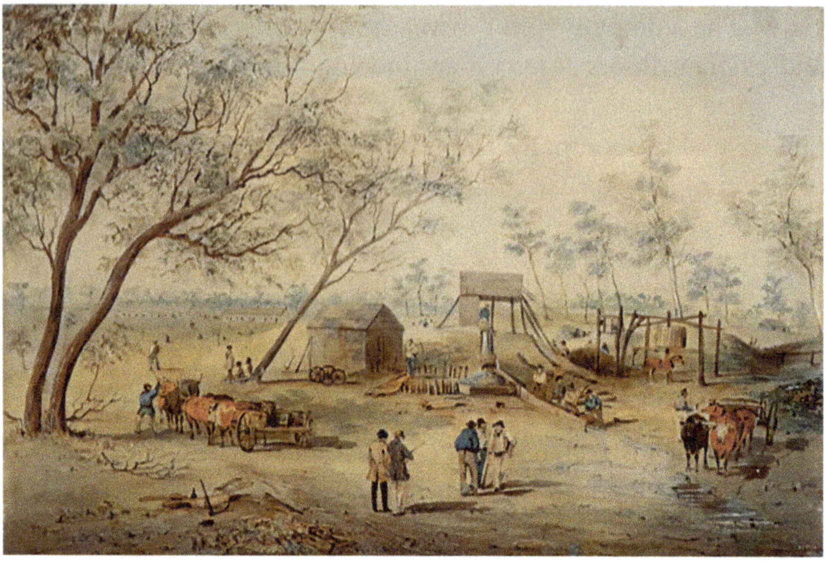

Kapunda Mine 1845
(Dixon Library, State Library of New South Wales, FL8815009)

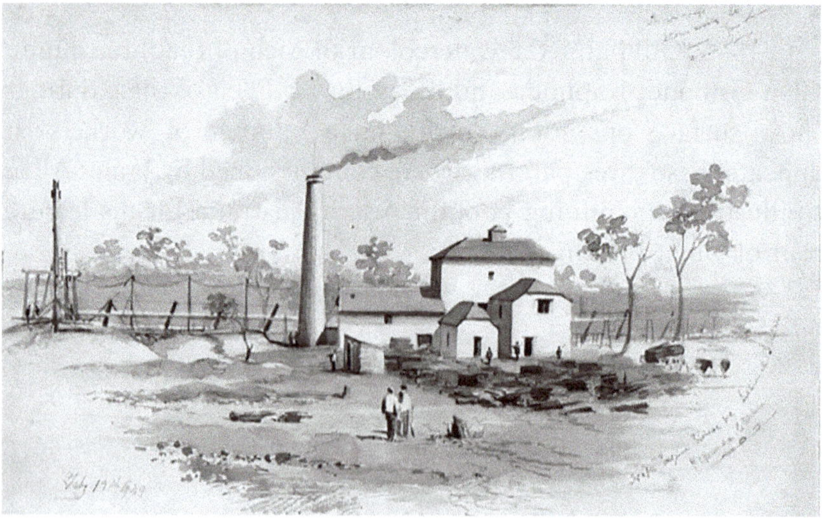

Kapunda Mine Works (State Library of South Australia)

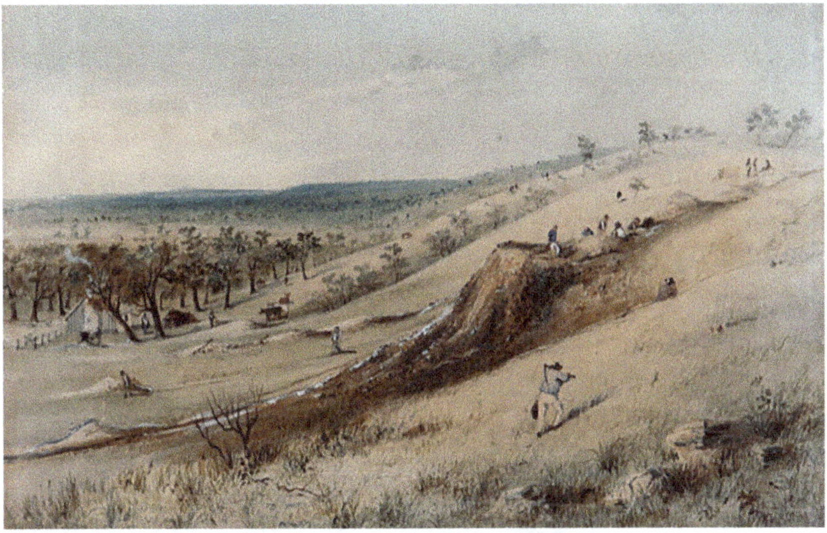

Glen Osmond Mine 1845 (State Library of Victoria)

These discoveries really ushered in Australia's first mining era, and they brought new immigrants to the colony, more capital, and generally had a positive effect on economic growth. Cornish miners and their families poured into South Australia to take part in the great copper boom. They brought with them their mining expertise to help extract the rich ore that gave South Australia the title of *The Copper Kingdom* by virtue of mines of world significance. While the Cornish were a major part of the South Australian mining workforce, there were also a significant number of German Lutherans, and even some Irish working in the mines and associated activities. The *South Australian Register,* in a report on 24 October 1846, was optimistic about the quality of the copper and the future of mining in the colony:

A stone taken promiscuously, from a quantity shipped per the Taglioni, from the Burra Burra Mine, was found on assay to yield 47 per cent. We do not hazard a random assertion, when we say, that the discoveries already made in South Australia (irrespective of future discoveries, which are in the highest degree probable), will affect the copper trade throughout the world. This is for the present encouraging enough, and such was the impression produced, by the facts which had leaked out on Saturday, that the shares were again going beyond the £100 quotation. The ores from Kapunda were more than sustaining their high repute; and the samples received from the South Australian Company's mine were spoken of in the most encouraging terms. Other accounts concur as to the estimation in which the copper and lead of the colony are held in England; and the ores of both metals from Rapid Bay participate in this high repute. The general impression in England was that the means of laying down railways of our own hard timber to the northern mines would soon be forthcoming. The Barossa Range Mining Company had been finally organised in England, and operations are to be forthwith commenced.

As the mines progressively became deeper, more sophisticated water extraction equipment was required. In 1848, the first Cornish engine house arrived in the colony and was constructed to handle the water from underground.

S. T. Gill was commissioned by the South Australian Mining Association to paint a series of watercolours at two guineas a painting. The association specified that the paintings were to comprise four of the Burra Burra underground operations, two surface views, and one of the township of Kooringa. All seven paintings were done in 1847. They were the subject of comment in the *South Australian Register* on 14 August 1847:

Mr Gill the artist has made seven interesting drawings at the Burra Burra Mines ... The drawings...have been so much admired for their truthfulness and the artistical talent displayed, that several sets of copies have been ordered from the artist by the Burra Burra proprietors.

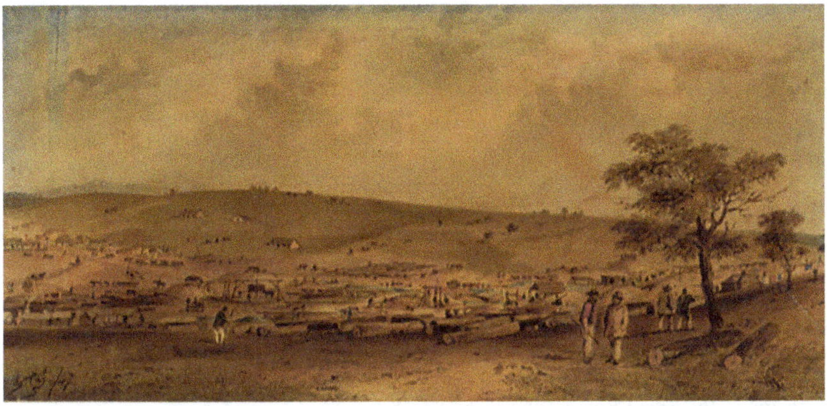

The Burra Burra Mine 1847
(Mitchell Library, State Library of New South Wales, FL3269731)

This panorama of the mine, facing towards the south-west, is a busy scene, with the pumping engine house and its flue the central and main feature of the painting. The launder (trough) from the engine house is supported by timber pylons and extends to the hill on the left, where water is discharged. A couple with a child are placed in the middle foreground and a number of horse whims (used for hauling material to the surface) are visible in the scene. A powder magazine is located in the far left of the painting. This painting is typical Gill style, with plenty of detail for the viewer to explore.

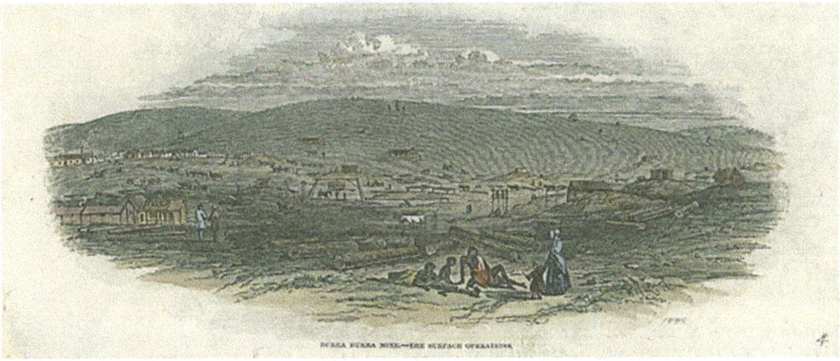

Burra Burra Mine - the Surface Operations[62]

62 Hand-coloured engraving made from a 1847 watercolour by S. T. Gill for use in the *Illustrated London News*, December 2, 1848.

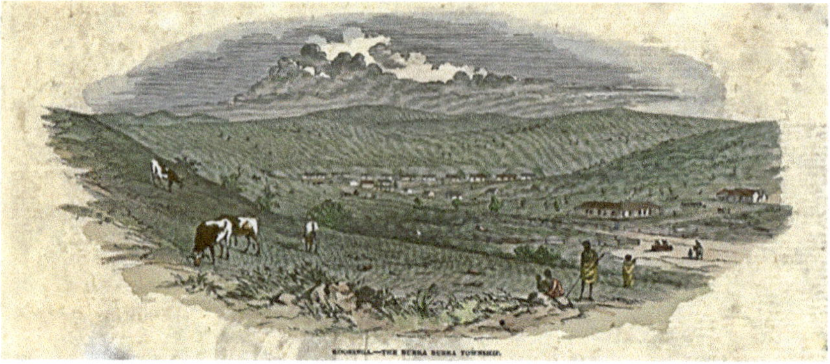

Kooringa - the Burra Burra Township 1847[63]

The four subterranean paintings were challenging and are very valuable, as they dramatically illustrate the underground life of the miners:

... you descend and find it is only twenty fathoms; you follow on through galleries dotted with copper, down little shafted passages and into great vaults and chambers, and caverns like Vulcan's forge, where men are seen with candles in their hats or stuck on rocks, hewing away at the most splendid copper ores that eyes have ever beheld.[64]

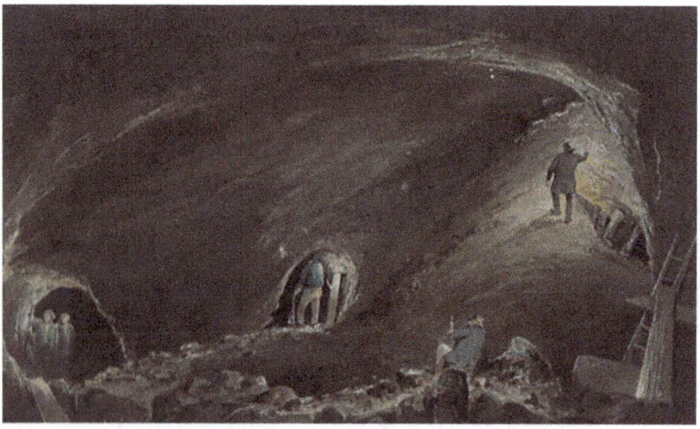

Leading from Stokes to Paxton's Lode, Burra Burra, 1847 (National Library of Australia, nla.obj-134373231)

63 Ibid.
64 *South Australian News*, London, July 1, 1848, p.248a.

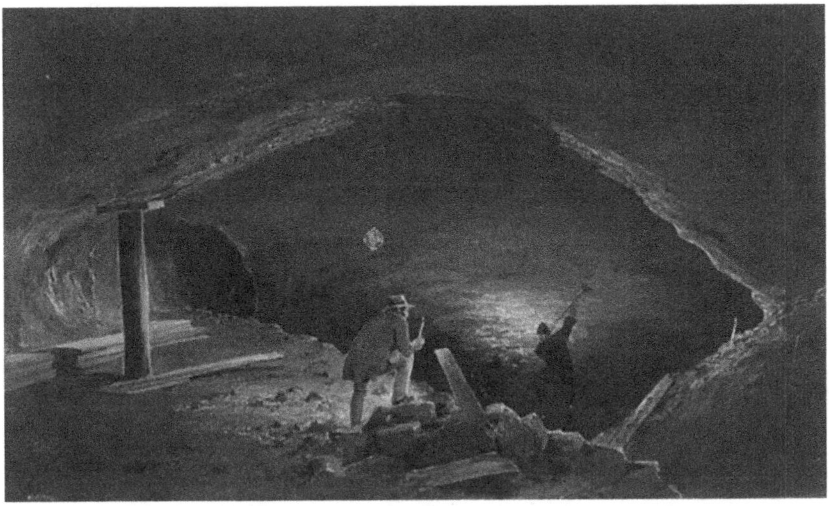

The opening of lode in Stokes' air-hole, 1847
(National Library of Australia, nla.obj.-134373070)

Some of S. T. Gill's Burra Burra pictures were reproduced, unacknowledged, in the *Illustrated London News* at the end of 1848.

Gill developed an interest in and painted the bullocks and their teams and drays, without which the mines would not have been able to operate. By 1848, more than 1200 bullock-drays were on the road, taking supplies to the mines and returning with ore to Port Adelaide. Transport was a nightmare for the Burra company. In winter, the tracks were a bog and almost impassable for heavy drays.

The bullock drivers often felt unappreciated and undervalued, as illustrated in a letter to the *South Australian Register* on 14 October 1848, by a teamster protesting against the intention to lower wages:

Does the poor bullock-driver, this poor 'pariah' of Australian society, does he ever have any rest? Look at him on the road, belted and bearded, covered with dust and perspiration. Where does he get a comfortable meal, a wash, a shave or a Sabbath?

Perhaps he has to walk a hundred miles to find lost bullocks.

By 1850, South Australia was the third largest copper producer in the world; the value of mineral exports exceeded wool and wheat combined and its mines had added financial stability to an almost bankrupt colony.[65] Directly or indirectly, at least during the period from 1845 to 1851, South Australian mining and smelting probably employed most of the adult population. There were some 49 mines (38 mining copper) in operation by 1850. These mineral deposits had a profound effect on settlement in the new colony. Land was surveyed for mineral tenements, mining townships, and agricultural purposes. Basic road networks were established during this period to cart ore to Port Adelaide for shipment to Wales, and to deliver heavy machinery and supplies to the mines.

By 1851, there were some 5,000 people living in the five townships associated with the Burra Burra operation. Many of the mine-tradesmen, artisans, and skilled underground miners were accommodated in the rented company homes in Kooringa, and the remainder in Redruth, Aberdeen, Hampton and other nearby villages. In 1850, Gill had been asked to produce further views of Kooringa and the surface operations at Burra Burra. The paintings were again undertaken for the South Australian Mining Association to record the development that had taken place since 1847. A feature of this work was the central placement of the large smelter, which was established in 1849 and had nineteen furnaces.

65 Ian Ahul and Denis Marfleet, *Australia's Earliest Mining Era, South Australia 1841-1851*, Rigby, 1975, p.10.

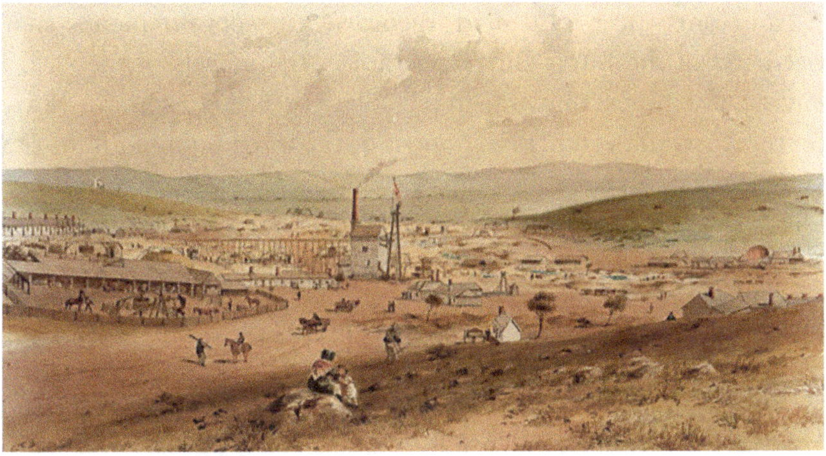

Burra Burra Mine, South Australia, showing chief portion of surface operation 1850 (National Library of Australia, nla.obj-134355627)

The Burra Creek was subject to flooding, and 1851 was a particularly bad year for flooding and dislocation for the people of the area. Extremely bad floods occurred in May, causing major problems in Kooringa, as reported in the *South Australian Register* on 15 May 1851:

The Creek presents a fearful sight; the water rose in half an hour to an unprecedented height, and those occupying huts excavated in its banks are at this moment floating their furniture out of the holes they have lived in. Livestock, in the shape of fowls, ducks and pigs, are going down the Creek; and men are seen carrying little pigs, women and children in all directions…

There were further and even more severe floods in June that year. When not in flood, the creek became a source of disease. The original clear waters of the creek became sluggish with debris from mining and rubbish, and sewerage found its way into the creek. There were outbreaks of illness resulting in some deaths from such diseases as dysentery, typhus, and typhoid fever.

Not long after Gill had recorded the developments that occurred in the Burra Burra operation, the wheels of the steam engine, the largest machine in the colony, ceased to spin. In 1851, South Australian miners and most of the male population of the colony joined the rush to the Victorian goldfields. By the end of 1852, mining operations had been suspended at Kapunda and Burra Burra and the extraction of ore from all South Australian mines had virtually ceased. S. T. Gill packed his bags and joined the exodus to the goldfields of Victoria. He left a very important record of the days when 'Copper was King' in South Australia.

The people of South Australia were alarmed by the exodus of so many men to the Victorian goldfields. This feeling was recorded by nineteenth-century diarist Emily Clarke:

We hear nothing but gold. People are leaving here by the hundreds and houses and land are being sold for half value. Trade is very bad, shopkeepers are in despair... Fifty went from Kensington last week and there are no less than twelve vessels advertised to sail for Melbourne.[66]

As in most of the states, the exodus of males from South Australia to the Victorian goldfields decimated the labour force and had an enormous impact, not only on mining but also rural industries. On January 19, 1852, the *South Australian Register* lamented:

...It is sufficient to repeat, that in losing the whole of our able-bodied population, we lose the very bone and sinew of the colony... It is computed that upwards of 8,000 persons have already left the colony for the gold-diggings, and of those that remain there are but few who do not intend to go... Nothing, we fear, will now stop this emigration but the discovery of prolific goldfields within our own territory.

66 Emily Clarke, cited in Elizabeth Kwan, *Living in South Australia: A Social History, Vol. 1*, SA Government Printer, 1987, p.44.

To assist the ailing economy, Adelaide sent shiploads of flour and wheat to Melbourne to feed the diggers. In March 1852, South Australia implemented a scheme to escort gold from the Mount Alexander diggings 400 miles to Adelaide, where it was cast into ingots. In less than two years, £1.2 million of gold was transported to Adelaide under police escort. While these measures helped the economy, they were no substitute for the discovery of gold locally. Some of the locals felt there must be rich gold in the Adelaide hills.

After the Victorian gold rushes, and the return to South Australia of experienced, but mostly unsuccessful diggers, copper and silver mines were in production again within a short time and some small deposits of gold were discovered. Later, there were many mines in the Flinders Ranges. The great copper mines at Burra Burra and Kapunda reopened and resumed operations after 1856. However, their best ore had been exhausted by the 1860s, but as they were winding down, even larger and richer deposits were being discovered.

It was across the water from Adelaide on Yorke Peninsula, where these large deposits of rich copper ore were located. The first mine to open, known as Wallaroo, was only five miles from water and a port, which became known as Port Wallaroo. Ships were able to anchor offshore and deliver coal from Newcastle as well as Cornish miners and Welsh smelter men. By 1861, the chimneys of the copper smelters were a beacon to the ships. A further discovery of very rich ore led to the opening of the Moonta mine. The ore for both mines was treated at the Wallaroo smelters, which, by 1866, had thirty-six furnaces. By 1872-3 Wallaroo employed around 1000 men and Moonta over 1400. A triangle of copper towns developed on the peninsula; Moonta and Kadina were the biggest and probably the largest towns outside Adelaide. Both mines were very profitable and the Moonta mine became the first Australian mine to pay a million in dividends to its shareholders. These mines provided work, stability and settlement, particularly in the arid north of South Australia.

By the 1870s, South Australia had replaced Cornwall as the largest copper region in the British Empire. Once more, copper had revived the economy and South Australia again became the copper colony.

Historian Geoffrey Blainey concluded, at that time in the history of the colony of South Australia, copper was extremely important:

To the colony copper was like a huge flywheel, generating wealth and activity.[67]

Clearly, the story of mining in early South Australia was a very significant part of the state's and indeed Australian history. We were fortunate that S. T. Gill was there to capture the people, places, processes and the development that took place on the surface and underground.

67 Geoffrey Blainey, *The Rush that Never Ended: A History of Australian Mining*, Melbourne University Press, 1963, p.125.

Chapter 6—
Charles Sturt's Final Expedition 1843

In the direction I was about to proceed, nothing was to be seen but the gloomy stone-clad plain,... Ignorant of the existence of a similar geographical feature in any other part of the world, I was at a loss to divine its nature.

—Captain Charles Sturt, 1849[68]

In December 1826, after a brief sojourn in England following duties in France, Charles Sturt embarked with a detachment of his regiment in the *Mariner* in charge of convicts for New South Wales and arrived at Sydney on 23 May 1827. He showed a keen interest in exploring the as-yet unmapped country and its rivers. With Governor Darling's approval, he set out to solve its mysteries. In 1828, while hoping to find a great inland sea, he discovered the Darling River and in January 1830, the Murray River, which he followed until he reached the location of present day Goolwa, South Australia.

With the assistance of the local Aborigines, Sturt and his party progressed to reach the Murray mouth. They had hoped to get

68 Charles Sturt, *Narrative of an Expedition into Central Australia Performed Under the Authority of Her Majesty's Government During the Years 1844, 5 and 6, Together With a Notice of the Province of South Australia in 1847*, Corkwood Press, 2001. The comment was a description of an immense flat plain of gibber stones, later named Sturt's Stony Desert.

their boat out into the sea but were unable to, and Sturt had to walk across the dunes to see the river flowing into the ocean. However, he had seen enough good land, and it was his report of this journey that later influenced the decision in England to establish the Colony of South Australia. After his exploring, Sturt served for a short time as Commander on Norfolk Island before returning to England, where he left the army and married Charlotte Greene in 1834.

In 1835, Sturt returned to New South Wales to take up 5,000 acres of land granted to him for his military service. He failed as a farmer, and the overlanding of cattle to the newly established colony of South Australia in 1838 was not a financial success either. Moving large numbers of cattle overland became common practice in and between the colonies. This was later observed and recorded by Gill during his movement about the colonies of South Australia and Victoria. Gill returned many times to this subject and made a number of paintings of the overlanders. This was possibly a statement by him about his evolving philosophy and appreciation of rural life in the colonies. The painting below is typical of Gill's overlander paintings, with the men sitting loosely in the saddle as they stop to water their horses; one lights his pipe, while the cattle, pack horse, and provisions wagon move slowly in the background.

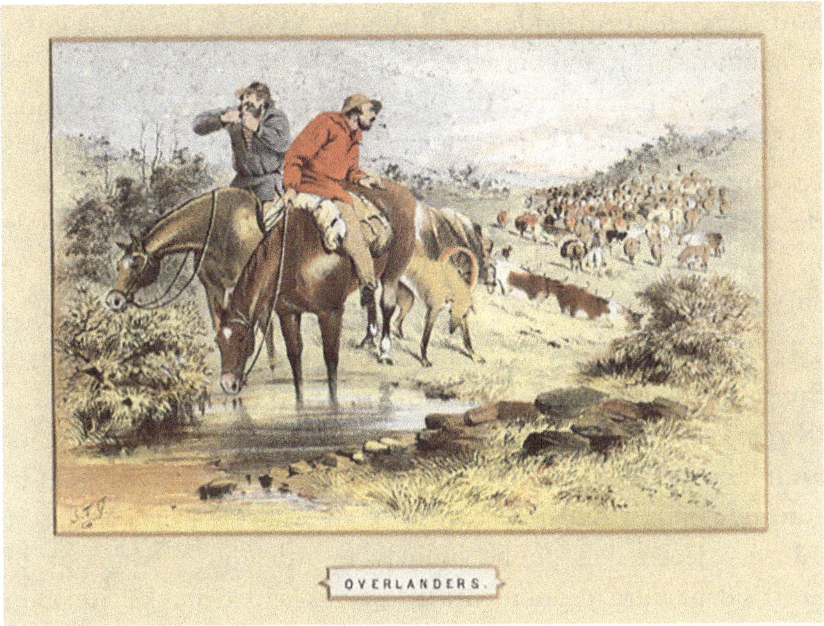

Overlanders (State Library of Victoria)

While Gill was eulogising the stock riders in his overlander paintings, recognising the long distances they travelled in remote parts of the colonies, Adam Lindsay Gordon was writing bush ballads describing the life of the stock rider in glowing terms:

'Twas merry in the glowing morn, among the gleaming grass,
To wander as we've wandered many a mile,
And blow the cool tobacco cloud, and watch the white wreaths pass,
Sitting loosely in the saddle all the while.
'Twas merry 'mid the Blackwoods, when we spied the station roofs,
To wheel the wild scrub cattle at the yard,
With a running fire of stockwhips and a fiery run of hoofs;
Oh! the hardest day was never then too hard![69]

69 From *The Sick Stockrider, Poems of Adam Lindsay Gordon*, Melbourne, 1880.

Sturt arrived in Adelaide on 28 August 1838, and was the guest of honour at a special dinner on September 7. On the eleventh, he left for the Murray River and Lake Alexandrina with T. B. and G. Strangways and Henry Inman. During his absence, Sturt was appointed a Justice of the Peace. On their return, Sturt wrote a detailed report, which was published in the local papers. While in Adelaide, he bought several blocks of land and did some surveying for the South Australian Company.

In 1843, having settled his family at the Reed Beds, Grange, Sturt set out on another exploration. This time, he was determined to finally settle the debate about the existence of an inland sea in the centre of Australia. His party assembled in Adelaide and included John McDouall Stuart. Saturday August 10 was declared a public holiday in Adelaide, in honour of Sturt's departure. A public breakfast was held at Stocks' Stores in Grenfell Street, attended by leading citizens, including Governor Grey. The procession departed at 2.00 P.M. and proceeded down King William Street and out along the Great North Road.

S. T. Gill was on hand to capture the excitement and atmosphere of the occasion. He recorded the activities in three watercolour paintings and a wash drawing of the expedition departing. One of the paintings shows the explorers, dressed in formal suit and top hat, mounted on a white horse, accompanied by citizens, turning from Grenfell Street north into King William Street (there was also a second smaller version of this painting). A second painting shows the procession, led by Sturt and Governor Grey, moving north along King William Street (viewed from the north-west corner of Hindley Street). Gill included lots of activity and movement in the foreground, with Sturt and his party relegated to the middle distance. Without the inclusion of life, movement, and a range of people by Gill, the event would otherwise have been depicted as a monotonous parade. Another of Gill's works recording the event shows a bullock dray transporting the boat that was to be used on the inland sea.

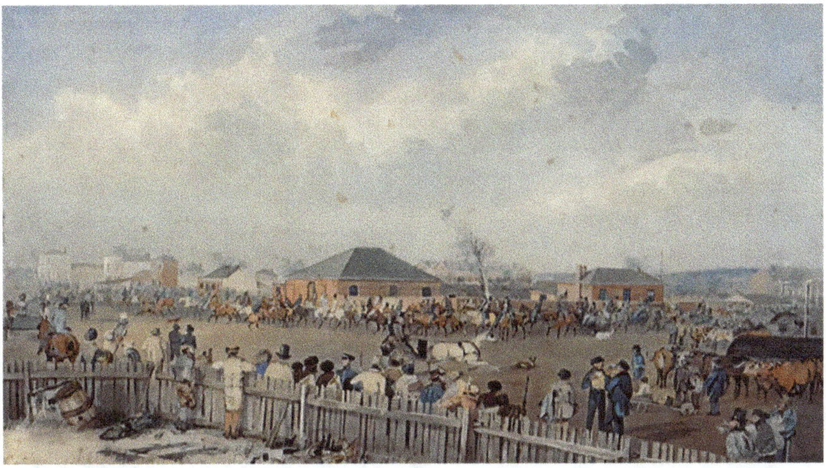

Sturt's Overland Expedition Departing, South Corner of Currie and King William Streets (National Library of Australia, nla.obj-135642533)

Art critic John McDonald, felt this watercolour of Gill's demonstrated his unique style and ability to create a sense of the viewer being present and part of the activity, familiar with the things of everyday life:

Gill accumulates apparently trivial detail in a way that downplays the great moment of the explorers departure. We watch the action from behind a paling fence, where we keep company with a broken carriage wheel, a barrel and a basket of empty wine bottles. People talk amongst themselves, dogs scamper around the horses' hooves, the ambience is festive and good humoured. And so it is with almost all Gill's work... [70]

70 John McDonald, *Arts of Australia, Vol. 1*, Pan Macmillan, 2008, p. 158.

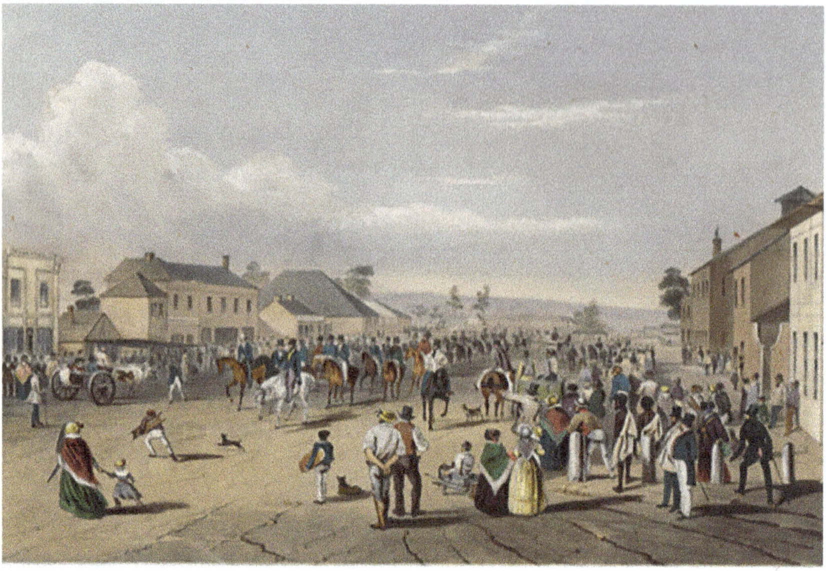

Sturt's Overland Expedition Departing North Along King William Street (State Library of South Australia, B15276/54)

Sturt left Adelaide with fifteen men, six drays, a boat and 200 sheep. He and some of the party journeyed as far as Dry Creek and then returned to Adelaide (time to change out of the formal attire) while the slow-moving drays continued. In eight days, the party reached Moorundie and then followed the Murray River to its junction with the Darling, and up the Darling to the vicinity of Lake Cawndilla, where they camped for two months, making several scouting expeditions into and beyond the Barrier Range.

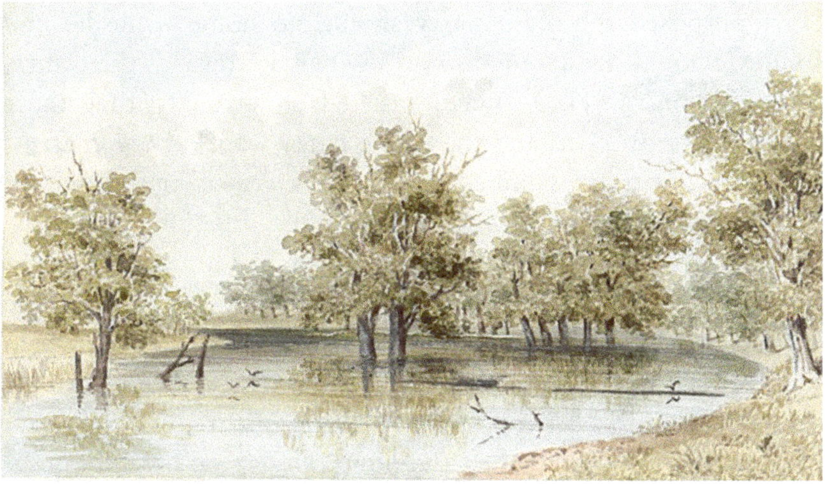

Anna—branch of the Darling
(National Library of Australia, nla.obj.-134794925)

In December, the party was short of water and some of the men showed signs of scurvy, but they moved further north into the Grey Range. There they made a camp on permanent water, fortunately found at Depot Glen on Preservation Creek. By that time, summer heat had dried up all other water within reach, and from 27 January to 16 July 1845 they were literally trapped in inhospitable country; men and equipment suffered terribly from the heat and Sturt's second-in-command, James Poole, died of scurvy.

In July, they were released by heavy rain. Sturt moved his party in a north-westerly direction to Fort Grey, whence he made a series of reconnoitring expeditions culminating in a 450-mile journey towards the centre of the continent. Repulsed by the sand dunes of the Simpson desert, he at last, reluctantly, abandoned the idea of an inland sea.

Sturt and his party returned exhausted to Fort Grey, and after another trip to the Cooper's Creek area from October 9 to November 17, they found the waterhole was rapidly drying. Return to the River Murray became imperative, nevertheless,

Sturt proposed the main party should go home while he and John McDouall Stuart made a do-or-die trip towards the centre. The surgeon, J. H. Browne, resisted so strongly that these heroics were dropped and the whole party went off together. At this point, Sturt succumbed to a serious attack of scurvy and Browne took command through the most difficult part of the journey. By using Aboriginal foods, Sturt had almost recovered when the expedition reached Moorundie on January 15. He arrived at Adelaide on 19 January 1846 ahead of his party, which followed a few days later. It had been a very difficult journey, with temperatures often above 115 degrees Fahrenheit. It wasn't until he had finally reached the Stony Desert and the Simpson Desert he was convinced there was no inland sea.

In Sturt's absence, Grey had been replaced as governor by Major Robe, and Sturt had been appointed Registrar-General and Colonial Treasurer, at £500 a year. His position was now more comfortable and early in 1847, he applied for leave. He left for England on May 8 and arrived in London just too late to personally receive the gold medal of the Royal Geographical Society; but was able to complete and publish an account of the expedition (*Narrative of an Expedition into Central Australia)*. It is not clear when Gill first met Sturt, but it seems a friendship had developed. As a consequence, a number of the illustrations of Sturt's journey were engraved from watercolours developed by S. T. Gill from sketches made during the journey (Sturt illustrated his field journals with sketches and his draftsman, John McDouall Stuart, also did some sketching). Sturt presented drawings and ore specimens to Queen Victoria in 1849. On his return to Adelaide in August 1849, he was soon appointed colonial secretary, but unfortunately his sight began to fail and at the end of 1851, he retired on a pension of £600.

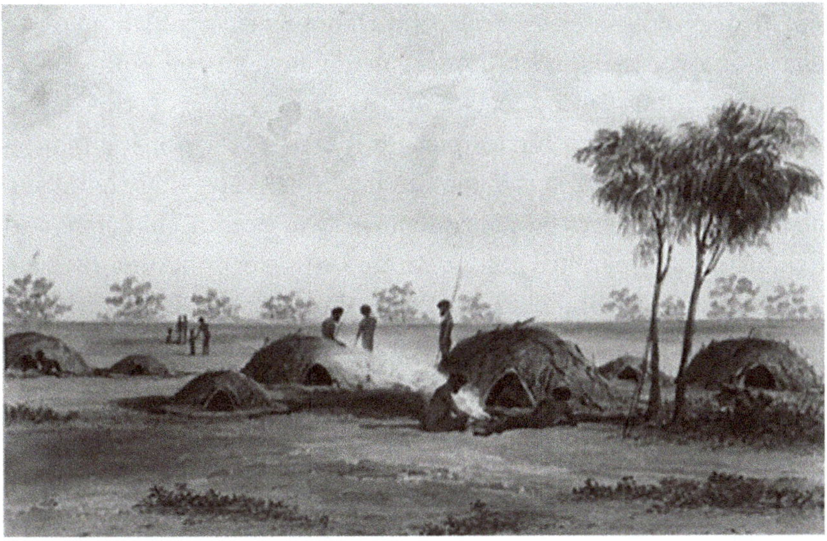

Aboriginal Village Northern Interior (State Library of South Australia, B16061/1)

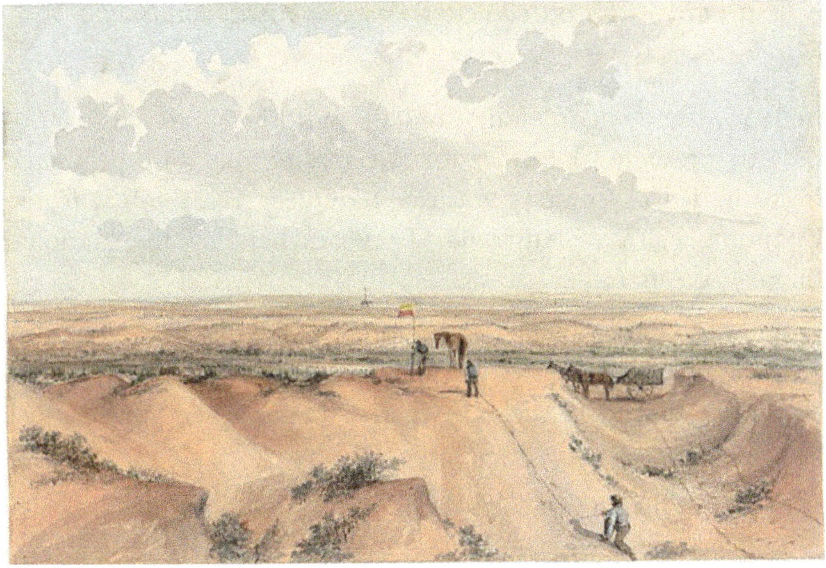

The Sandy Ridges of Central Australia (Chaining Over the Sand Hills to Lake Torrens) (National Library of Australia, nla.obj.-134371152)

The original sketch by Sturt of the above scene, which involved chaining over the sand hills, was made close to the point where the expedition turned back. Gill's watercolour of this scene presents us with a vivid picture of the laborious chaining process involved in surveying at that time. Carrying the heavy chains required for the process must have been a challenge and exhausting. Apparently, Sturt wanted to determine the distance between a lake (Blanche, which he thought was Lake Torrens) and the Darling River. Gill's exposure to parts of the outback possibly equipped him to capture the true nature of the desert which Sturt encountered. Historian Roslynn Haynes felt Gill's paintings of the Sturt expedition scenes:

...captures brilliantly the surface glare, the deceptively flat horizon of terrain that is actually row upon row of parallel sand dunes, and the desolation of a country where the only vegetation is a spattering of spinifex bushes...His expeditioners are tiny but gallant individuals pitted against a vast, hostile landscape.[71]

In 1956, three watercolours by Gill and other material, part of the gift presented by Sturt to Queen Victoria, were presented from the Royal Library, Windsor by Queen Elizabeth II to the Commonwealth of Australia. They are held by the National Library of Australia.

There is a monument to explorer, Captain Charles Napier Sturt, in Victoria Square, Adelaide, which was described as 'the most alive' statue in Adelaide when it was unveiled in December 1916.

The front inscription is as follows:

71 Roslynn D. Haynes, *Seeking the Centre: the Australian Desert in Literature, Art and Film*, Cambridge University Press, 1998, p. 95.

Captain Charles Sturt
Explorer
Born April 28th, 1795 - Died June 16th, 1869

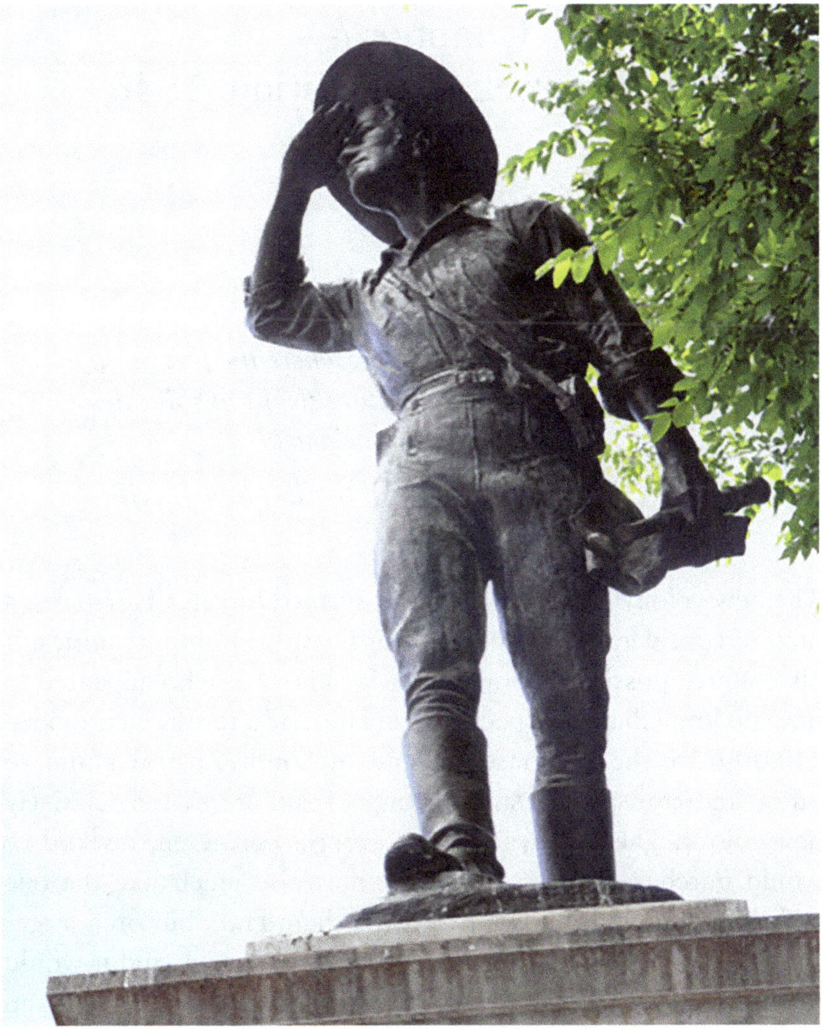

Monument to Charles Sturt, Victoria Square, Adelaide (Photograph by author)

Gill's work here helps us understand and visualise the enormous difficulties faced by Sturt and his party.

Chapter 7—
The Horrocks Expedition, 1846

Deserts thorny, hot and thirsty, where the feet of men are strange, And eternal Nature sleeps in solitudes which know no change.

—Henry Kendall, The Fate of the Explorers, c.1862

The new colony of South Australia seemed to Peter Horrocks, a man of considerable means, to offer investment opportunities. It also offered possible opportunities for his sons, who appeared to have no immediate prospects in England. As a result, he provided £10,000 for the purchase of land in South Australia and to outfit and transport a small group of settlers to the relatively new colony. The plan was for the group to settle on the land he would purchase and establish an enterprise much like the one he had in England, known as Penwortham Hall, but on a larger scale. Two of his sons were to be part of the group and it would be led by his eldest son, John Ainsworth Horrocks. The group largely comprised people who had worked for Peter Horrocks at Penwortham Hall. On 20 October 1838, the group departed from St. Katharine Dock in London for South Australia on board the *Catherine Stuart Forbes*, a 457-ton ship.

John Ainsworth Horrocks, aged 21, and the other members of the group, arrived in South Australia on 22 March 1839. The group included a family servant, a blacksmith, shepherds, four merino rams, sheepdogs, tools, sufficient clothing for five years, and a church bell. Unlike many, John Horrocks was impatient to move into new parts of the colony and did not wait in Adelaide for the completion of land surveys. On the advice of explorer Edward John Eyre, he travelled to land near the Hutt River north of Adelaide, and established Penwortham village. Other pastoralists followed him into the area. In 1841, the long-awaited special survey provided a frustrated Horrocks with title to only some of the fertile land he had been occupying. Nevertheless, he built up a flock of 9,000 sheep and is believed to have established the first vineyard in the Clare district.

By 1846, Horrocks was bored with farming and he rented out most of his properties and proposed an expedition to search for new agricultural lands near Lake Torrens. Explorers Edward John Eyre and Charles Sturt had returned from their respective expeditions completely dispirited by their experiences of the salty Lake Torrens and surrounding countryside. Yet Horrocks was not deterred, and in fact, he was enthusiastic and positive in his belief he would penetrate the region reached by the other explorers and find good grazing land. An appeal for government assistance was unsuccessful and a public appeal for support was launched. It was strongly supported by the *South Australian Register*, with a piece on page 2 on Saturday, 4 July 1846, urging people to subscribe:

The names of many of our merchants, our landholders, our sheep owners, and our speculators, are already on the subscription list. They ought to be all there. It is a small matter for Adelaide to raise a hundred or two hundred pounds. In this instance it should be done at once, that the enterprising party may not miss the winter rains… The spirit of the colonists should furnish forth such an exploring party which will do its work far better unfettered by Government instruction... We are glad therefore that Government has nothing to do with it.

The appeal raised over £140 in private subscriptions. An association was formed in Adelaide to support Horrocks in what was being called his 'Northern Expedition'. With this financial support, it was then left to Horrocks to decide who would travel with him on the expedition.

The first person selected was John Henry Theakston who would be his second in command and who had expedition experience with the ill-fated Drake exploration[72]. The second person approached by Horrocks was S. T. Gill, a friend of his, who readily agreed to join the expedition, as he was keen to document what it might find. Gill was clearly caught up in the enthusiasm shown by Horrocks. It was reported enthusiastically in the *South Australian Register* on page 2 of 4 July 1846, that Gill was to be part of the expedition:

... talented artist Mr Gill, a gentleman of whom, as of true South Australian breed, the colony has a right to be proud. It was only the other day that we had the opportunity of seeing some of his recent drawings of bush scenery. They are the most vivid and lifelike of any that have been before presented to us. He gives the true idea of South Australian scenery—nothing is exaggerated nor any point lost. His sketches of the yet unknown districts he is to visit will be invaluable. He goes only as an amateur for the purpose of filling his note book. We shall have a rich treat on his return...

The *Register* also reported on July 15 that Gill gave a parting supper to a few friends, where he indicated that he hoped:

... to give a full, true and accurate report of his adventures with... faithful scenic representations.

72 On an expedition into the Gawler Ranges via Port Lincoln, John Drake died, in October 1844, as result of wounds inflicted by Aboriginal people. He was buried at the foot of Drakes peak, Eyre Peninsula.

Three others made up the party for the expedition: Bernard Kilroy, William Garlic, and a young Aboriginal boy, Jimmy Moorehouse, who would look after the animals (cattle, dogs, horses, goats, and a camel).

S. T. Gill was looking forward to joining Horrocks and saw this as an adventure, an artistic opportunity, and possibly a challenge, to accurately record the experiences and sights the expedition would encounter. Gill felt the expedition would provide an opportunity for him to create images of parts of the colony not previously recorded by a European artist.

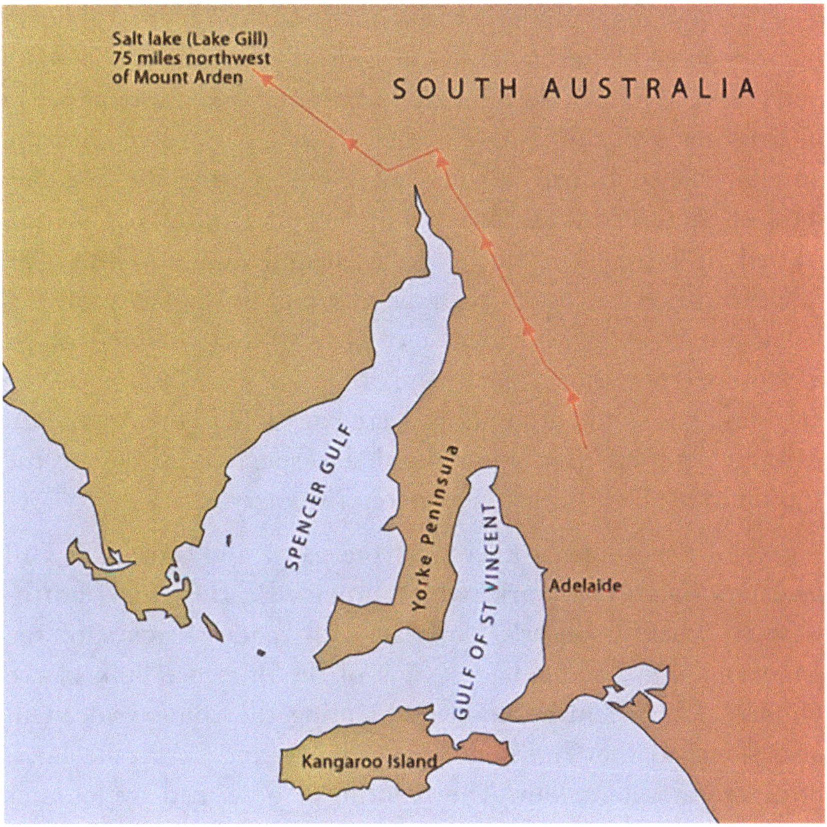

Horrocks Expedition Map (National Library of Australia, nla.obj-5517999)

Leaving Penwortham on 29 July 1846 for a planned four-month absence, the party of six travelled with a camel, two drays, six horses and twelve goats. Other expeditions had taken sheep with them for food, but Horrocks decided goats would be a better proposition, as they were more suited to the type of country they would encounter. The first few days they travelled in a north-westerly direction, moving at a fairly easy pace, gradually easing into the expedition. They initially had some problems with equipment, one of the drays and a horse, which required one of the party, Theakston, to backtrack and obtain replacements from the nearest station. A problem was also encountered with the camel named Harry. He was stubborn, bad-tempered and even vicious at times (biting one of the goats and Garlic). None of the expedition members had any experience in working with camels. Nevertheless, they persevered with the animal and continued moving north-west during the first few days of August into the Lower Flinders Ranges, onto a station owned by brothers Samuel, Frederich and Edwin White. The White brothers had established the property in 1844 and called it 'Charlton' after their home village, Charlton Marshall in Dorset. The property later became the site of the town of Wirrabara. The original house and outbuildings were later sold to the Australian Mining Company. The party decided to spend a rest day on the station to enable Theakston to rejoin the party.

One of the White brothers met the party and took S. T. Gill to a prominent landmark, which provided a clear view north-west to where Spencer's Gulf lay. Gill made sketches of the panorama and he also had a view of the immense bulk of the Flinders Ranges. In addition to painting the countryside, Gill also sketched the Charlton Station scene and sometime later, produced a watercolour. The painting is described by Jennifer Carter;

It could be called a 'typical' Gill of the period: a rudimentary homestead with outbuildings in the middle distance, trees indicating meandering creek beds beyond, with a nod of local flora, this time in the shape of sheoaks... and various tussock grasses. The Aboriginal figures in the foreground are a frequent device used by Gill to create a modicum of human interest...[73]

It's interesting that this painting (*Charlton Station near Mount Remarkable, South Australia, 1848*) must have been purchased by Samuel White and taken back to the home country when he, his wife and two children departed Australia in October 1852, following the birth of their son. It's even more interesting that the painting returned to Australia in 2002 after it was acquired at a London auction for £4000. It is held by the National Library of Australia in Canberra.

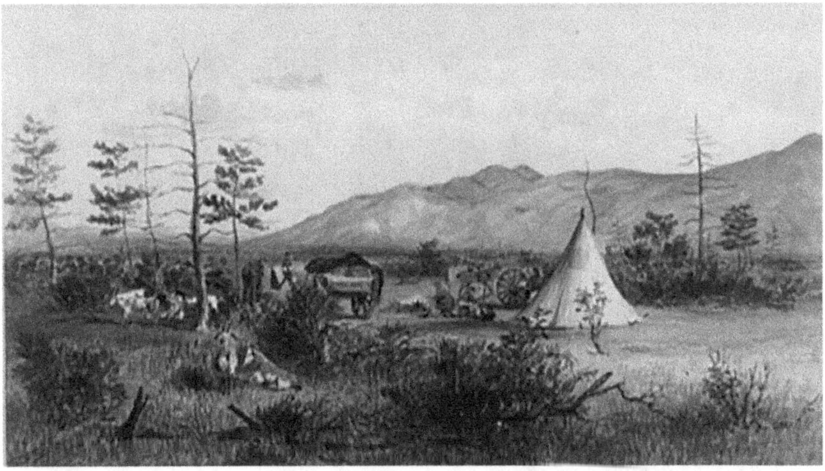

Mount Brown at the Head of Spencers Gulf (State Library of South Australia, B16060/4)

By August 9, the party had moved further north and camped at the base of the Flinders Ranges. They now needed to find a way through the ranges so they could get on with the real task of exploring. After some exploration, they found a pass that

73 Jennifer M. T. Carter, *Mr White's Station at Charlton. NLA News*, April 2004, Vol. XIV, No. 7, p. 18.

appeared to provide access to the heart of the ranges. The party moved into a valley Horrocks had located on August 11. The main valley had many small side valleys. The terrain, involving dry creek beds, created mobility problems for the drays. The supplies and equipment had to be moved in stages by using the horses and the camel. This took several days. While in the area, Horrocks climbed part of the Flinders Ranges to view the country to the north-west. On a separate occasion, Gill and Jimmy Moorehouse also climbed to the top of a hill, where Gill made some sketches. By August 18, they had finally reached the plain beyond the ranges. Looking back at the large gulley they had ascended, they decided this passage through the Flinders Ranges would be called Horrocks Pass.

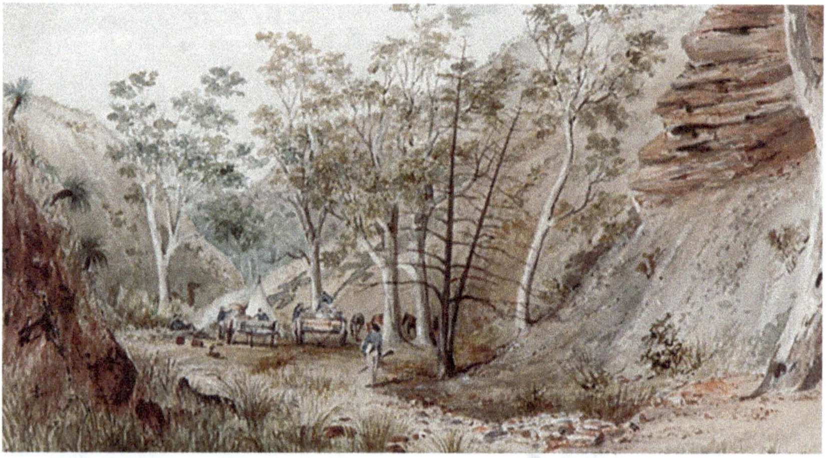

Creek Bed Camp, Flinders Rangers
(National Library of Australia, nla.obj-134371955)

Horrocks found that although the camel was temperamental, and had bitten both humans and goats, it was essential, as it could carry up to 350 pounds, vital for the anticipated treks through waterless country. Beyond the pass, they kept finding traces of explorer Edward John Eyre's old tracks.

The horses had been without water for two days when, on August 21, the party reached Depot Creek, a permanent spring discovered by Eyre in 1839, some 16 miles north of Spencer Gulf, and used as a campsite by Eyre's party. The Horrocks party had taken 26 days to travel 125 miles. The slow progress was partly due to stoppages needed to repair and replace equipment and move supplies by hand. Gill utilised the stoppages along the way to wander around and sketch the countryside. From the Depot Creek campsite, several exploratory trips were made.

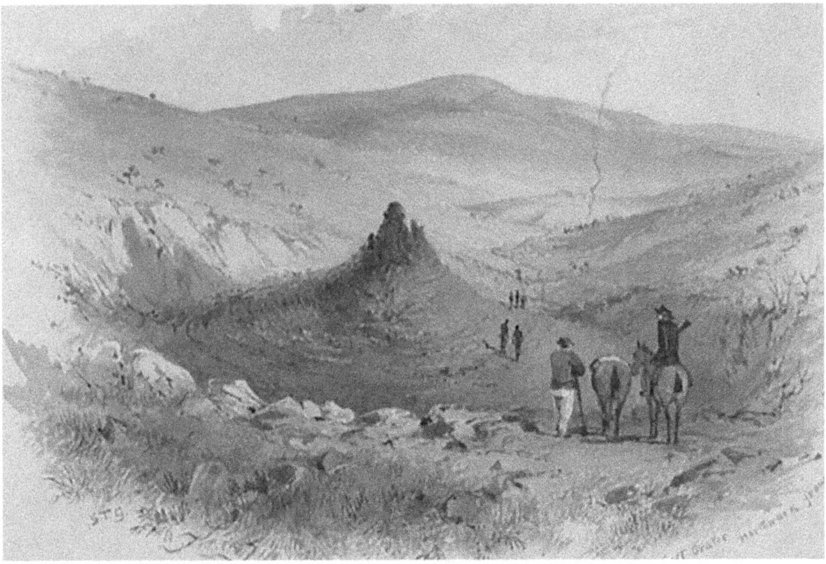

Extinct Crater, North of Spencer Gulf (State Library of South Australia, B72815/1)

The push north-west began in earnest with the first exploration on August 22 and 23, when Horrocks and Gill made a journey west-north-west on horseback. The main objective was to find a base for the main party with water. They were unsuccessful, but had several confrontations with the Aborigines, which Gill recorded in his diary. It appears the Aboriginal people were unimpressed with such 'marvels of civilisation' as tobacco and firearms. Gill noted they were not particularly friendly, and on one occasion, the party fired a few shots into the ground, which did not appear to trouble the natives. In the image below, Gill and Horrocks are asking for directions to water (Gill is partly obscured by the taller Horrocks, with his pistols and telescope at his back).

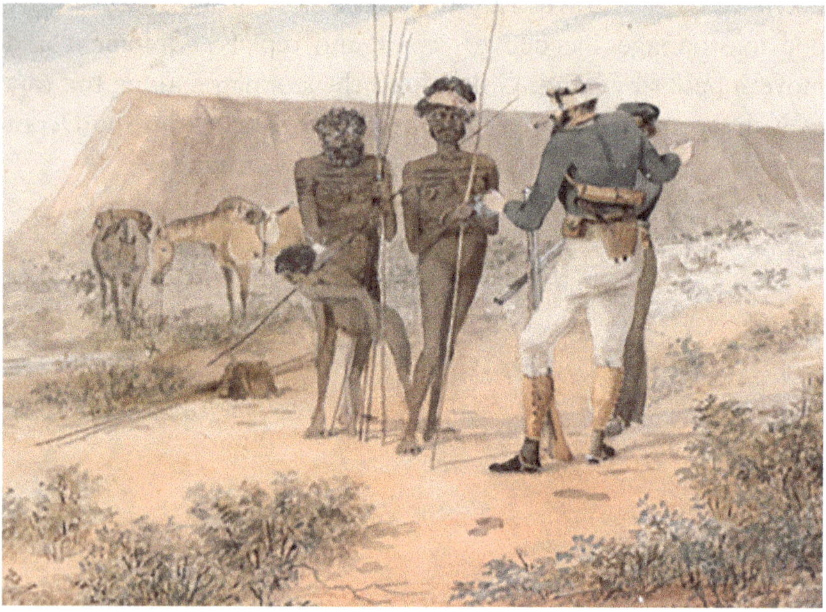

Encounter with two Barnggarla Men, Uro Bluff (State Library of Victoria)

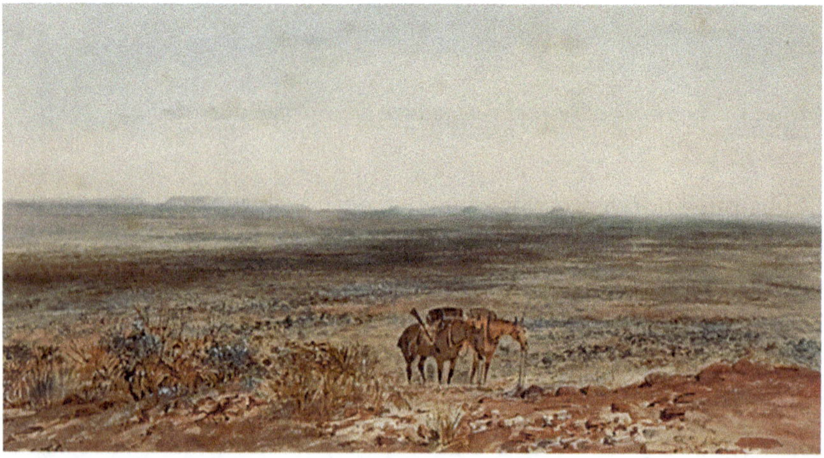

Looking South West from Table Land (22 August)
(National Library of Australia, nla.obj-134371631)

The vastness of the country is recorded by Gill following the viewing of a panorama that he and Horrocks witnessed on climbing a hill:

Mr H and I climbed the hill, which was excessively stoney and steep, taking with us the spy-glass to look over the north-west country, which presented a most desolate aspect, - one immense space of dry sandy country, covered with low, dry, crisp scrub, without the slightest vestige of grass or possibility of water. I took a sketch of this uncheering scene, which shows the distant bit of elevated land.[74]

Gill's sepia watercolour painting, *Country NW of Point Encounter*, depicts this panorama. He included two figures, Horrocks and himself, seen from behind, contemplating the vastness of the view.

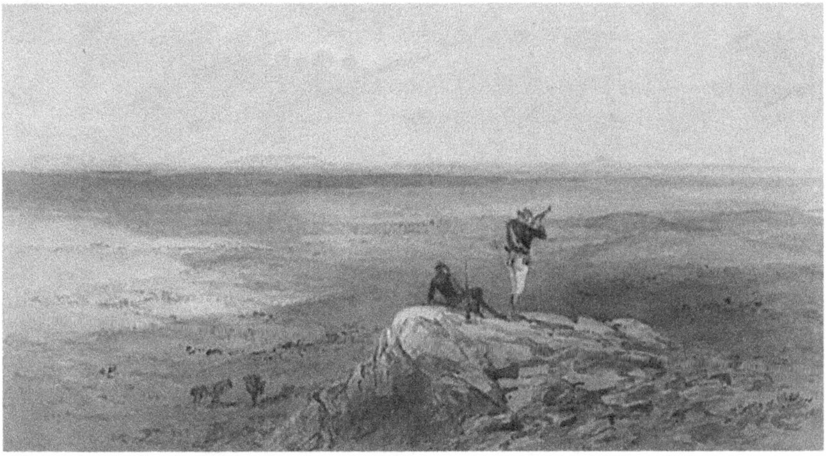

Country N.W. of Point Encounter, 1846
(State Library of South Australia, B72811/1)

74 The Diary of S. T. Gill Kept on the Horrocks Expedition, Progress and Discovery—Expedition to the North-West. *South Australian Gazette and Colonial Register*, October 10, 1846. (see Appendix II for a copy of Gill's Diary).

This view and the sheer vastness clearly had an impact on Gill. He also produced a slightly different sketch of the event, showing Horrocks and himself standing together with their backs to the viewer, which he called *Desert Interior.* In that sketch, Horrocks is holding a gun and Gill a sketchpad. Gill later produced a watercolour of this scene (*Country NW of Tableland*).

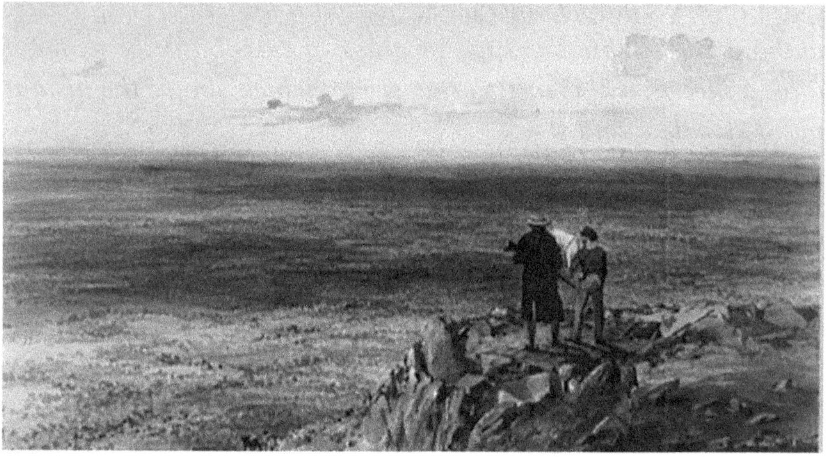

Desert Interior (State library of South Australia, B19060/5)

Horrocks decided they would continue to use Depot Creek as a base and further exploration would be made from there. Because of the uncertainty of finding water, the expedition would be made on foot. On August 28, on a wet and windy day, he set out to the north-west together with Gill and Kilroy and the camel, laden with three weeks' supply of food and water. Theakston was left in charge of the Depot Creek base.

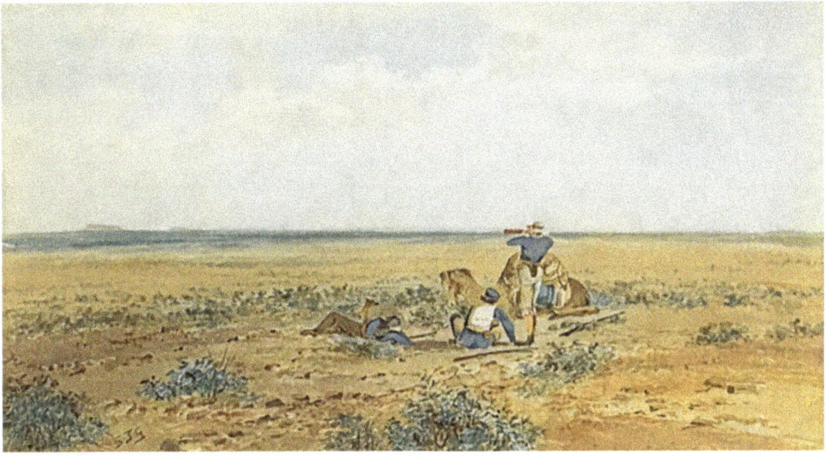

Halt on Stony Ground (31 August)
(National Library of Australia, nla.obj-134354182)

On the first day, they travelled through scrub and red sand hills covered with oaten grass. The next day, there were more red sand hills, scrubby country, and a stony area. On August 31, they crossed a sterile stony plain; they could see their planned destination ahead, a tableland rising above the plain. Gill wrote:

...could distinctly see the rising land we were making for, towering out of dense scrub...[75]

On September 1, the three men reached a salt lake now known as Lake Dutton (which Horrocks named Lake Gill shortly after it was reached by the three of them). They could see water in the centre of the lake bed. The three men walked to the water's edge and tasted the clear liquid, which they found to be exceedingly salty. They rested while Gill sketched the lake.

75 The Diary of S. T. Gill Kept on the Horrocks Expedition, Progress and Discovery—Expedition to the North-West. *South Australian Gazette and Colonial Register*, October 10, 1846. (see Appendix II for a copy of Gill's Diary).

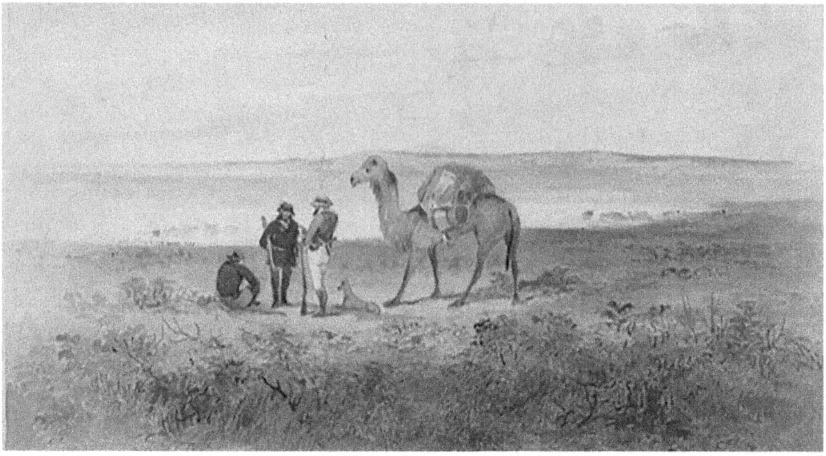

Salt Lake North West of Mount Arden (State Library of South Australia, B72813/1)

One of Gill's sketches from the expedition features what has been claimed as the first camel in Australia. Sadly, two hours after this sketch was completed on September 1, there was a shooting accident, which Horrocks later described in a letter:

Bernard Kilroy, who was walking ahead of the party, stopped, saying that he saw a beautiful bird that he recommended me to shoot to add to the collection.

My gun being loaded with slugs in one barrel and ball in the other, I stopped the camel to get at the shotbelt which I could not get without his lying down. Whilst Mr Gill was unfastening it I was screwing the ramrod into the wad over the slugs standing close alongside the camel. At this moment the camel gave a lurch to one side and caught his pack in the cock of my gun which discharged the barrel I was unloading, the contents of which took the middle finger off my right hand and entered my left cheek by my lower jaw, knocking out a row of teeth from my upper jaw.[76]

76 *South Australian Register*, Tuesday, May 29, 1888, p. 7.

Gill's sketch is annotated with the following information about the incident: '*The camel was imported into South Australia from the islands of Madeira & was shot after the accident*'. This was the furthest point the expedition attained.

Gill nursed Horrocks, while Kilroy walked about 75 miles back to Depot Creek for help. Kilroy returned with horses in the afternoon of September 4. On September 5, they started their journey in stages back to Depot Creek where they planned to wait for a doctor. They were hopeful that the doctor would arrive at the camp by September 8.

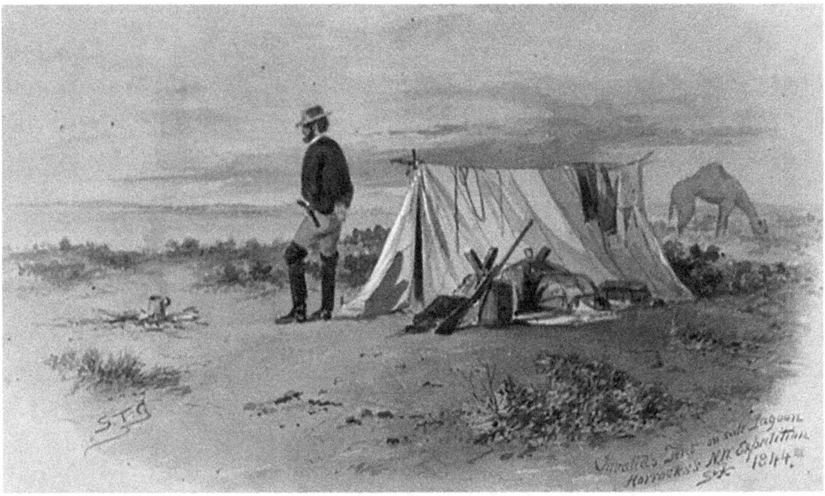

Invalids Tent on Salt Lake (State Library of South Australia, B34381)

In Gill's image of the invalid's tent, he stands looking to the left waiting for help to arrive, and possibly contemplating the desolate salt lake and his feeling of helplessness in assisting Horrocks as they wait to be rescued. There is a sense of isolation and aloneness created with the salt lake in the background. It's interesting he includes the rifle and the camel (feeding calmly) which are the combined cause of Horrocks's injuries. John McDonald felt the content of Gill's image clearly indicated the drama that was taking place:

... it is the methodical accumulation of detail that is impressive in a scene that invites all the trappings of a high tragedy.[77]

A doctor did not arrive, and so on September 10, the party travelled south. On September 11, Kilroy left the party with Horrocks, in order to reach Penwortham as quickly as possible. Gill, Theakston and Jimmy, the native, followed, possibly by a different route. They reached Penwortham on September 19, by which time Horrocks was very ill. The doctor arrived that evening. Horrocks appeared a little better on the 20th, but that night his condition declined and by the 21st, Gill reported he was 'dangerously ill'. Horrocks died from his wounds on the evening of the 23rd, some three weeks after the accident, and was buried the following day in land at Penwortham that he had given to the Church of England for a church.

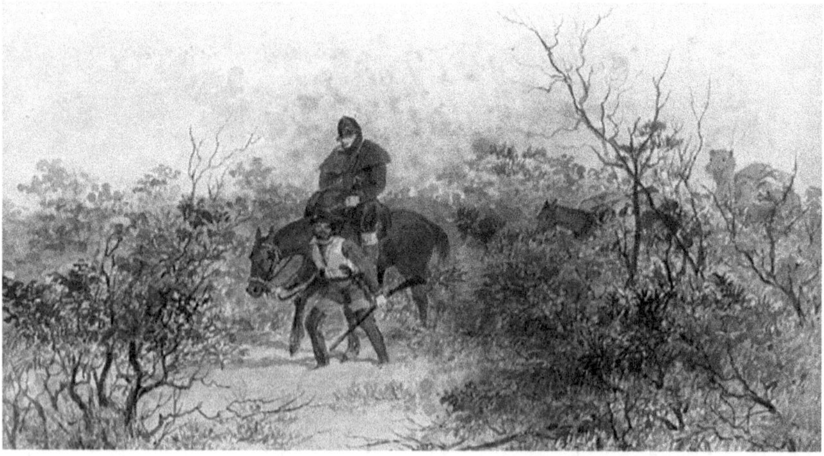

Transporting the Wounded Horrocks, 1846 (State Library of South Australia, B 475)

77 John McDonald, *Art of Australia*, Pan Macmillan, 2008, p. 172.

Horrocks wrote about Gill and his work:

Mr. Gill showed himself to be a brave and steadfast companion by remaining with me. He has taken several sketches of this country which will show to those interested how very impossible it is that any stations can be made to the west of Lake Torrens.[78]

Although the expedition had ended so prematurely and so tragically, and failed to find any new agricultural country, Gill had made a series of drawings illustrating the type of country over which they travelled and the activities and incidents along the way. His sketches and paintings were the first ever to be made by a professional European artist of the Flinders Ranges, three-quarters of a century before Hans Heysen, and he was therefore possibly the first to show both the delicacy and desolation of the saltbush plains and the salt lakes.

Gill sketched assiduously throughout the trip, often taking his paper and painting materials to a high point in order to draw a panoramic view of the surrounding country or the next day's prospect. The resulting watercolours and sketches are very much a narrative of the journey, and often include identifiable portraits of both men and animals, as well as dates of execution and details of dress and behaviour. Gill often included himself in the scene, and the accuracy of the colour and form with which he depicted the topography and vegetation demonstrates his acute observation and recording skills.

On his return to Adelaide, he quickly set to work developing his sketches. Within three months, he produced 33 watercolour paintings documenting the doomed expedition. He also produced a diary of the expedition which was published in the *South Australian Gazette* on 10 October 1846. It's clear from the diary the journey was very strenuous and Gill was very conscientious in sketching the country throughout the journey.

78 Geoffrey Dutton, *Paintings of S. T. Gill,* Rigby, Adelaide, 1962, p. 6.

His diary emphasises the deep sense of alienation that he and his companions experienced, assailed by the heat, flies, lack of water and hostile Aborigines. Gill's diary and artwork of the expedition provide an intimate and detailed encounter of the moment-by-moment day-by-day story of what took place. Gill is there as an eyewitness, incorporating himself into a number of the scenes.

I believe the Horrocks expedition had a considerable impact on S. T. Gill and was responsible for shaping his thinking and understanding of the uniqueness and vastness of the Australian landscape, the Australian Aboriginals, and possibly, a deepening love of the bush. It's clear from the newspaper accounts prior to the start of the expedition Gill was looking forward to participating, seeing this as an opportunity for adventure. It wasn't long before the difficulties of the project became apparent. The expedition was unable to find water and was faced with extinction in an unfamiliar and alien environment. The encounters with the Aboriginal people were not what was expected, based on experiences with the Aboriginal people living around Adelaide. These people were proud, competent, comfortable in their environment and clearly unimpressed with the white intruders and their trinkets. These experiences, I believe, changed the way Gill understood the land and the people and how he painted. This was not only a formative time for Gill, but there were possibly long-term consequences for his physical and mental health. He undertook to participate in the expedition at his own expense, and clearly, short of money on his return, he was forced to organise a subscription raffle of some of his Horrocks expedition paintings. As noted in the previous chapter, two of the paintings were purchased by Charles Sturt and were part of the gift he made to Queen Victoria. Gill's funds were depleted and he was tired after his adventure. McDonald felt Gill's watercolours were the only good thing to come from the expedition:

Hardship and death were the full complement of his discoveries, with Gill's watercolours being the only positive outcome of the ordeal.[79]

At least one resident of South Australia appreciated the efforts of Kilroy and Gill in assisting Horrocks after the accident, as expressed in a letter to the editor in the *South Australian Gazette and Colonial Register* on October 3, 1846:

TO THE EDITOR OF THE SOUTH AUSTRALIAN GAZETTE.

Sir—I am not aware whether the Royal Humane Society take cognizance of anything beyond the limits of the United Kingdom; but if such be the case I trust that the devoted heroism of Bernard Kilroy in the melancholy termination of the late Mr Horrocks's expedition may not pass unrewarded. I feel assured that my fellow-colonists will unite in offering to the whole party, and especially to Mr Gill and to Kilroy, some fitting testimonial of the esteem their gallant conduct has so well merited.—I am, Sir, yours, &c., Civis.

The two paintings which Sturt acquired (*Looking South-West to Spencers Gulf, August 10, 1846, and Country North-West of Tableland)* show the expeditioners in a confident pose looking towards what might turn out to be new grazing country (they were probably still optimistic at that stage and feeling that what they saw held no fear for them). However, the situation changed, and this was reflected in Gill's later images, where the small human figures were juxtaposed against the featureless desert landscape. By that stage, they had probably come to the conclusion there was no land worth occupying. This may have been the intended message to the people of South Australia.

79 John McDonald, *Art of Australia*, Vol. 1, Pan Macmillan, 2008, p.172.

Positive comments on his work were contained in a piece in the *South Australian* on 5 January 1847, under the title, The Arts in South Australia:

> *Mr Gill has politely favoured us with an inspection of his series of views, depicting the most remarkable scenes met with by the expedition under the conduct of the late Mr Horrocks. The series comprises no less than thirty-three views, the execution of which, as faithful transcripts of nature and in some instances a territory untrodden by white men, reflects much credit on the talented artist. Some of these pictures are possessed of a peculiar interest, as, for instance, one representing the extreme point attained by the party.*

One of Gill's most dramatic landscapes was painted as part of the Horrocks expedition series and depicts rocky mountain views of the Flinders Ranges. The painting entitled *Mount Remarkable Survey, from above the falls* shows starkly angular, rocky outcrops which form a dark ravine. Several Aboriginal people are placed in the painting, to draw your eye to them and then into the ravine. Possibly one of the most stark and desolate paintings in the series is the *Invalid's tent, salt lake.* A small tent dominates the foreground and Gill is reclining at the tent entrance where Horrocks lies dying inside (the version I have included above has Gill standing). It clearly shows isolation, loneliness and tragedy. Gill produced several versions of this image, including a watercolour.

By 1847, a number of artists were working in Adelaide. In that year, 23 artists, including Gill, banded together and held South Australia's first general exhibition, entitled *Exhibition of Pictures: The Works of Colonial Artists.* Gill displayed 62 works, among them a dramatic series of the 33 pictures of the Horrocks expedition, arranged chronologically and depicting the rugged Flinders landscapes, the hard country through which they had travelled and the tragic return with the dying Horrocks.

The exhibition ran from February 10 to 17; the venue being the Council Room in North Terrace (a similar exhibition was held in 1848, and although Gill exhibited at least ten works, full details are not available).

Even though Gill had moved quickly on his return to paint many scenes of the expedition, it clearly had been a traumatic time for him. In his diary, he mentioned problems with his feet and legs; he had found it a physically gruelling experience. By 1850, he was still unwell, and for a period of three months at the end of 1850 into early 1851, he was unable to paint because of a swollen and painful right hand. I believe the expedition had a long-lasting negative impact on Gill's emotional wellbeing and health.

A memorial to John Horrocks can be found at Penwortham in the north-west corner of St. Mark's Cemetery. It was unveiled on Sunday, 22 September 1946, and bears the following inscription:

John Ainsworth Horrocks

Pastoralist and Explorer.

A Prominent Pioneer of this District.

Left Penwortham 28 July 1846 with

Theakston, Gill, Kilroy, Garlic and a Native

To Explore Country North of Mount Arden.

Horrocks was Accidentally Wounded 1 Sept. at

Lake Dutton, and Died 23 Sept. at Penwortham.

Erected 1946

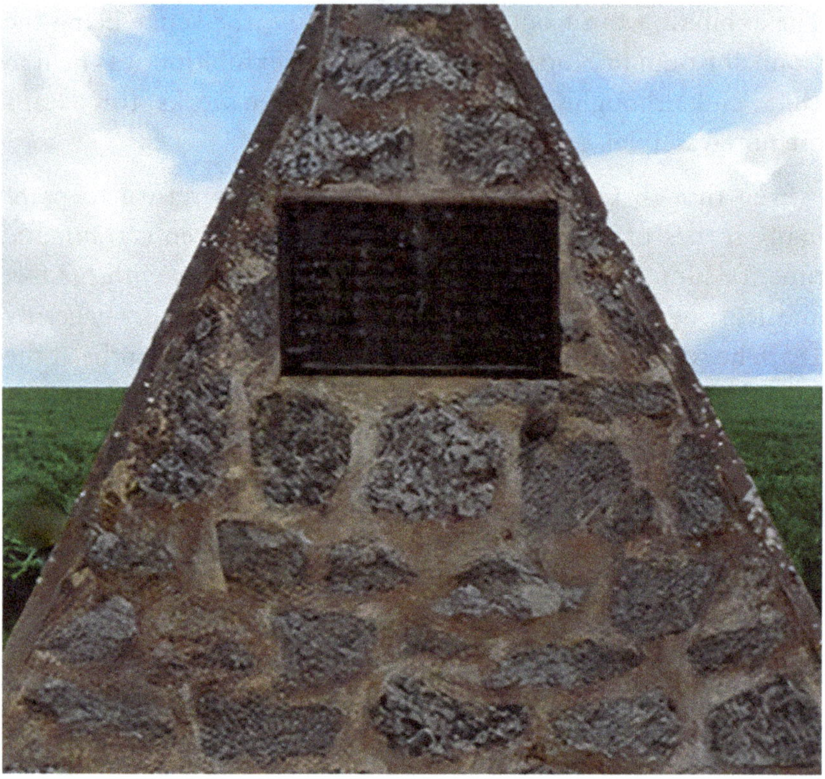

Memorial to Horrocks, Penwortham, South Australia

Despite the failure of the expedition to achieve its goal of locating new grazing land, it did result in the production of some wonderful images of parts of South Australia that had not previously been recorded by a European artist. We particularly see, through Gill's images, the vastness and beauty of the land previously known only to its Aboriginal inhabitants. The experience changed the way Gill defined and painted the Australian landscape. Twenty-five years after the expedition, Gill continued to produce variations of the event and the landscape of the Flinders Ranges. This demonstrates how popular this theme was in the total body of Gill's work compared to his earlier pieces in South Australia, such as the *Seasons* and *Months* style of painting, which it appears were never repeated.

Chapter 8—The Gold Rush, 1851

When first I left Old England's shore,
Such yarns as we were told,
As how folks in Australia
Could pick up lumps of gold.
So, when we got to Melbourne town,
We were ready soon to slip
And get even with the captain —
All hands scuttled from the ship.
—Anonymous

From 1849, the gold rush in California attracted thousands of Australians. Prior to this time, there was no interest in New South Wales in supporting exploration for gold in the colony, as it was feared that a discovery would lead to social and economic dislocation. However, the loss of so many men from the colony led Governor FitzRoy to offer a generous reward for anyone who discovered a commercially viable deposit in New South Wales. The reward was claimed by Edward Hargraves, who had returned from an unsuccessful time on the Californian gold fields.

The rush was now on, and men from all vocations became gold miners and headed for Summer Hill Creek. They carried with them digging implements of every kind, as blacksmiths couldn't keep up with the demand for picks. Prices for basic commodities doubled overnight. FitzRoy, being afraid of the impact on the colony, imposed a miner's tax of 30 shillings a month to be paid, regardless of whether the prospector found gold or not. He reasoned the unsuccessful miners would quickly return to their former employment as they would not be able to afford to pay the tax without a source of income.

The discovery of gold in New South Wales disturbed those in the newly independent colony of Victoria. Late in May 1851, the startling news of the gold rush over the Blue Mountains in New South Wales reached Port Phillip. Distance and the wintery weather deterred many, but within a couple of weeks, at least 200 men had packed a swag and departed on the three week trudge to the Bathurst area of New South Wales. It's likely that as many as 1000 eventually joined the rush overland or by sea.

It was feared that Victorians would continue to desert the new colony in large numbers and join the gold rush in New South Wales. To counter this, in June 1851, Lieutenant Governor Charles La Trobe offered a reward of £200 for the discovery of gold within 200 miles of Melbourne. William Campbell had discovered gold at Clunes north of Ballarat in 1850 but did not disclose the discovery until a month after La Trobe had offered the reward. This was followed by a discovery at Andersons Creek, near Warrandyte in July. In September, a richer field was discovered at Golden Point Ballarat, a mere 75 miles from Melbourne. The Victorian gold rush was now on, and within a month, between six and ten thousand men had arrived to search for the yellow metal.

Further discoveries followed, including the huge area around Castlemaine known as the Mount Alexander field. This fifteen-square-miles-field proved to be the richest and most easily worked of all the alluvial diggings. Around 20,000 people had arrived at the diggings by Christmas 1851.

The diggings presented an extraordinary sight, as described by the *Mount Alexander Mail* in an article about the gold rush of the 1850s, published on 24 October 1908:

... bearded, begrimed men were feverishly burrowing like moles into the earth, scarring the face of nature; the air filled with.... Discordant shouts... the noise of the cradle and the reports of firearms. At night, as far as the eye could see, the camp fires... were burning in two long, irregular string of luminously iridescent beads.

Melbourne and Geelong were deserted as the rush to the goldfields intensified. Houses were left unoccupied, businesses shut down and even some schools were closed. It was impossible to hire servants at any wage. Boats lay idle in the harbour, because their masters were unable to keep their crew. Pastoralists were left without men. The shearing season had arrived, but the shearers had thrown down their blades to prospect for gold and the Geelong stevedores, who customarily loaded the wool bales into ships' holds, had quit their jobs.

Large numbers also arrived from other colonies. By late 1851, 7000 gold seekers had arrived by sea and hundreds more trekked across the colonial borders. The flow of mostly men continued into 1852, with ships bringing 14,000 from New South Wales, 19,000 from Tasmania, 15,000 from South and Western Australia, and 1000 from New Zealand.[80]

By the end of 1852, 88,000 people had left the United Kingdom and arrived in the colonies (nine out of ten went directly to Victoria). More ships sailed to Melbourne than to any other port in the world. Another 63,000 arrived in 1853, followed by 83,000 in 1854.[81]

80 Richard Broome, *The Victorians*. Arriving, Fairfax, Syme & Weldon Associates, 1984, p. 67.
81 *Emigration Commission, Thirty-Third General Report of the Emigration Commissioners*, Appendix No. 1, pp. 48-9.

William Howitt, who spent time on the Victorian goldfields, commented on those arriving in Melbourne and heading to the diggings:

Yesterday as we went down to the ship, the steamers were coming in ... They were densely packed on the decks of the steamer, as you have seen Irish emigrants on decks of vessels setting sail from Liverpool for America. What men! and what costumes! Huge burley fellows with broad, battered straw or cabbage-tree hats, huge beards, loose blue shirts, and trousers yellow with clay and earth, many of them showing that they had already been digging in Sydney, where there is much gold, but according to fame, not so abundant or so pure as in this colony; almost every man had a gun, or pistol in his belt, and a huge dog, half hound half mastiff, led by chain. Each had his bundle, containing his sacking to sleep upon, his blanket and such slight change of linen as these diggers carry. They had, besides, their spades and picks tied together; and thus they marched up the country, bearing with them all they want, and lying out under a tree.[82]

Art critic, Robert Hughes, described the impact of the discovery of gold as follows:

In 1851 gold was discovered in Australia. Colonial society, sixty years stable in a pyramid from convicts through farmers, merchants, professional men and officers to the Governor was thrown into flux by the diggers. Adventurers, cranks, whoremongers, foreigners and three-pea men crashed through it, oblivious to what their proper level should have been. Gold caused the most profound social upheaval in sixty years; and between 1851 and 1861 Australia's population trebled.[83]

82 William Howitt, *Land, Labour and Gold or Two Years in Victoria*, Longman, London, 1855, p. 22.
83 Robert Hughes, *The Art of Australia*, Penguin Books Ltd., 1966, pp.18-20.

Following some health and financial problems, Gill decided to follow the large number who left from South Australia for the Victorian goldfields. It's not clear how he travelled, but it seems he arrived at the rich Mount Alexander diggings by July 1852. Some writers reported Gill travelled to Melbourne with his brother John and James Thompson in the brig *Hero*. However, shipping records show only John and James Thompson were passengers on the ship and they didn't depart Adelaide until mid-September 1852.

In the Mount Alexander area of central Victoria, the surface and shallow workings, especially at Forest Creek, were very productive. It was reported that, in nineteen days, three diggers had uncovered 360 ounces of gold, and another group had obtained £1000 worth of gold in a mere two weeks. The yield was so rich that diggers even deserted Ballarat for the Mount Alexander field. This was at a time when more than two tons of gold were arriving in Melbourne each week from Ballarat and the new diggings around Castlemaine and Bendigo.

As a veteran bushman and explorer, Gill was able to identify with the environment of the goldfields. By 1852, the goldfields were a labyrinth of roads, tracks, and bog holes, and conditions were frightful. Winter and summer, the tracks were thronged with human and animal traffic. Trees quickly vanished and the scene became one of an environmental disaster. This is evident from a number of Gill's goldfield images.

In his watercolour, *Diggers on the way to Bendigo, 1852,* Gill depicts prospectors on the road from Melbourne (he produced several versions of this work). In one version, they are carrying their blankets, a gun, a kettle, and the basic mining equipment of tin dish and an axe, accompanied by a dog. In another version, there is the addition of a shovel and a cradle. In both versions, there are two men and a boy. On the way to the diggings, the prospectors had to pass north through the Black Forest, where travellers were sometimes waylaid by highwaymen. Hence, they were often well-armed, and frequently had a fierce dog as added protection against thieves and bushrangers (as described above by Howitt).

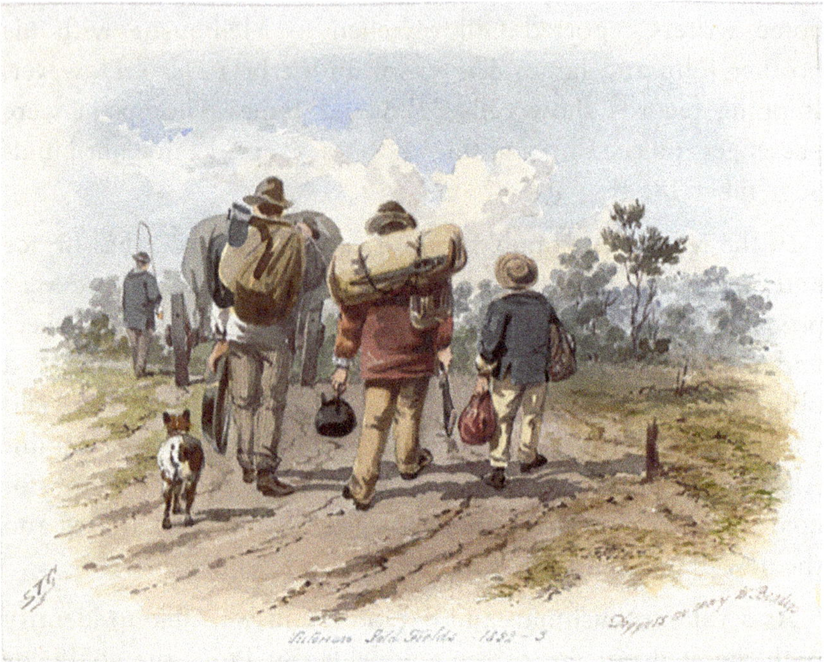

Diggers on the way to Bendigo, 1852 (State Library of Victoria)

Typhoid was common on the goldfields and became known as 'colonial fever'. The conditions on the goldfields were conducive to the rapid spread of illness, aided by the fact that most miners were ignorant of elementary hygiene and took little care. Insect plagues were common. This generated plenty of business for the doctors, as depicted in several of Gill's paintings.

Gold miner and writer, Howitt, commented on the health of the diggers:

We see the most frightful effects of cramps and rheumatism, of fever and dysentery. With the camp and the dysentery we have had our struggle; but our constitutions are intact, and our health good; whilst around us we see the strongest men racked and crippled, and others cut off by fevers with fatal rapidity.[84]

The work was extremely arduous, suitable for young, fit men. Disputes over claims were common and often led to fights. Shopkeepers attracted Gill's eye. Shop keepers often made more profits from the diggings than the diggers. Discoveries of large nuggets were relatively rare, although three years after Gill drew miners at work at Fryers Creek, two young men turned up a 1000 ounce lump of gold worth more than £4000 at that time. Most diggers were lucky to earn between five and ten pounds a week.

S. T. Gill may have dug for gold at Pennyweight Flat, near Castlemaine on Forest Creek, where many Adelaide diggers had gathered. It's assumed he teamed up with brothers, John and James Thompson, but he may in fact have teamed up with other Adelaide friends. Because of the large number of men who had come from South Australia, Gill may have found a number of familiar faces on the diggings. Forest Creek, in fact, had its Adelaide store, Adelaide restaurant, and Adelaide gold office, where South Australian diggers could deposit their gold for safe escort home. However, regardless of whom he dug with, Gill soon gave up mining to indulge his passion for recording all aspects of life and work around him in sketches and watercolours. The diggings were, no doubt, an irresistible and inexhaustible source of inspiration for him. He clearly started recording the scenes soon after arriving on the diggings, because he had his first set ready for publication as soon as August 1852. Therefore, he must have spent his first few months on the diggings, working mostly with a pencil than a pick and shovel.

His images of Forest Creek are strong in detail and topographic in style. The viewer is treated to detailed mining scenes with intimate glimpses of diggers as they maintain a semblance of normal life in these unfamiliar circumstances.

---

84 Howitt, William. *Land, Labour and Gold or Two Years in Victoria*. Longman, London, 1855, p. 181.

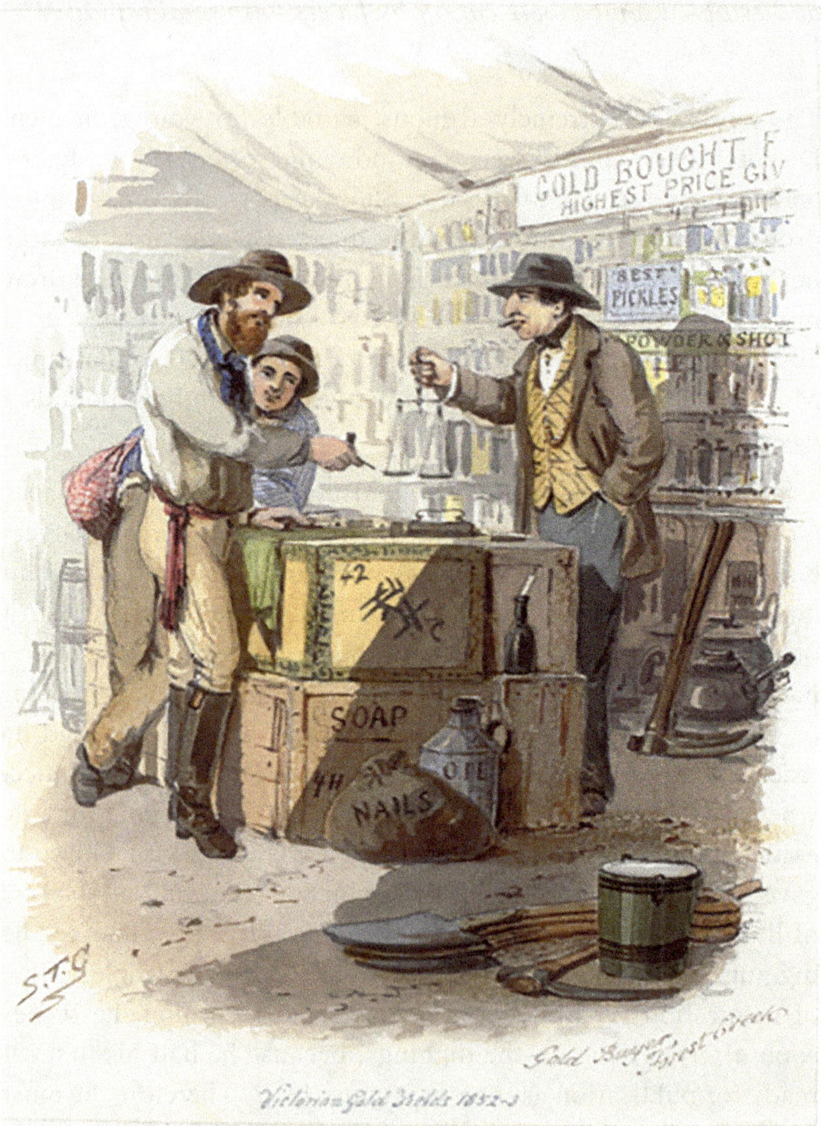

Gold Buyer Forest Creek (State Library of Victoria)

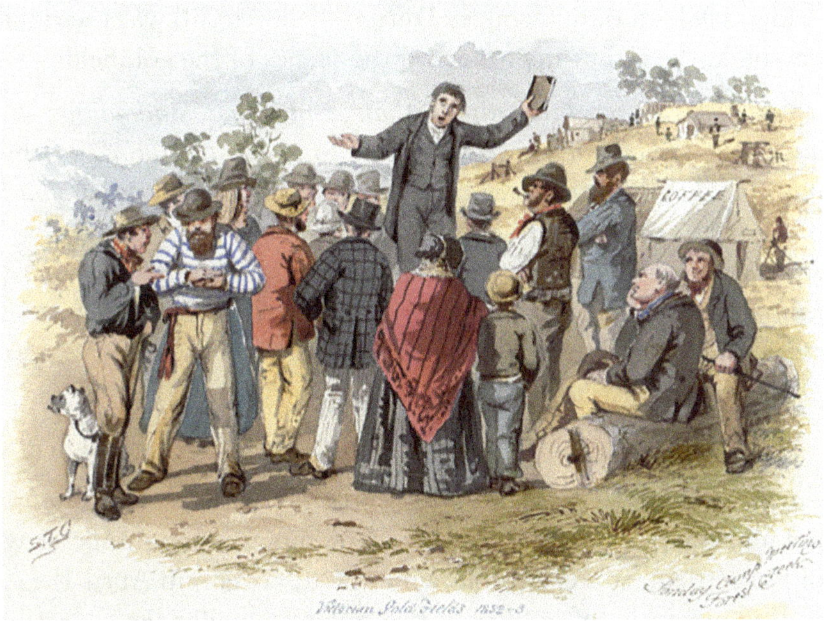

Sunday Camp Meeting Forest Creek (State Library of Victoria)

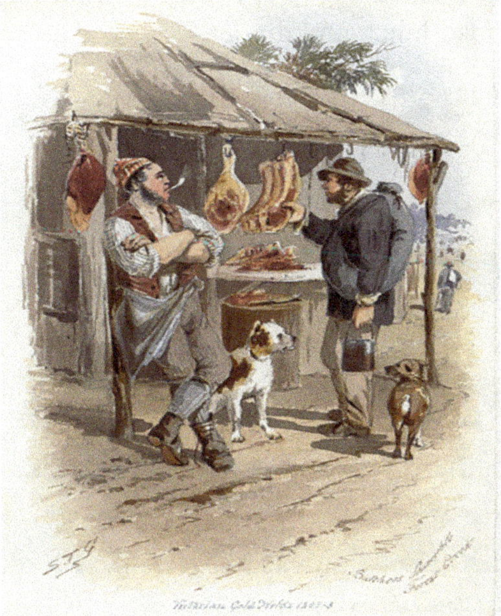

Butchers Shamble Forest Creek (State Library of Victoria)

Literary historian, Geoffrey Dutton, believes Gill was the right person at the right time to record the scenes of the goldfields:

Gill was a humanist rather than a moralist, and above all an artist; his characters are allowed to speak the words of the human comedy themselves. This gentle, convivial man, who had nursed wounded Horrocks and painted the young gardens of Adelaide, who knew horses and bullocks, who lived on hard rations and slept in the cold of the outback nights under the stars, was exactly fitted by fate to record one of the greatest peaceful convulsions of human history.[85]

Eagle Hawk Gully, Bendigo is possibly one of Gill's most popular goldfield paintings. This work shows a panoramic view of the settlement created following the discovery, in April 1852, of large deposits of gold only five miles from Bendigo. Hastily erected board and lodging tents usually contained rough stringy-bark camp stretchers available for five to ten shillings a night, and for a further five shillings, lodgers were supplied with mutton, damper, and tea for breakfast, lunch and dinner.

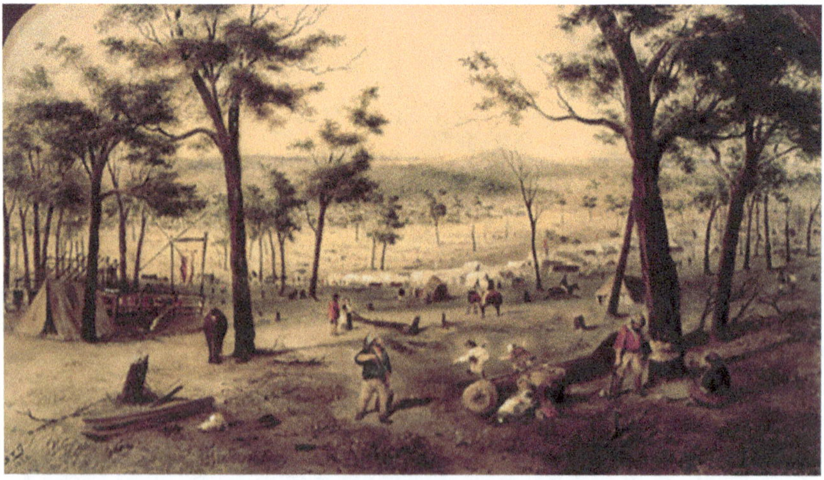

Eagle Hawke Gully, Bendigo, 1852 (State Library of Victoria)

85 Geoffrey Dutton, *S. T. Gill's Australia*, Mead & Beckett Publishing, 1981, p.28.

The sly grog trade flourished on the goldfields, where it was illegal to sell liquor, and if discovered, the vendor was fined £50 and his tent burned down. The proprietors simply moved on to another location. They were often called 'coffee shops', as seen in Gill's paintings. Sly grog sellers did a roaring trade from what they also called their 'lemonade' tents, sometimes paying the police to look the other way while they served spirits and other alcohol to diggers. Some of the vendors were women. Very little of the activity of the goldfields escaped Gill's keen eyes. His depictions of the miners evoke dry digger humour and illustrate the lively entertainments on the goldfields, the hated commissioners, the naivety of freshly arrived 'new chums' and the despondent many who did not strike it rich.

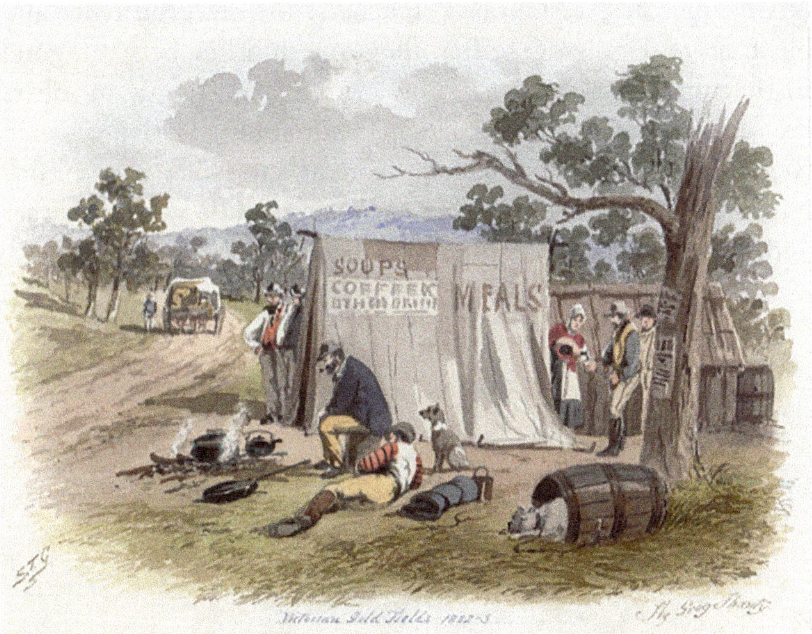

Sly Grog Shanty (State Library of Victoria)

In historian Lesley Blakes exploration of the goldfields, he commented on how Gill captured the goldfields scene:

Gill's drawings of the mining fraternity, touched with caricature, and his authentic depiction of the pock-marked countryside in the vicinity of any diggings momentarily stilled and fixed unique seconds in the ceaselessly changing goldfield scene.[86]

S. T. Gill went to the diggings many times over a four-year period, recording the experiences of diggers and their families through his art. He was constantly in the saddle between Melbourne and Ballarat, Mount Alexander and Bendigo. Gill was fascinated by all he saw. There was so much human interest as he rapidly sketched the population at the diggings. He produced detailed illustrations of gold mining techniques and daily life, including boxing matches, restaurants, butchers, the sly grog tents and much more. His images often show the thin line between good fortune and ruin. In his sketches, women and family members are often shown as active participants in mining activities, as in *Zealous Gold Diggers*, where a woman nurses her baby in one hand while she rocks the gold-extracting cradle with the other and her little boy ladles water into the cradle.

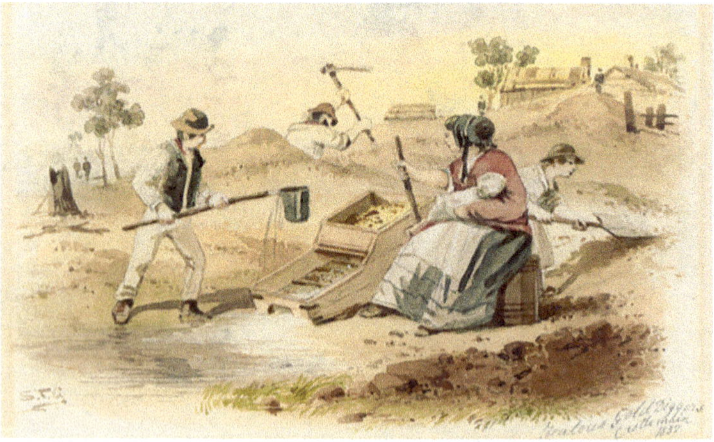

Zealous Gold Diggers, Castlemaine (State Library of Victoria)

86 L. J. Blake, *Gold Escort*, Hawthorn Press, 1971, p.134.

Gill had a particular interest in painting themes relating to illness and death, such as the doctor's tent, invalids and unlucky diggers (a skeleton and rotting clothes). It's possible this was a reflection of his own state of health.

Gill wasn't afraid to depict the darker side of life on the goldfields. He was very conscious of the existence of racial tension between local diggers and Chinese and Indigenous people, the environmental impact of mining, and the many types of people who came to the goldfields hoping for riches, only to find terrible living conditions, and often, death. Over time, he changed the way he portrayed a number of these situations. For example, on the matter of race relations with the Chinese, he portrayed the miners as the aggressors. Some of his works also present a picture of harmony, such as in his various drawings of John Alloo's Restaurant, where he shows diggers interacting with the Chinese workers. It seems Gill recognised the injustices perpetrated against the Chinese and he wanted to show that they were diligent, hard-working people.

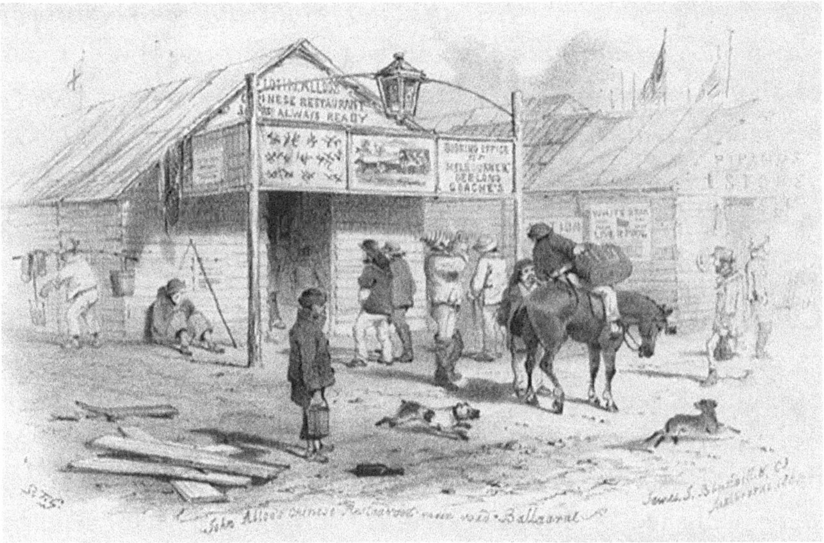

John Alloo's Chinese Restaurant Main Road Ballarat (State Library of Victoria)

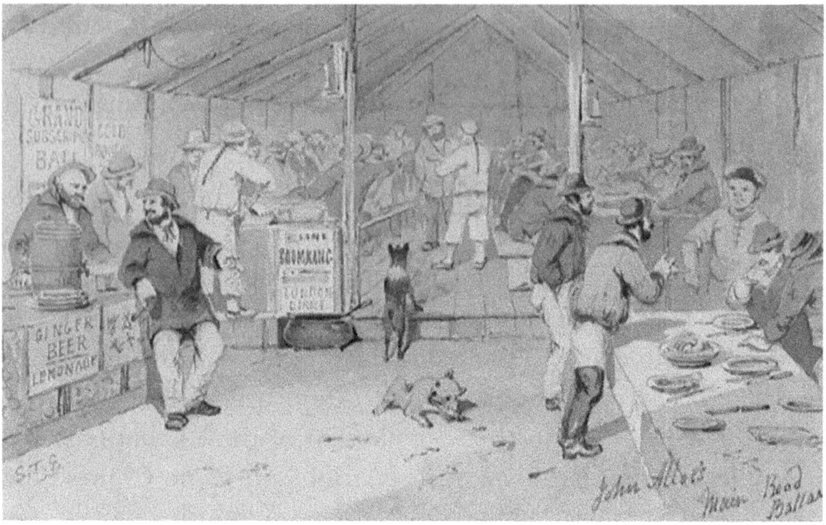

Interior of John Alloo's Restaurant Ballarat (State Library of Victoria)

Robert Hughes felt S. T. Gill was exactly the right type of artist to record the activities of the gold rush:

Everything on the goldfields was grist to his mill; in landscape, the scrubby gums, dark shafts and sunlit bullock-heaps, red clay banks, streams and sluices; the washing-troughs and racks of shovels, the furnaces and weighing-stations where miners brought their dust and watched out for rigged scales; the fights over claims, the diggers swinging picks or sleeping at the bottom of a shaft; the honky-tonk pubs ...[87]

Gill sold many copies of his gold rush sketches and watercolours as small lithograph booklets, much like modern postcards. As a result, he became one of the best known and most popular Australian colonial artists of the time. His first two series of lithographs of Victoria, each of 24 black and white sketches, were published by Macartney and Galbraith in Melbourne in 1852 as *Sketches of the Victorian Gold Diggings and Diggers*

87 Hughes, Robert. *The Art of Australia*. Penguin Books Ltd., 1966, p.21.

As They Are. The first series of 24 sketches also appeared in London in August 1853 under the imprint of H.H. Collins & Co., and Piper Brothers & Co. It is largely from these works, some of which were also reproduced in England and Germany, where there was a great demand for knowledge about the new discoveries, that Gill earned the reputation as the 'artist of the goldfields'. His success was so great that his work was pirated in both England and Germany. John Sherer's *The Gold-Finder of Australia; How He went, How He Fared, and How He Made His Fortune* (published by Clarke Beeton, London in 1853) contains forty-eight engravings attributed to W.A. Nicholls, but they are clearly Gill's work.

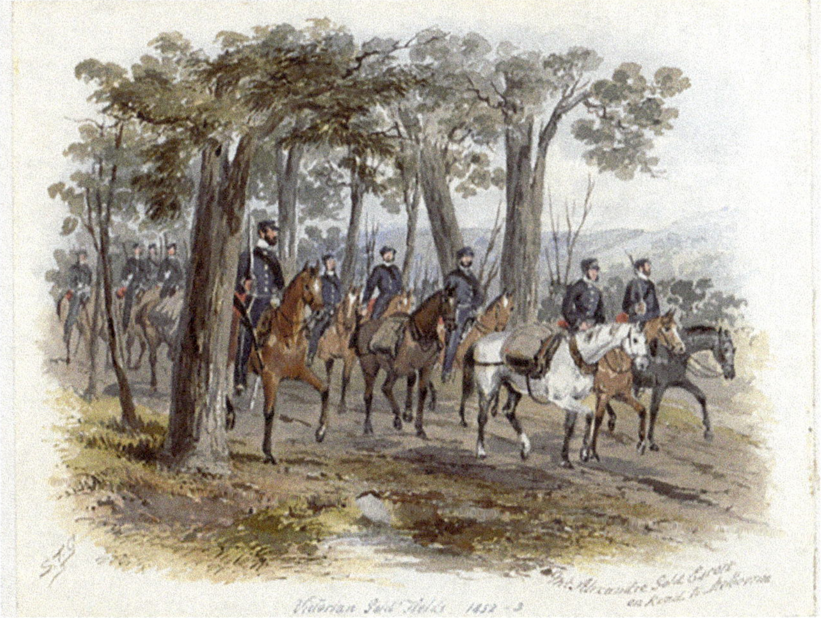

Mt. Alexander Gold Escort en Route to Melbourne (State Library of Victoria)

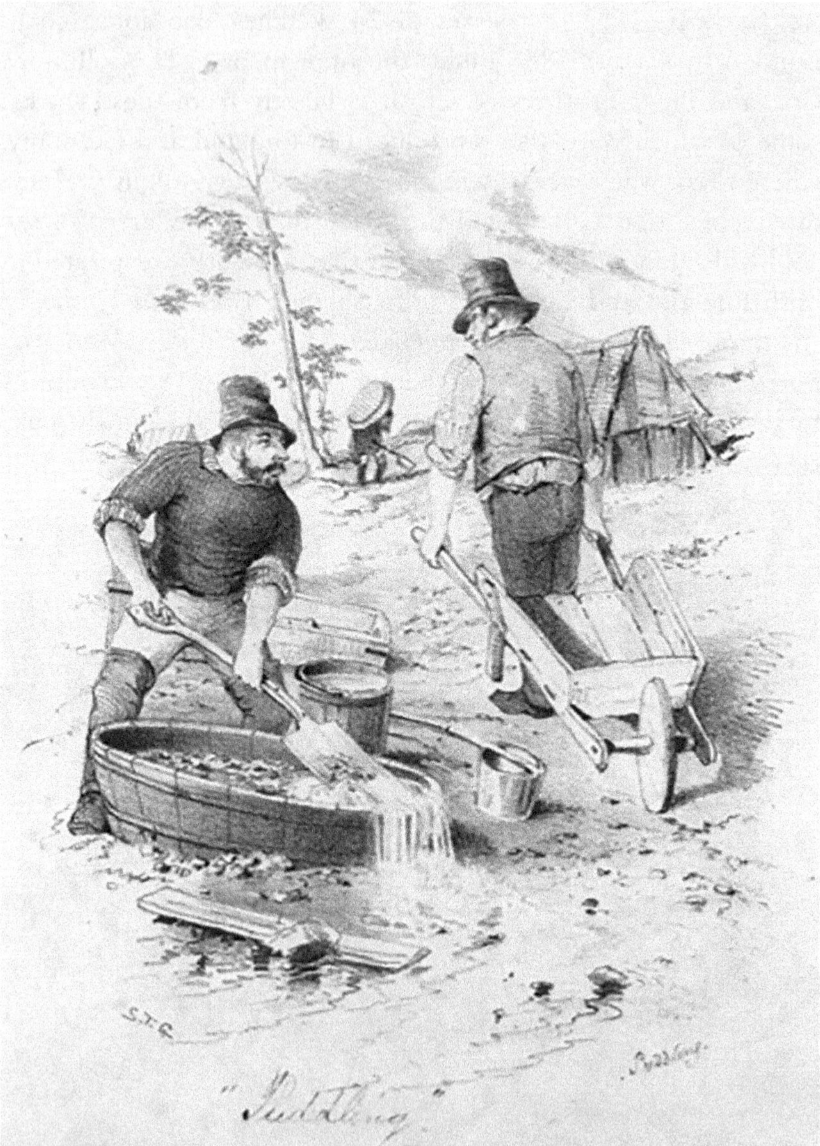

Puddling (State Library of Victoria)

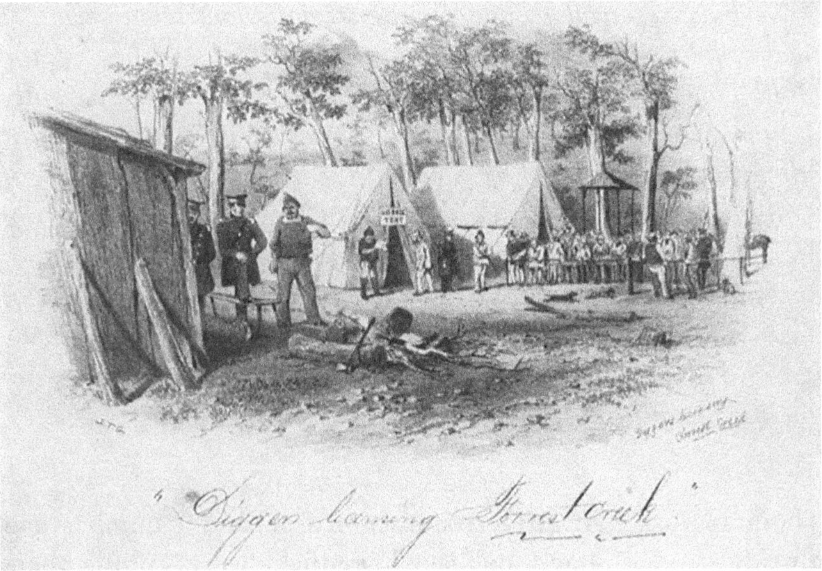

Diggers Licensing Forest Creek (State Library of Victoria)

The image, *Diggers Licensing Forest Creek,* is one of a number produced by Gill on this subject. It's possible he produced many images of this subject, because it illustrated the highly unpopular practice of requiring diggers to be licensed to look for gold and the practice of employing standover thugs to enforce the law. As time went by, social tension on the goldfields grew, and this was exacerbated by the licensing system and the rough treatment of diggers by the license inspectors. This unpopular system was not assisted by the replacement of La Trobe by the temperamental Sir Charles Hotham as Lieutenant-Governor in June 1854. It's likely that this contributed to the Eureka Stockade uprising by diggers in Ballarat on 3 December 1854. It's interesting that Hotham died in office a year later, in December 1855.

In 1852, Gill was unknown in Melbourne and his 1852 lithographs were the city's first opportunity to view his work. This was clear from an editorial in *The Argus* on 26 August 1852:

We have received from some mysterious quarter a series of twenty-four very spirited and well-executed sketches of the Gold Diggers and Diggings of Victoria. They are apparently drawn by some gentleman signing himself S. T. G. and are most admirably lithographed by Messrs Macartney and Galbraith, of Collins Street. Some of the sketches of Diggers, evidently from life, are not the most pleasing in the world, but there is an air of evident truthfulness about them, combined with a vigour and dash of humour which should lead to a very extensive sale. We have no idea of their price but the very cover in which they are enclosed is quite a gem in its way.

The gold rush had attracted other artists, and a number had already produced and published goldfield work. While there were a number of artists active in the goldfields, the publication of their work relating to the goldfields was, according to art historian and critic Alan McCulloch, fleeting or short-lived.[88] McCulloch compared Gill's goldfields paintings with the work of other artists working on the goldfields and commented on the differences in style between Gill and another goldfields artist's interpretation of a goldfields scene:

... it is still the work of a detached, clinical observer. The artist records the salient details of the diggers' meeting but his figures have the rigidity of soldiers. Gill doesn't show the meeting at all, but he captures the atmosphere of the shanty-town with a wit and precision that brings the scene alive. All the participants in the picture are imbued with personalities.

A number of commentators point to Gill's ability to observe and be detached. It's interesting to speculate whether Gill's capacity for detachment and observation was due to his temperament or as a result of the tragedies in his family and private life (or possibly a combination of both).

88 Alan McCulloch, *Artists of the Australian Gold Rush*, Lansdowne Editions, 1977, pp.84-5.

While Gill was observing and sketching activities on the goldfields, an entertainer named Charles Thatcher had arrived, tried gold mining, but decided that entertaining the diggers was more rewarding. He was referred to as the 'Colonial Minstrel' because of his ability to put new words to popular songs in order to comment in a humorous way on contemporary issues. He commented through song on many of the same subjects that Gill illustrated through his artwork. Gill painted a lively watercolour of Charles Thatcher performing titled *Concert Room, Charles Napier Hotel, Ballarat.*

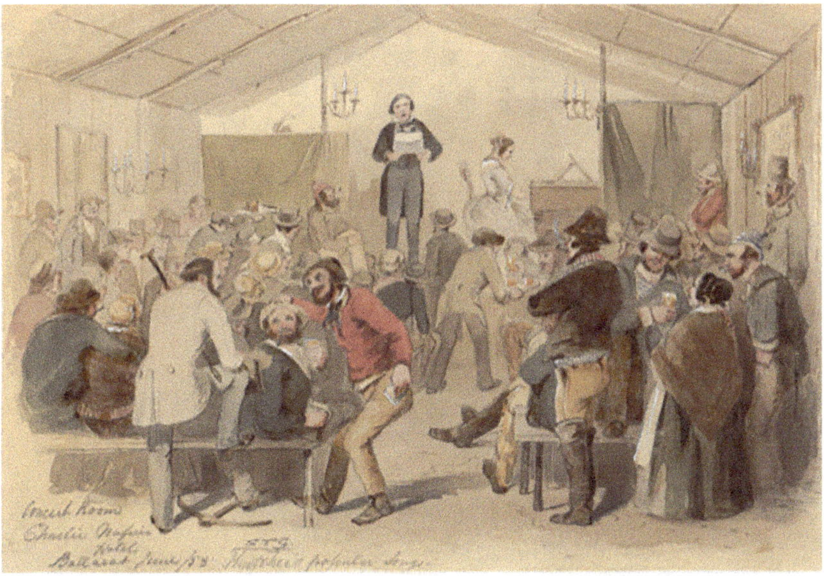

Concert Room, Charles Napier Hotel, Ballarat, June 1855, Thatcher's Popular Songs (National Library of Australia, nla.obj.-134363212)

Over his years visiting the diggings, Gill's drawings captured diggers in many different ways, including as travelling diggers, celebrating diggers, and fighting diggers. There were drawings of Eaglehawk, Forest Creek, Fryer's Creek, Ironbark Gully, and drawings showing all the goldfield processes, including cradling, puddling and fossicking. He was particularly interested in the human face of the gold rush and tried to capture the movement and activity.

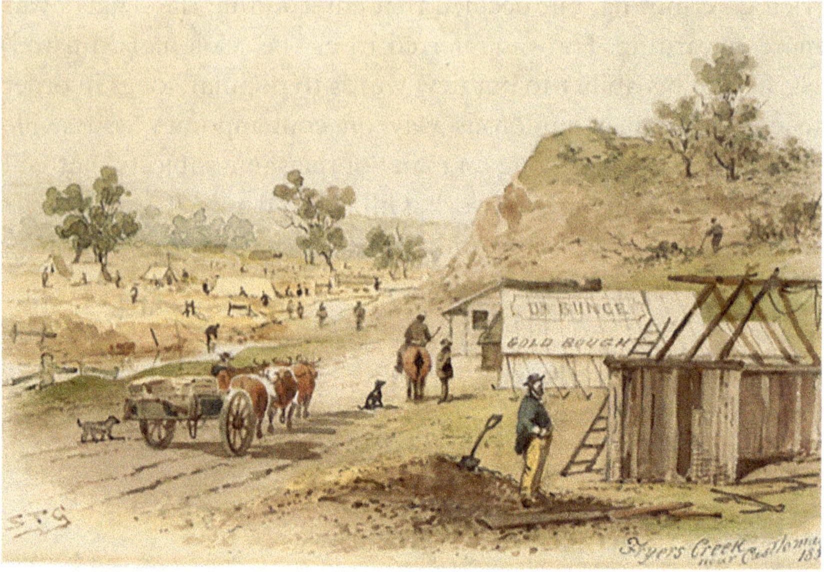

Fryer's Creek, Near Castlemaine (State Library of Victoria)

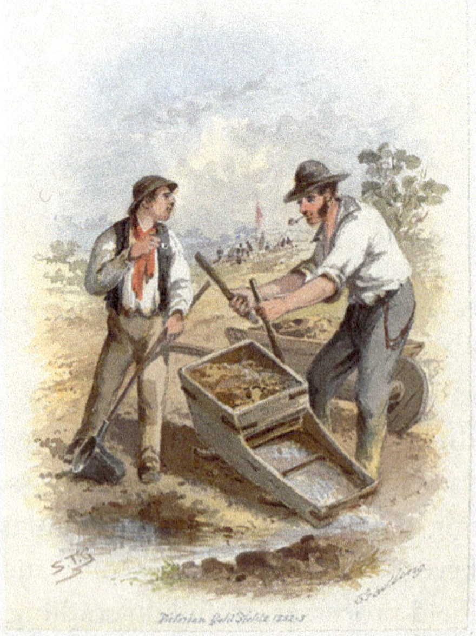

Cradling (State Library of Victoria)

There was constant activity on the goldfields, blended with a sense of noise and excitement. James Bothwick, a contemporary of the goldfields, recorded the atmosphere in 1852:

Occasionally a rush gives animation to a gully. The seizure of a grog-tent, a squabble about a claim, the horn of a news-vendor, a visit from the commissioner, give a diversion to the scene.[89]

Gill's lithographs of the goldfields clearly show this movement and activity and provide the human narrative of the diggers and those who came for a different purpose. McCulloch says of Gill's work in the diggings that:

The drawings of the diggers are extraordinarily observant but never critical. There is sadness and sympathy in his wit, but no cruelty. His art derived unique humanism from its objectivity and the understanding it revealed of living things.[90]

In 1855, James Blundell & Co. announced the publication of a new set of goldfield lithographs entitled *The Diggings & Diggers of Victoria as They Are in 1855*. This new series recorded the considerable change that had occurred in three years since the 1852 series was published, and was also issued as lithographed letterhead papers, the same as had taken place with the 1852 series. The series of letterhead paintings became very popular and were widely used by colonists writing to family in the home country. The major transformation in the three-year period was the disappearance of tent settlements and their replacement with thriving and well-established townships. Gill's work includes views of Ballarat, Castlemaine, Kyneton and Keilor.

89 James Bothwick, *Notes of a Gold Digger and Gold Digger's Guide*, R. Connebee, 1852, p.17.
90 Alan McCulloch, *Artists of the Australian Gold Rush*, Lansdowne, 1977, p.84.

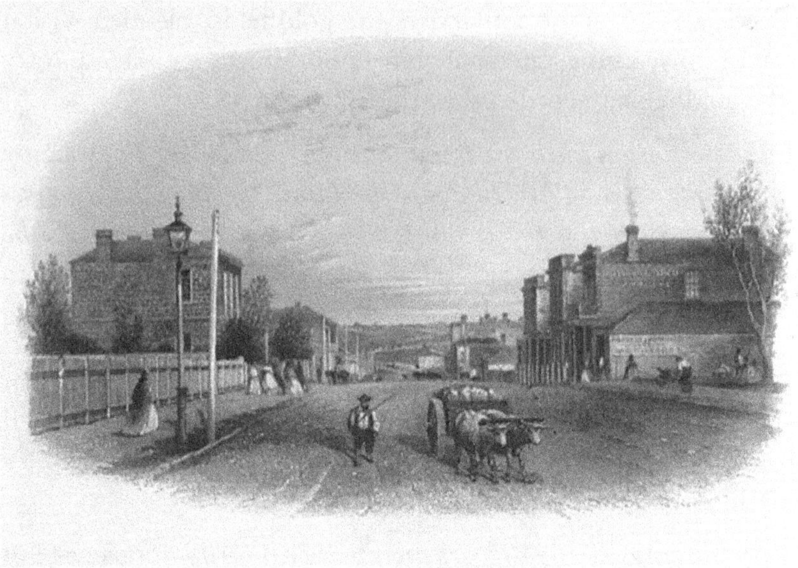

View of Kyneton Looking Towards the Bridge (State Library of Victoria)

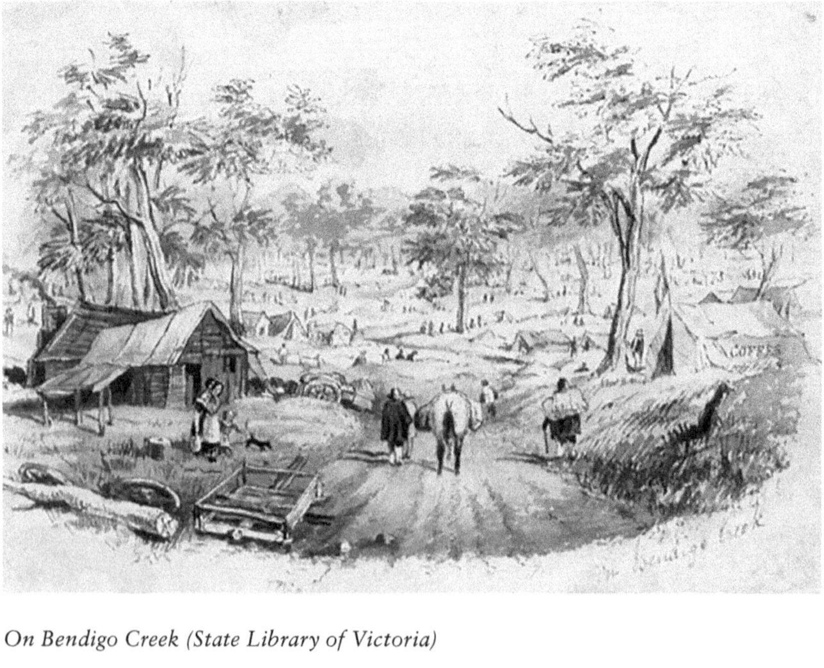

On Bendigo Creek (State Library of Victoria)

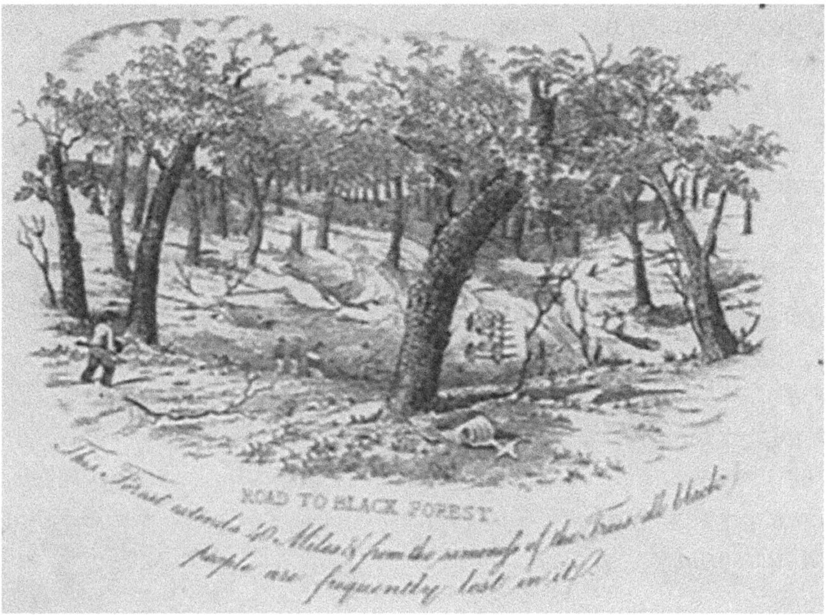

Road to Black Forest (letter head series) (State Library of Victoria)

The speed with which buildings and amenities in these places appeared was even more astounding than the growth of Melbourne. This new series also showed the substantial increase in mechanisation that had taken place. Deep pits and mechanised quartz-crushing were common. These changes meant the nature of mining had moved from claims worked by individuals to pits worked by teams. Gill's 1855 images also show an increase in the number of Chinese in the goldfields. By this time, gold was becoming harder to find and mine. The decline in income was clearly the main cause of resentment against the Chinese, although many other charges were made about them. Demands were made for the number of Chinese permitted to immigrate be restricted. In 1855, the Victorian government passed legislation[91] enabling the imposition of a poll tax of 10 pounds on each Chinese immigrant, with ships forbidden to carry more than one Chinese person for every ton of the ship's weight. To avoid these

91 An Act to Make Provision for Certain Immigrants 1855, Victoria, June 12, 1855.

requirements, ships dropped their passengers at Robe, just over the South Australian border and the Chinese passengers walked overland to the Victorian goldfields. Vitriol continued to be heaped upon the Chinese from many quarters. When nineteenth-century writer and traveller, Sara Aspinall, visited the goldfields, she was surprised and felt some sympathy for the Chinese:

Whilst I was up the country I saw some thousands of my Celestial fellow-creatures. I believe there are about fifty thousand of them in Victoria, chiefly at the 'diggings'... I came to the conclusion they are a very much abused race... I must confess to having taken rather a fancy to the poor Chinamen... I thought they betrayed more equanimity and meekness of disposition than do many of my own countrymen. They are patient and industrious.[92]

It seems from Gill's paintings he also had some sympathy for the Chinese and thus often depicted them as diligent and hard-working people. His two paintings of John Aloo's Restaurant in Ballarat (above) show a scene of hard work, frenetic activity and racial harmony. There were, nevertheless, periodic outbreaks of violence against the Chinese on the goldfields.

S. T. Gill had a way of getting in among the action, smells, noises, and activities, and of recording the big picture as well as an incredible amount of detail. Journalist and art critic, William Moore, saw Gill's approach on the goldfield as follows:

... who with a singular facility, depicted the men and the manners of the time. In his numerous sketches he has preserved the life of the whole period. He adopted the admirable method of drawing a perspective view of a goldfield and then sketched everyday scenes at close range.[93]

92 Clara Aspinall, *Three Years in Melbourne*, L. Booth, London, 1862, pp. 176-7.
93 William Moore, *The Story of Australian Art. Volume 1*, Angus & Robertson, 1934, p. 126.

One of the impacts of the discovery of gold was that it led to development of a set of social, cultural and economic opportunities in Australia that, for many, was not available in mid-nineteenth-century England and Europe, or, for that matter in late Qing Dynasty China. Hence, gold not only provided opportunities and moved the colonies away from dependence on wool and wheat, but also created a new image abroad that helped distance the colonies from their penal origins. The change in image helped foster one of the colonies as places of opportunity and wealth, employment and commerce. This made emigration to the colonies even more attractive and created an era of mass migration from all over the world. The people who came represented a cosmopolitan and multicultural group, and the diggings were a melting pot of cultural complexity, ideas, ideals, and political dissent. This group of people formed a generation that had a major impact on shaping Australia in the future.

Through this mix of people who came as a result of the discovery of gold, combined with the first generations of native-born Anglo-Celtic Australians, there began to emerge more clearly an identity that was uniquely Australian. The emerging culture differentiated it from the British. It embodied a clear sense of egalitarianism and a code of conduct that became known as mateship. This idea of mateship was much more than friendship and demanded a solidarity that was necessary to survive in the harsh Australian environment. It was clearly present on the goldfields.

Cannon believes S. T. Gill's work, which was so widely available in Britain and in many European countries, played a significant part in changing the image of Australia and attracting people to the colonies:

S. T. Gill played a significant although largely overlooked part in this change in attitude towards Australia.[94]

94 Michael Cannon, *The Victorian Gold Fields 1852-3. An Original Album by S. T. Gill*, O'Neil Publishers, 1982, p.12.

It's clear why Gill has been called the artist of the goldfields. His goldfield images were popular, they were published and widely available; they were exciting and colourful, and there were so many of them. His contribution to our understanding of life on the goldfields is enormous. He was, however, so much more than the artist of the goldfields.

Chapter 9—Melbourne 1852-56

This is an age of marvels, and of all the marvellous facts of the nineteenth century, the rapid growth of the colony of Victoria is not the least marvellous. The metropolis is a fair index of her extraordinary development.

—William Kelly, 1857[95]

Of all the colonial cities, Melbourne exhibited the most dramatic growth. Having only been founded in 1835, it already had a population of 29,000 at the start of the gold rush. Within a decade it had grown fourfold, overtaking Sydney, which had been established for almost half a century. Between 1851 and 1861, Melbourne's population grew to 125,000—an annual rate of increase that averaged an incredible sixteen per cent.[96] It grew rapidly as a commercial and residential hub.

While Melbourne grew in importance in the middle of the century as a commercial centre, this growth was dependent on its development as a port. The growing rural industries required livestock, supplies and equipment, which were landed there before being sent to the country. A major export, wool, destined

95 William Kelly, *Life in Victoria or Victoria in 1853 and 1858*, Chapman and Hall, London, 1859, p.38.
96 Tony Dingle, *The Victorians.* Settling, Fairfax, Some & Weldon Associates, 1984 p.152.

for distant markets, required ships, shipping agents, warehouses, merchants, insurance and financial facilities. No matter how productive the pastoralists, farmers and miners might be, their produce was unable to reach the consumer without the assistance of these city-based services.

In 1854, the first Australian railway (only three miles long) was opened in Melbourne by the new Governor, Sir Charles Hotham. Telegraphic communications were introduced, and the University of Melbourne and the Melbourne Library were founded. Until 1858, the chief item of government expenditure was road construction. With better roads came improved transport and the era of Cobb and Co. coaches, with expert drivers and teams of thoroughbred horses that earned a reputation for speed and punctuality.

Having emerged from the activities of the goldfields, Gill quickly produced a large number of sketches. He moved to Melbourne to prepare his images of the goldfields for publication, many showing the contrast between diggers at work in the goldfields and those at play in Melbourne. Work on the diggings was extremely hard, and it's no wonder that after months of toil, and for some a rich reward, they should seek a spell in Melbourne. In fact, hundreds came, giving a tremendous impetus to business. Not all successful diggers came to Melbourne to squander their gold; there were some who came seeking investments (as in Gill's *Provident Diggers)* while others were foolish with their money *(Improvident Diggers*). Others returned home to take up former occupations, reunite with families, and live comfortably in Melbourne or elsewhere. Gill painted several versions of the diggers who returned home to a loving wife and children. It's possible that he was idealising family life, something he didn't have.

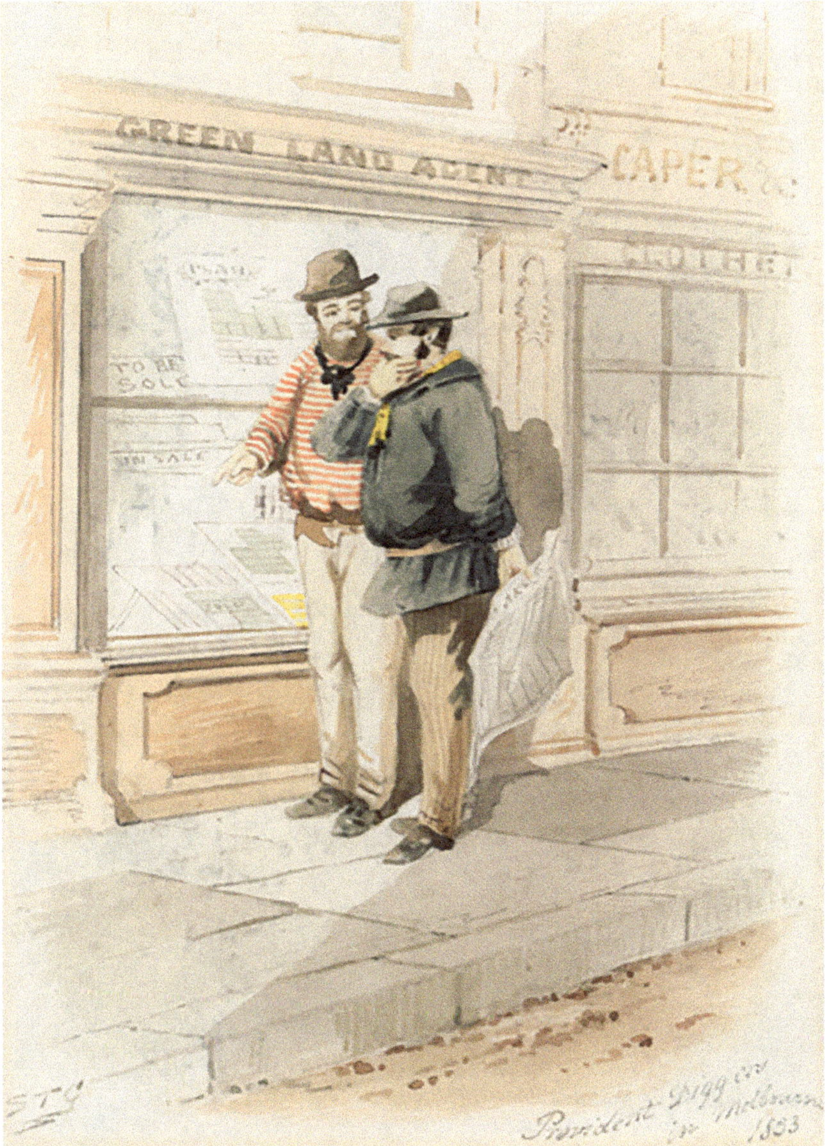

Provident Diggers (State Library of Victoria)

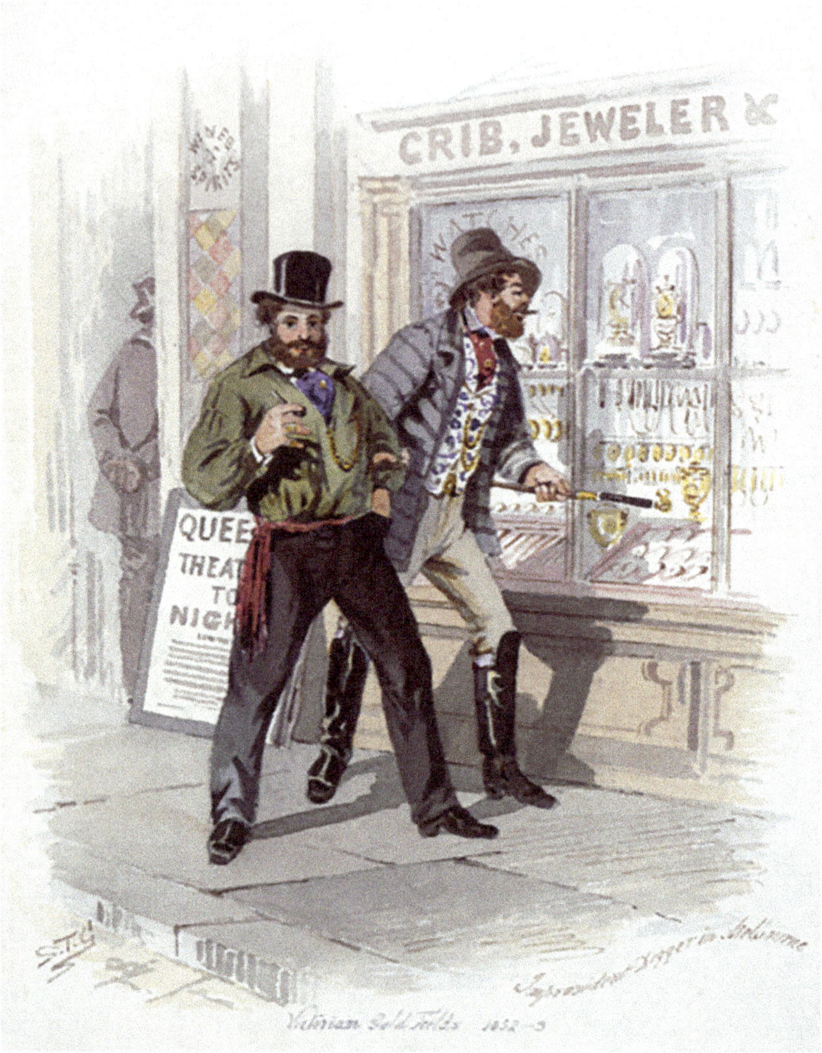

Improvident Diggers (State Library of Victoria)

Gill quickly recognised that Melbourne provided a number of opportunities for him. He set about recording life and happenings in this rapidly growing city, where more curious scenes awaited his paintbrush. He settled into Melbourne life very quickly, and it's possible he felt more at home there, because it was a much larger city than Adelaide and he could blend in—one among many.

As indicated in the previous chapter, his first work to be published in Melbourne occurred in 1852 as *Sketches of the Victorian Gold Diggings and Diggers As They Are.*

1n 1853, J.J. Blundell & Co. took over the bookselling business at No. 44 Collins Street, not far from lithographers Campbell & Ferguson at 30 Collins St. Between them, they were to issue Gill's next three books. Gill apparently used a room above the bookshop as a studio, where he worked his designs onto the lithographic stone. The stones then went to Campbell & Ferguson.

In 1852, Gill was commissioned to produce a large, tinted lithograph of the Mount Alexander Goldfields, based on one of his watercolours. It was a Gill-type street scene with diggings in the background, showing that the deforestation of the area was almost complete. The work was published in March 1853 and received praise in *The Argus* on 9 April 1853:

... admirably executed... from the able pencil of Mr. Gill, the gentleman of whose graphic representations of the diggers and diggings we have before had to make most complimentary comment. This sketch is on a large scale and is well worthy of the reputation of the artist.

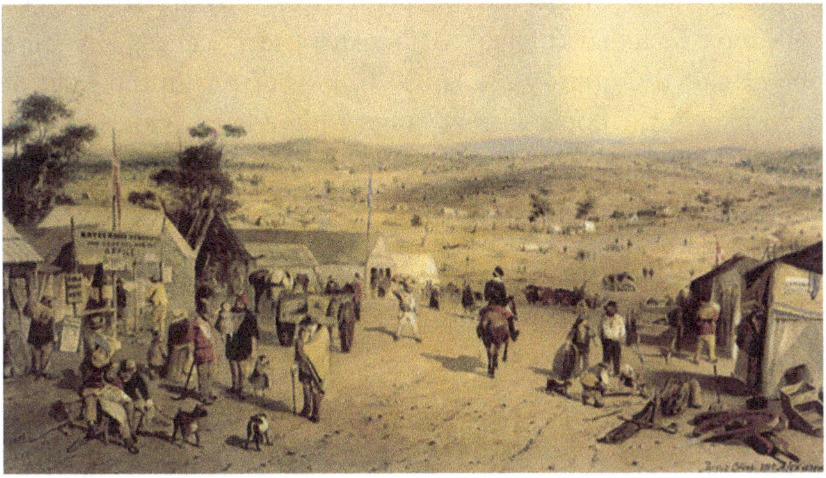

Forest Creek, Mount Alexander Diggings 1852 (State Library of Victoria)

Gill's father died intestate in December 1852, and as the eldest son, he inherited the property at Coromandel. He apparently mortgaged the property in order to settle Adelaide debts. While Gill had a number of reasons for departing Adelaide in 1852, it's interesting to speculate if one of the reasons was to place some distance between himself and his father. While he respected and admired his father, it's possible he found living up to family standards and expectations too difficult.

On 4 February 1853, Gill had his first exhibition in Melbourne at the Exchange Room of the Royal Hotel. The work he displayed was largely from his South Australian watercolours but did include some Victorian scenes and some work in sepia. *The Argus* was impressed and commented on 4 February 1853, that his work:

> *... must meet with high approval from all who can appreciate their merit as works of art, and as truthful delineations of bush life and scenery.*

In June 1853, he published the first of his lithographs in his series entitled *Views in and around Melbourne.* It was a street scene entitled *Collins Street looking west from Russell Street.* The collection included further Melbourne street scenes, including one he called *Criterion Hotel, Gt Collins Street* (in the right of this image is the book shop of James J. Blundell & Co., showing the area above where Gill had a studio). This series was followed rapidly by eight new lithographs under the title *Colonial Sketches.* They were largely a reworking of some of his South Australian work. By 1853, H.H. Collins of London had issued a set of coloured plates of his goldfield pictures for half a guinea (marking the start of Gill's celebrity in the home country).

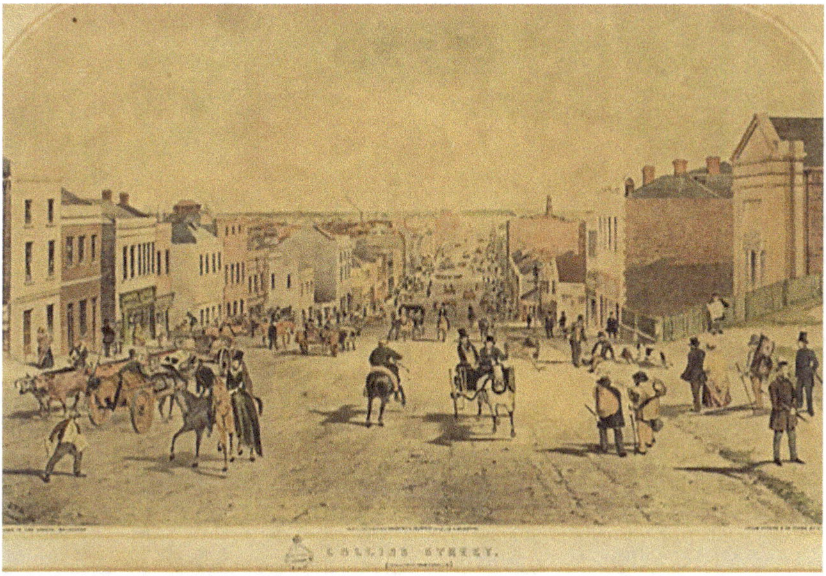

Collins Street, looking west from Russell Street
(Mitchell Library, State Library of New South Wales, FL3270184)

In a fine watercolour, *Dress Circle Boxes, Queen's Theatre, Lucky Diggers in Melbourne, 1853*, the interior of the theatre, completed in 1845, is vividly portrayed, packed with miners and their 'lady' friends at an evening performance. The viewer observes the interaction between the more prosperous miners in the boxes and the more impecunious diggers in the stalls. This picture is similar in many ways to his later *Subscription Ball, Main Road, Ballarat, 1880*.

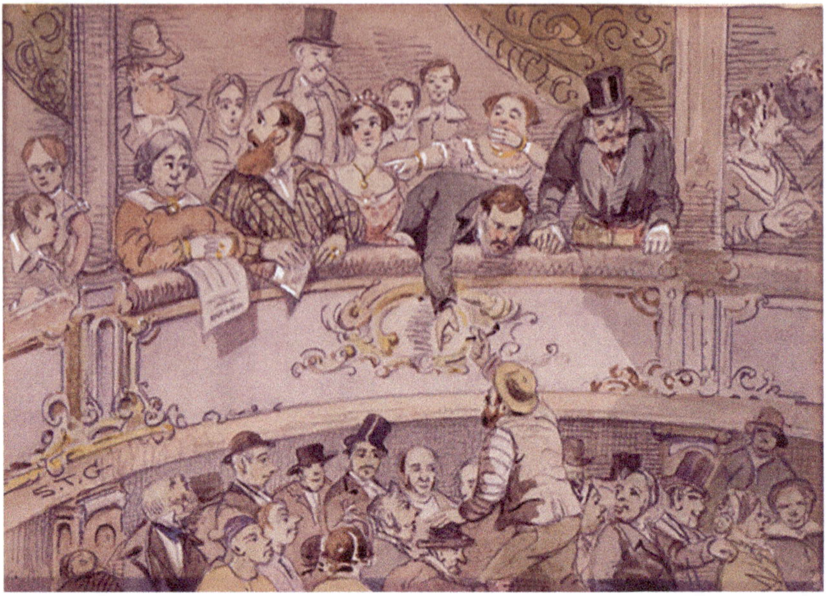

Dress Circle Boxes, Queen's Theatre (State Library of Victoria)

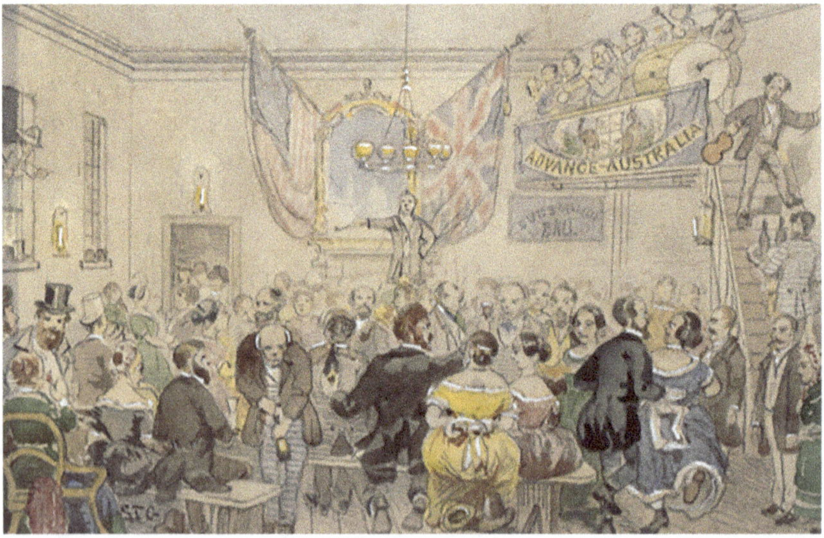

Subscription Ball, Main Road Ballarat (State Library of Victoria)

Gill's *The Digger's Wedding* captured the euphoria of the successful gold miner who returned to the city to establish himself in metropolitan life. Bride and groom are seen driving through the streets in an open carriage, the best man quite overcome from celebrating, and offering a glass, or possibly a bottle of champagne, to the bemused carriage driver. The hire of a carriage was six pounds a day, and champagne cost at least three pounds a bottle. Often the cost of such celebrations amounted to £100 or even £200. In 1853, he produced a number of scenes of diggers celebrating in Melbourne.

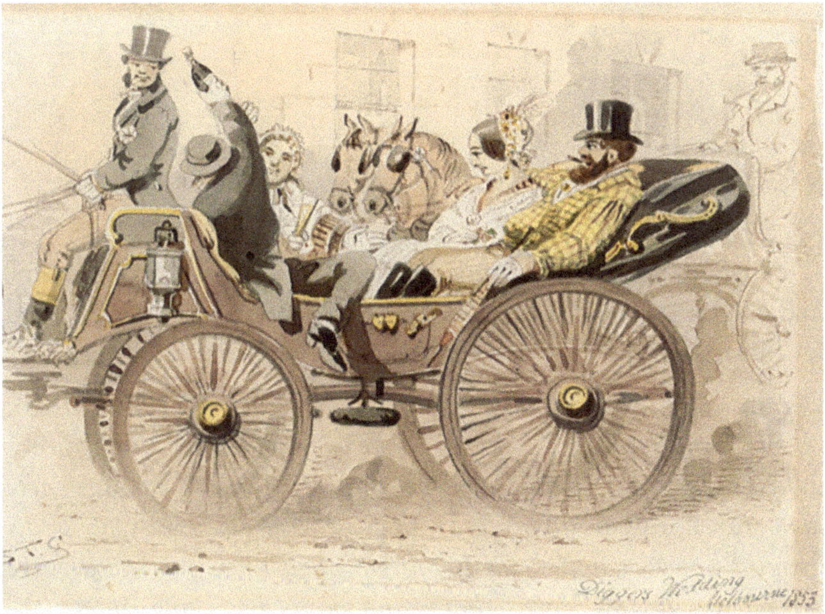

The Digger's Wedding (State Library of Victoria)

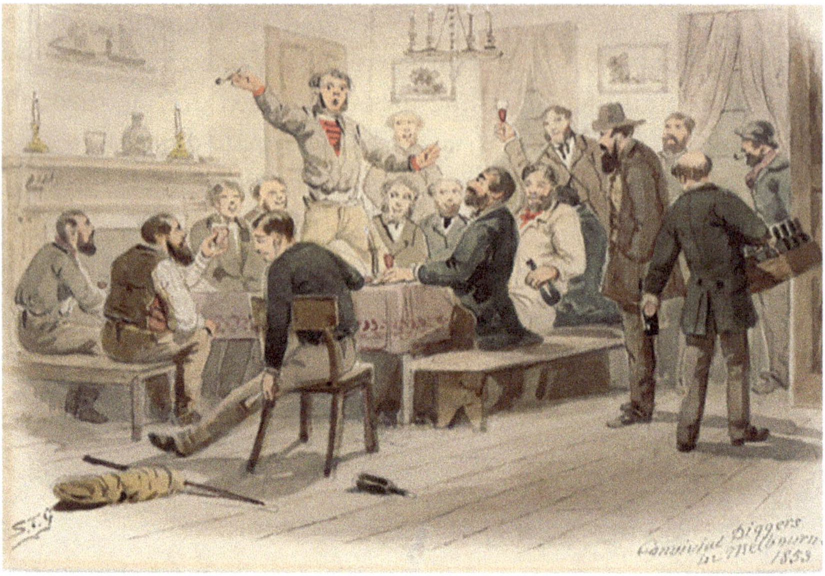

Diggers Celebrating (Convivial Diggers) in Melbourne (State Library of Victoria)

It's clear that diggers found many ways to spend their money and celebrate when in Melbourne. William Howitt commented on this in 1855, during his time in the prosperous city:

Yesterday, I watched the "successful diggers" in Bourke Street. At the top of this street there is a large yard, only railed round, which seems to belong to a horse-dealer. There are various carts also standing there for sale to diggers. You can rarely pass this ground without danger of being galloped over, for the diggers are always trying horses there, and come headlong out of the yard into the street, and gallop and rampage about the street in a famous way. The whole street swarms with diggers and diggeresses. Men in slouching wide-awakes, with long untrimmed hair and beards, and like navvies in their costume. Some have heavy horsewhips in their hands and are looking at the exploits of other diggers on horseback with a knowing air. Others are swearing about the doors of pot-houses; where others, again, are drinking and smoking. Others, with a couple of bundles or a pair of huge boots swung over their shoulders, are lighting their pipes at a candle or cheapening digger apparatus. The whole street abounds with second-rate shops, which supply tools, kettles, tin-ware, boots, clothes, and so on. You are amazed at the price of every article.[97]

By 1853, Gill was clearly at a high point in his artistic career. He had received substantial praise for his work, and his reputation had sky-rocketed in a relatively short time. Gill's work, possibly his style, had struck a chord with the colonists of Melbourne. In 1853, he entered into a relationship with a new illustrated weekly newspaper called the *Arm-Chair*. The editor, Edward Butterfield, announced the arrival of this new weekly in the first edition on page one on 3 September 1853, in rather flowery terms with a particular pitch to women:

Gentlest of readers, take your seat. Our legs and arms are of the finest Spanish mahogany. Cover the bareness of the former with your snowy skirts: suffer the cordial Platonic embrace of the latter. The stuff we are made of is pure merino —our skin real morocco. Our garment is the most delicate crochet, and our entire 'personnel' the essence of refinement. We desire you to be at home with us at once, ladies, for we are your friends and champions to the death.

Butterfield continued for over a page, extolling the aims, principles and objectives of this new paper, promising it would soon become, to every lady and gentleman of talent in the colony, a refuge, a source of pleasure, solace and enjoyment. He also announced in the paper on September 3 it would provide high quality illustrations and the services of S. T. Gill had been acquired:

97 William Howitt, *Land, Labour, and Gold, or Two Years in Victoria*, Longman, London, 1855, p. 22.

> *... the best artist in the country is laid under contribution for our reader's benefit. This gentleman's sketches have been universally admired, distinguished as they are for raciness and ease, and that perfect 'vraisemblance' which gives a good picture its peculiar merit. Some of the caricatures "prepared expressly for this publication" are perfect gems, and we are sure that if our readers were to see them, they would soon run up our circulation...*

From the outset, the paper was confident it would become a force in Melbourne and had aspirations of emulating the London *Punch*. This was not to be, but while it had a short life, it used satire to trumpet a range of issues. The style suited Gill, who had used satire in his artwork in Adelaide. The best example was possibly his *Heads of People* series. The Anti-Vice League, an organisation staunchly supported by temperance reformers, was ridiculed by the paper from the outset as intolerant and bigoted. Gill supported this stance, as he was comfortable in his lifestyle at that time, which included pipe smoking, beer drinking, shooting, and horse racing.

Melbourne, by this time, was possibly the brashest city in the world. Gill enjoyed the milieu of the city, and his art could match his lifestyle without fear of family rebuke. This probably exposed a dichotomy within Gill, with the pursuit of his new lifestyle on the one hand, while on the other hand he was conscious of the moral code his family had adhered to. An inability to live up to family expectations (even though his parents were dead and he had severed ties with his brother) would have meant guilt, self-deprecation, and probably, a search for solace. This was a time of new order in the colony, with much of the old being turned upside down. The paper saw this as a 'Young Australia', which it championed. While it projected an air of being radical, it was conservative on some issues. This was possibly a pragmatic decision to avoid litigation. At times, the *Arm-Chair* displayed some conservative moral values, such as promoting the values of worthiness and good character. Gill often used his work to support these values. As an example, his diggers were often linked with prudence and providence.

From the first issue, the paper promoted women's issues. While it wanted to be seen as the champion of the fairer sex, it actually projected a fairly conservative and traditional role for them. Gill's view was coloured by uncertainty, unease, and inconsistency and hence he opted for an idealised view, like the paper, of the civilising influence of women. His views were no doubt shaped by his idolisation of his mother. In some of his earliest work on the *Months & Seasons* series, women were shown in a family context, tending vines, roses, and caring for children. In his work on diggers, he had several versions of a theme of the digger who returned home. In each version, the digger is shown on a couch with a dog at his feet being looked after by an adoring wife and child.

Gill provided a number of sketches for the paper during its short life, including some that occupied a full page; interestingly, the paper, at one point, railed against those who had plagiarised his work. However, he did not do his own lithography for the paper, and the illustrations were clumsily executed. His last illustration for the paper appeared on page 42 of the final issue on 25 March 1854. He is shown smoking a pipe, holding an empty pannikin behind his back, facing a digger who is holding an uncorked bottle. The caption devised by the paper was its last criticism of the Anti-Vice League:

> *… that the man who wants his beer is entitled to have it, and that he who dares to have a partiality for spiritual comforts should not be utterly precluded from their enjoyment.*

In September 1853, Gill secured a prestigious commission to produce the official record of Melbourne's First Old Colonists'

Festival. Unlike his rather humorous representation of the Adelaide festival, he produced a version which depicted a respectable affair.

Gill sketched many scenes, showing the change in Melbourne from a colonial seaport to a modern metropolis. Melbourne's growth had been significant after its canvas-town period when the swelling population was accommodated in tents. His 1854 work, published in 1855, is proof of the substantial progress in Melbourne, showing scenes of the capital's new buildings and bridges, crowded shipping and wharves, busy hotels and theatres, arrival of the gold escort at the Treasury - full of the bustling drama of a boom city, and an individual record of human life still difficult to record photographically. In April and May 1855, Blundell issued two parts each of eight lithographs of *Sketches in Victoria*. These are all of Melbourne, followed later by two more parts of scenes in the country and/or near Geelong.

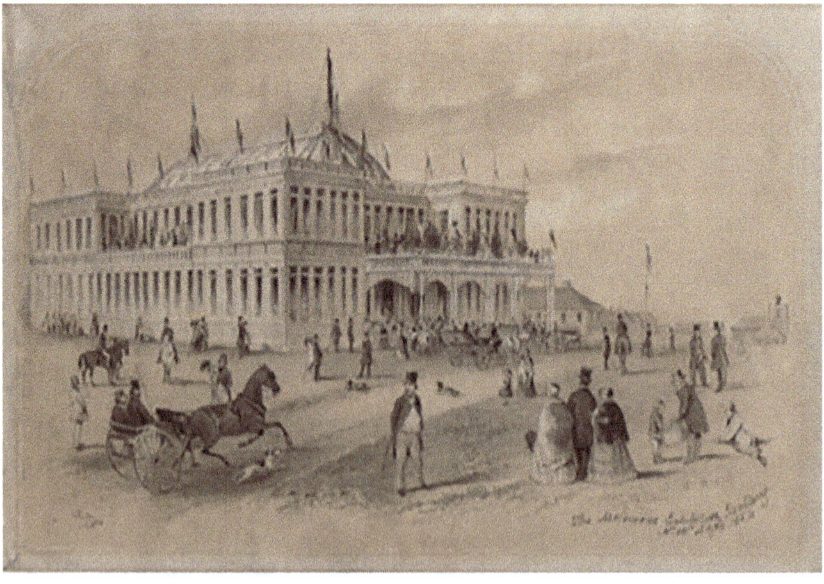

The Melbourne Exhibition Building (State Library of Victoria)

In 1854, Gill also produced a series of whimsical drawings dealing with various types of locomotion, including the first little steam engine and steamships on the Yarra.

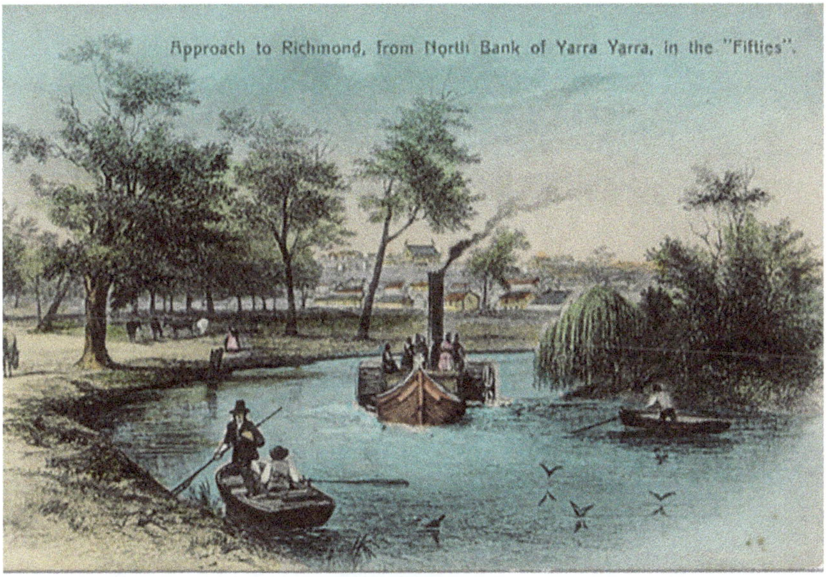

Approach to Richmond from North Bank of Yarra Yarra in the 'Fifties'
(State Library of Victoria)

As indicated in the previous chapter, in 1855, James Blundell & Co. announced the publication of a new set of goldfield lithographs entitled *The Diggings & Diggers of Victoria as They Are in 1855.*

A major production of Gill's work took place in 1856 with the publication of *Victoria Illustrated* by Sands & Kenny in Melbourne and Sydney and Thomas Brown in Geelong.

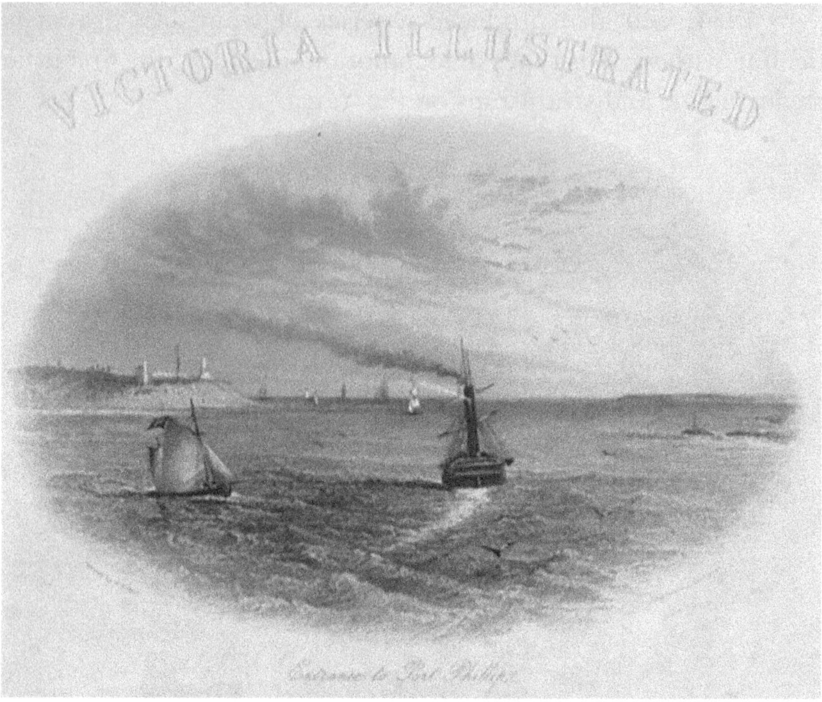

Victoria Illustrated (cover) (State Library of Victoria)

It contained 46 images by Gill. However, it's unclear what part he played in the project. It seems the publishers may have selected the artwork and then sent it to London for a professional engraver to do the engraving work. The cover, designed by Gill, was engraved locally. There is some confusion about the release date, as some of the plates are dated 1857, while it appears it may have been on sale towards the end of 1856. It seems the English engraver made some changes, particularly with trees and skies, to give them more of an English look. Australian viewers of this work were quick to see these changes. The Melbourne based weekly journal, *My Note Book,* published an analysis of *Victoria Illustrated* on 3 January 1857, making particular reference to the work of the engraver:

Everybody knows the initials S. T. G.; I mean everybody in Victoria who has the least feeling for pictorial art. From time to time there have been published with his signature, lithographs of various kinds... Sands and Kenny have selected from the best of them, and, together with some that have not been published, sent them home where they have undergone the process of steel engraving, and they now come to us as 'Victoria Illustrated', and a very elegant Book they make, bound up in scarlet and gold, ... I have little to complain of ... I could have wished, however, that the engraver had been himself intimate with Victorian scenery and Victorian usages, for there are here and there such manifest indications of these views having been engraved at a distance from the country of first production, as drawings, that some of the essential qualities are often wanting in consequence. Every artist who has lived in Australia, knows that one special quality of the foliage is a kind of raggedness, and that the masses are broken up into irregular patches, quite different from the large oval shaped forms which characterise the trees in an English landscape. The engraver of these views, evidently puzzled with this peculiarity of broken masses, has made a kind of compromise between the two kinds, and the result is neither gum tree, nor elm, nor oak, but trees of doubtful botanical character. So, too, in the skies; they are all too English ...But these are minor qualifications to the general excellence of the work, which I have no doubt will meet with an extensive sale, and repay the enterprising publishers ...

The more formal look of the images in *Victoria Illustrated* is evident from the following examples:

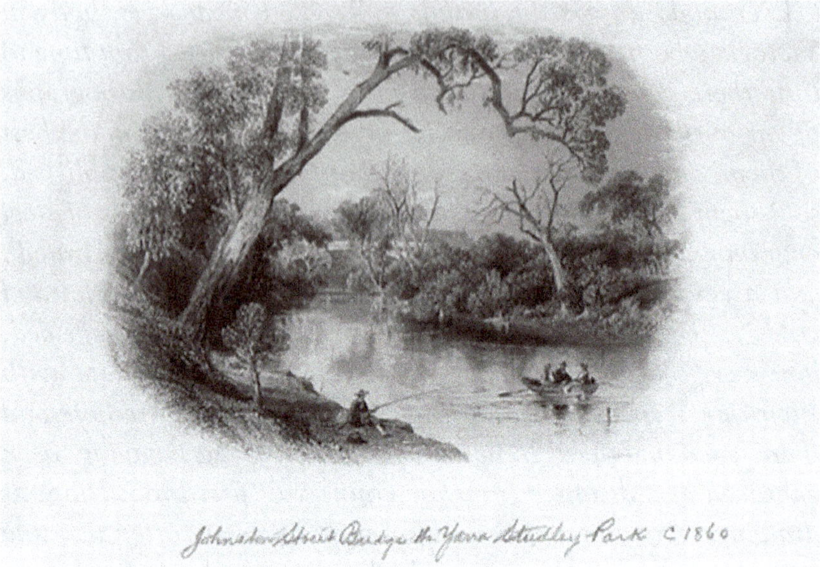

Johnston Street Bridge South Yarra (State Library of Victoria)

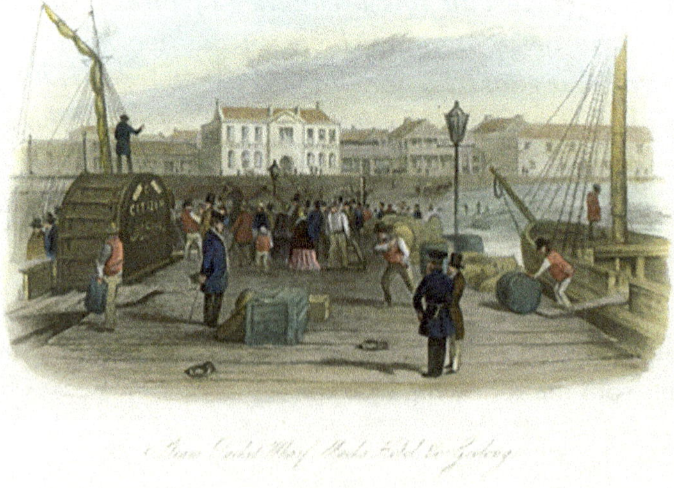

Steam Packet Wharf Geelong (State Library of Victoria)

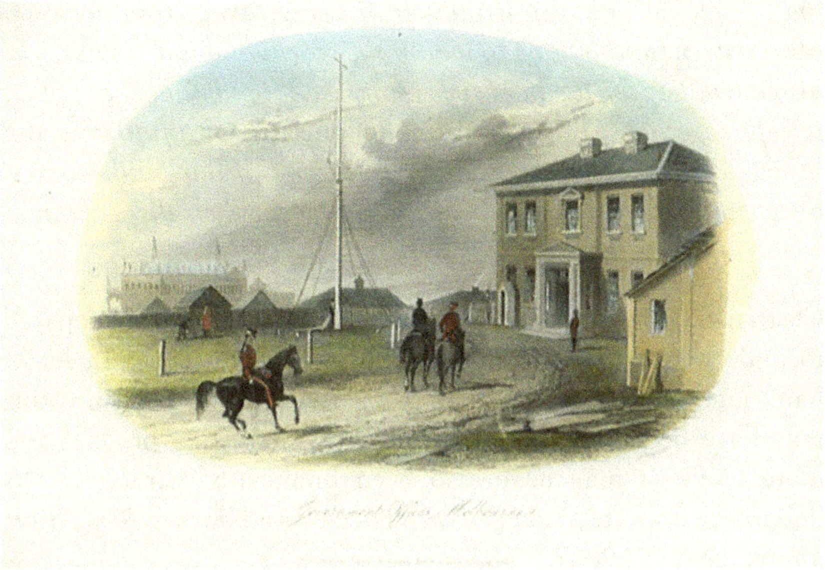

Government Offices Melbourne (State Library of Victoria)

By now, Gill's work had been published in Edinburgh and Hamburg as well as in London. The sheer volume of his published work must have generated a considerable amount of income. However, it is highly likely Gill wasn't particularly interested in the financial aspects and opportunities associated with his work. He had shown little interest in the business side of his affairs in the past, and as a result, found himself in financial difficulties, including insolvency in South Australia. A second series of *Victoria Illustrated* was released by Sands & Kenny in 1862.

Even with Gill's successes in Melbourne, it seems he was in need of money by 1856. *The Argus* in January announced enthusiastically in the Domestic Intelligence column:

Such an opportunity seldom occurs as that which will be afforded today at Tennent's Auction Room, where 12 magnificent watercolour drawings, by the pencil of the renowned S. T. G., will be offered for unreserved sale. Independent of their artistic merits, these masterly delineations of colonial scenery have the somewhat unusual attraction of being taken from personal observation, and by one to whom the stockwhip is as familiar as his pencil. For the credit of the colony we should hope that the set is kept together, for a more valuable nucleus for a future school of arts could not be devised. Surely, some of our 'millionaires' have sufficient taste and liberality to prevent their dispersion.

Clearly, STG was flexible in the design work he was prepared to undertake as at this time he was engaged to design a set of banknotes for the Colonial Bank of Australasia. For him, this may have been seen as a challenge, an interesting project, and quite likely, it may have also been financially attractive. His design incorporated a digger with his pick and bucket. *The Argus* announced on 1 March 1856:

The first proof of the note of this corporation was yesterday evening shown to us. The design is from the pencil of S. T. Gill... The design, as might be expected, is very beautiful and the engraving and printing are worthy of the design.

Geoffrey Dutton believes Gill demonstrated a sense of humour in his design work which was apparently not noticed by the media. It seems the rough-looking digger with his pick and bucket on the £1 note becomes decidedly more prosperous looking in the £50 and £100 notes.[98]

In 1856, Gill produced a humorous design depicting himself on a ladder nailing up a sign on a wall which read *Miscellaneous Sketches by S.T.G, 1856*. It's not clear why this colour lithograph was produced. It's possible it was intended as a frontispiece for a series of lithographs, but there does not appear to be any record of their publication. The scene contains a number of possible messages, such as clearing the decks of his work at sacrificial prices, and possibly a feeling that society was passing him by.

98 Geoffrey Dutton, *S. T. Gill's Australia*, McMillan, 1981, p.41.

This may have been Gill saying goodbye to Melbourne.

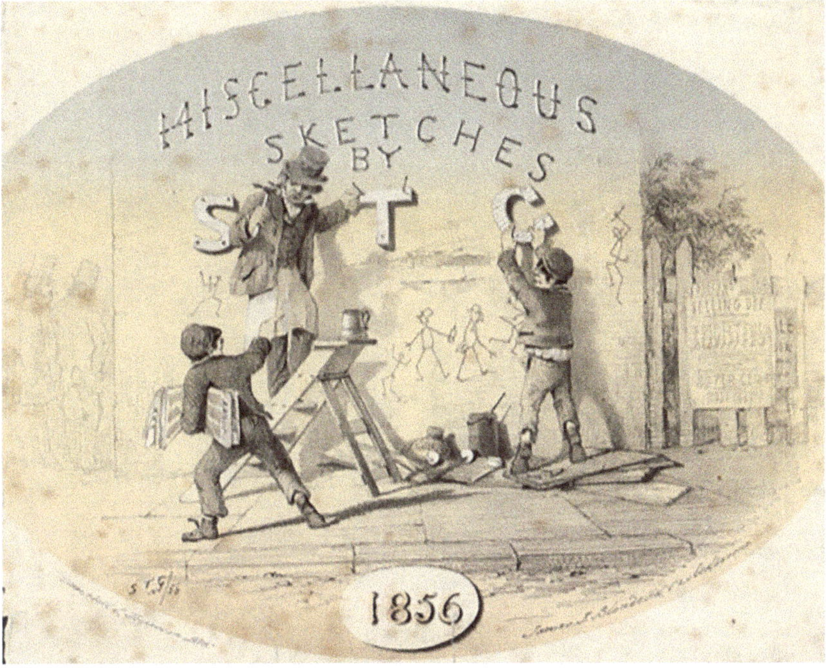

Miscellaneous Sketches by S.T.G. 1856 (State Library of Victoria)

By 1856, much of the early colonial life in Victoria, which appealed to Gill, was fading. It is possible the art-buying public was starting to take more of an interest in artwork portraying a more romantic image than the earthy work that characterised much of Gill's art. However, after the launch of the banknotes, he made another trip into the Victorian countryside he loved so much. On that occasion, he travelled to Portland in the *Queen,* a small coastal steamer, to visit the western district so he could paint the Wannon Falls and sketch the coastal towns of Port Fairy, Portland and Warrnambool. By this time, he had decided to leave Victoria (some of these scenes were lithographed and published in *Victoria Illustrated* in 1857). So, at 38, he departed for eight years, hoping his triumphs of Victoria could be repeated in Sydney. In May 1856 he sailed for Sydney in the *London.*

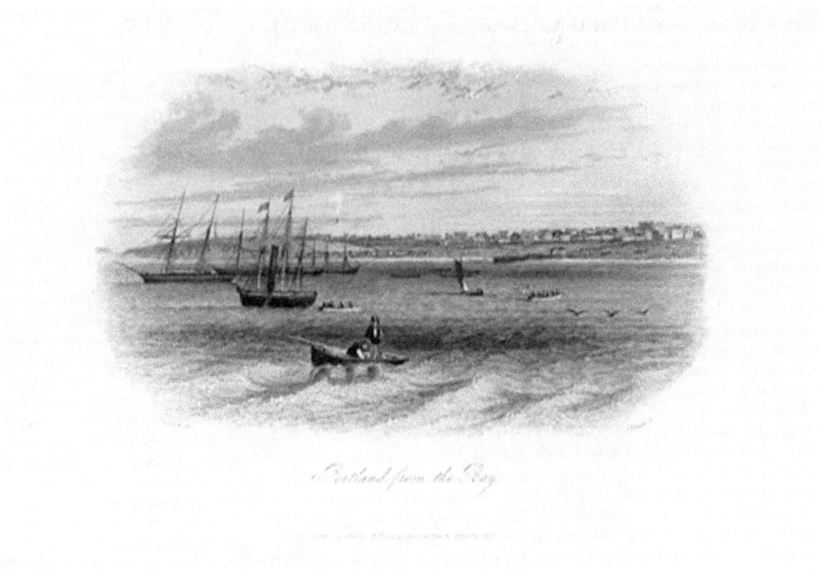

Portland from the Bay (State Library of Victoria)

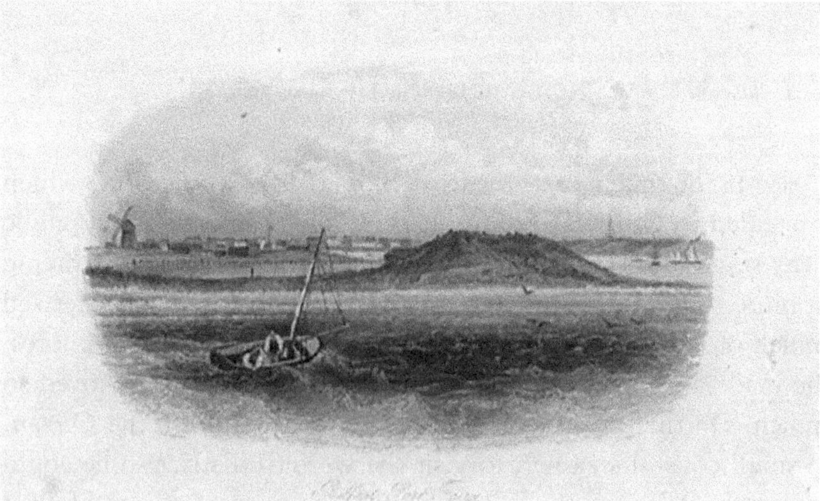

Belfast Port Fairy (State Library of Victoria)

Gill's time in Melbourne was probably the most productive time in his artistic career. He produced an enormous number of images of the city at a very formative time in its evolution, with such enormous and rapid change occurring. He also produced a wonderful record of rural Victoria and the change that occurred in the urban settlements outside Melbourne. All of this work was being produced when Gill was also creating an enormous number of images of life on the diggings.

Chapter 10—
Sydney and Beyond 1856-1864

Tiers of fine buildings seem to rise one above the other,
like the seats in an amphitheatre, and towering above them all,
is the tall spire of St James' Church.

—John Askew, 1857.[99]

In 1856, at the height of his fame, Gill travelled saloon class to Sydney on board the *London* with his de facto wife, Elizabeth,[100] hoping to repeat his Victorian success. They arrived on 20 May and settled in Woolloomooloo, which at that time contained extensive barracks, prisons and many windmills. Balmain and Pyrmont had established themselves as the home of shipbuilding in Sydney and the whole of Australia, for that matter. The newly developed wharves around Woolloomooloo Bay handled international trade, whereas Darling Harbour catered solely for coastal trade.

99 John Askew, A *Voyage to Australia and New Zealand*, Simpkin Marshall, London, 1857, pp. 185-6.
100 This is the first reference that I have found to Gill having a partner. There is no record in the Victorian Marriage Registers for the years 1852 to 1856 of a marriage between S. T. Gill and an Elizabeth (one record of a Samuel Gill's marriage to Ann Gale in 1852). There is also no record of a marriage between S. T. Gill and an Elizabeth in the New South Wales Marriage registers for the period 1852 to 1864.

The climate of the colony of New South Wales was often the subject of favourable comment, although dust and extreme heat (in English terms) were frequently mentioned. A visitor to Sydney in 1857, F.J. Hobson, was generally impressed:

> *... Its climate is hot in summer, but dry and salubrious; yet at times, terrific storms of thunder and lightning, rain and dust, sweep over the city... The evenings at Sydney were, at times, singularly beautiful. The moon was so bright and large that you could see to read by it. The stars too, were brighter and larger than ours in appearance, and seem to drop like pendant lamps of glittering crystal from the deep blue dome above... The change of heat and cold from day to night was sometimes sudden, the sudden changes in atmosphere have their effects upon the complexion and constitution of the weaker sex.*[101]

When S. T. Gill arrived, the main commercial streets in the city were George and Pitt. In the 1850s, when Pitt Street was extended to Bridge Street, the Tank Stream was covered completely. The finest shops were in Pitt Street, between King and Market streets. There was still, however, a motley mix of single-storey and multi-storeyed buildings. The northern end of the city (north of the General Post Office) was evolving into the financial centre. The opening of the Royal Exchange in 1853, on the corner of Gresham, Pitt, and Bridge streets, promoted this, as did the construction of solemn banks built in the various revivalist architectural styles of the Victorian era. As the city's commercial activity grew in the 1850s, the two main commercial east-west streets, Hunter and King, became the home of unusual and specialist shops and small businesses. The finest town houses, which were often grand and up to four storeys high, were located in Macquarie Street. In 1858, Sydney, Melbourne and Adelaide were linked by telegraph. Gill's watercolour below of the scene at the corner of George

101 Rev. F. J. Hobson, Australian, *With Notes by Way of Egypt, Ceylon, Bombay, & the Holy Land*, Homitten Adams & Co., London, 1862, p. 159.

and Margaret streets includes F. Mader's stationery shop, above which Gill found a studio.

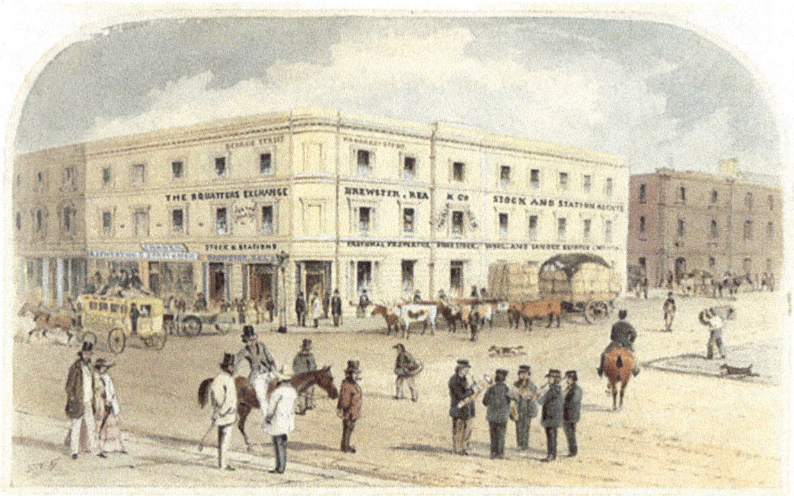

The Squatters Exchange: a view of the corner of George and Margaret Streets (Dixon Library, State Library of New South Wales, FL8804084)

A visitor to Sydney in 1849 commented on the markets:

Sydney possesses a very good market-place. Everything pertaining to a market is sold there, except fish, which are hawked about the streets. There is generally a fine display of fruit and vegetables. On the evenings of Saturdays the market is thronged, and, the buildings being lighted up with gas, the effect is pleasing; but take care of your pockets![102]

In 1858, a social survey, which included a study of Sydney housing, was undertaken by William Stanley Jevons, who was employed from 1854 by the relatively new mint as an assayer and became known in Sydney as a scientific observer and writer. He found that successful merchants, shopkeepers, and professional men lived in mansions or villas, usually on elevated land just

102 Joseph P. Townsend, *Rambles and Observations in New South Wales*, London, Chapman & Hill 1849, p. 267.

outside the city, such as in Paddington, Darlinghurst, Elizabeth Bay or Glebe, or in the middle of town in Macquarie Street or in Lower Fort Street. The people he called middle classes, which he defined as skilled workers, lived in four-to-five-roomed houses, clustered in districts such as Surrey Hills, Strawberry Hill, Redfern, Glebe, Pyrmont, Balmain and the higher area of the Rocks around Millers Point. He noted that the worst quality housing, which was much older, was located at the Rocks, the lower end of Sussex Street and around Druitt and Goulburn Streets.[103]

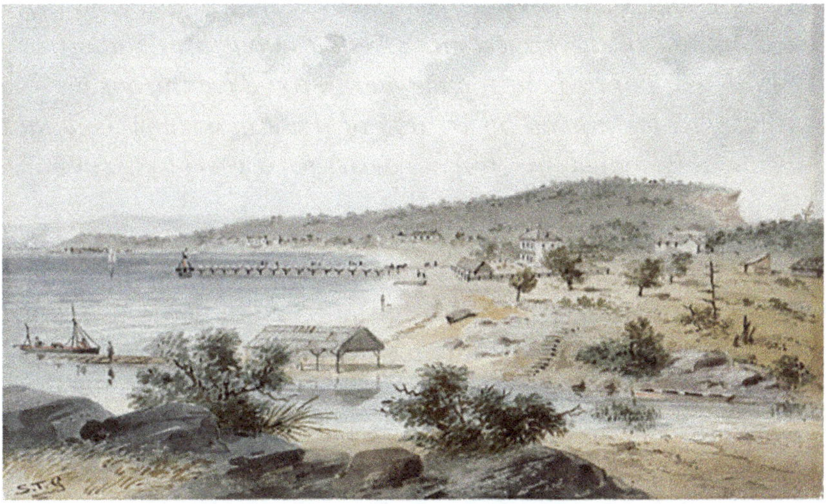

Watsons Bay, Port Jackson (Dixon Galleries, State Library of New South Wales, FL3270628)

Gill's reputation, established in South Australia and enhanced on the goldfield, had preceded his arrival in Sydney. Unfortunately Sydney, a conservative but charming seaport town, was suffering a depression due to a slump in wool prices. The economic climate was not only unkind to Gill but to Sydney artists generally. The best known of Sydney artists at that time was landscape painter Conrad Martens. Besides Martens, there were other painters of

103 W. S. Jevons, *Social Survey of Australian Cities 1858*, reproduced in the Sydney Morning Herald, Saturday November, 9, 1929, p. 13.

harbour and shipping subjects including Joseph Fowles, Frederick Garling and Frederick Terry. All were very active during Gill's time in Sydney. For these artists, a major focus for their work was the wonderful harbour and the many vessels arriving and departing. The harbour and the foreshore were also places for recreation. Even then, swimming in the harbour wasn't without its challenges. A local commented on swimming in Port Jackson:

> *As I strolled along the edge of the Domain near the Harbour, I came upon a hulk moored close to the shore... The said hulk, I found, had been converted into a bathing-machine, round which bathers could swim secure from sharks, which swam in Port Jackson, and of the largest size. A spot about fifty yards from the hulk was pointed out to me where a too adventurous person had had his leg nipped off by one of these monsters. This fact considerably cooled my growing desire for a good long swim.*[104]

Having quickly established a studio above F. Mader's stationery shop in George Street, Gill wasted no time in getting to work recording Sydney. Possibly his first work, dated 24 May 1856, was his drawing of the Government Domain. This was followed a few months later by a set of views around Sydney entitled Scenery in and around Sydney, which were advertised in the sporting paper, Bell's Life, on 18 October 1856. Six of the sketches were lithographed and printed by Allen and Wigley as Lithographic Sketches of Scenery in and Around Sydney. They soon followed with a second set of six lithographic sketches.

104 Rev. A. Polehampton, *Kangaroo Land*, Richard Bentley, London, 1862, p. 36.

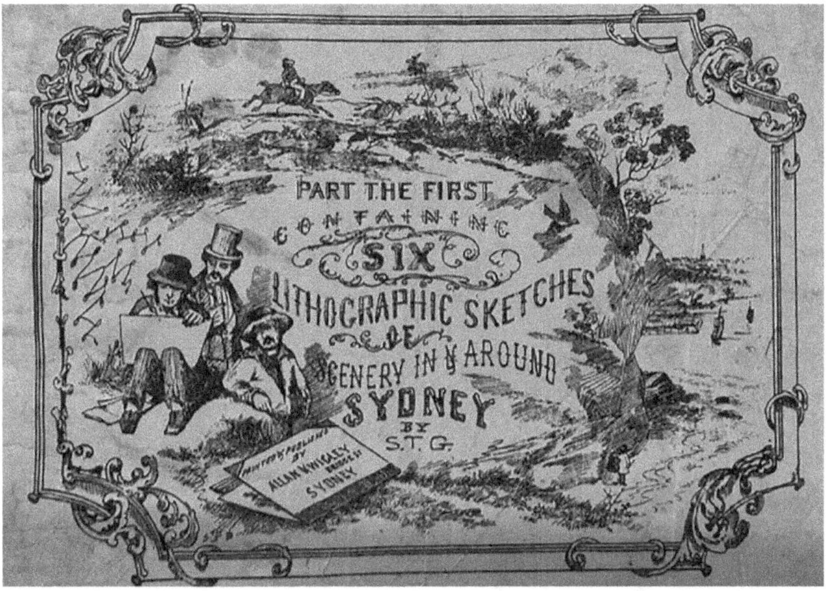

Part the first, Containing Six Lithographic Sketches of Scenery in and around Sydney, by S. T. G.
(Photograph of cover to set of images held by the National Library of Australia)

Twenty-four of the scenes were eventually published as *Sydney Illustrated*. His Sydney views are typical of his previous artwork, full of life and detail. The publishers advertised the set of sketches on page 7 of the *Sydney Morning Herald* on 11 September 1858:

… a series of Twenty-four Sketches about Sydney, comprising some of the principal buildings, churches, street, and harbour views, &c., drawn by Mr. S. T. Gill.

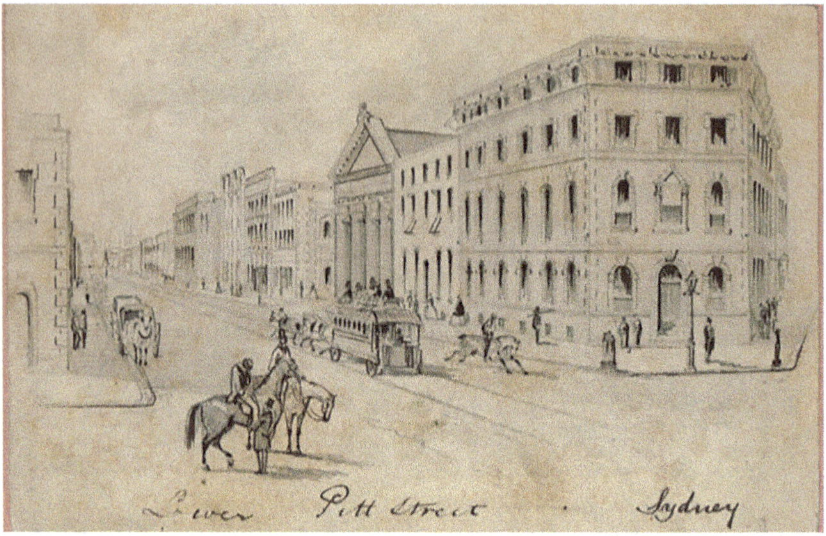

Sketch of Lower Pitt Street Sydney (State Library of Victoria)

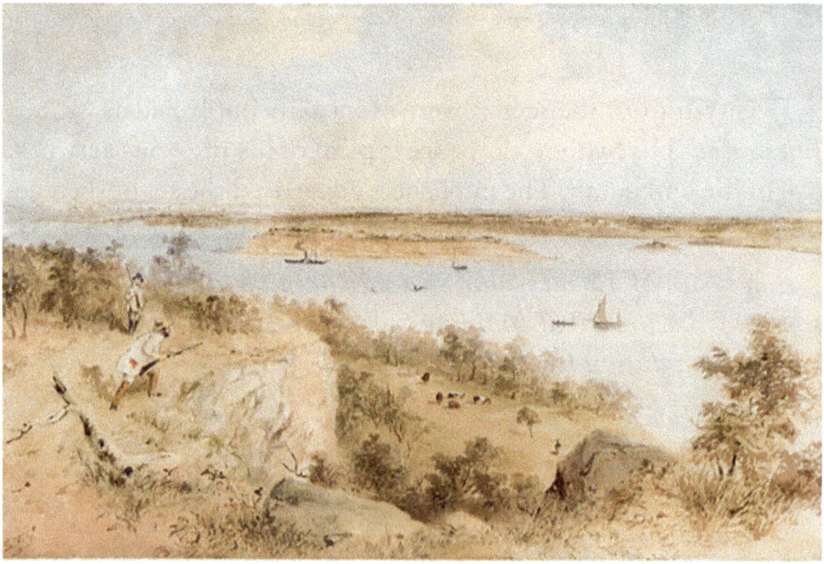

View of Cockatoo Island
(Dixon Galleries, State Library of New South Wales, FL513499)

Gill followed this work with four views of Sydney Harbour. These views were lithographed and printed as vignettes on a sheet of paper. In a vignette painting, the corners are left unpainted and the picture doesn't have a definite border, incorporating the beauty of the paper. They are sometimes used as a decorative design placed at the beginning or end of a book or chapter of a book or along the border of a page.

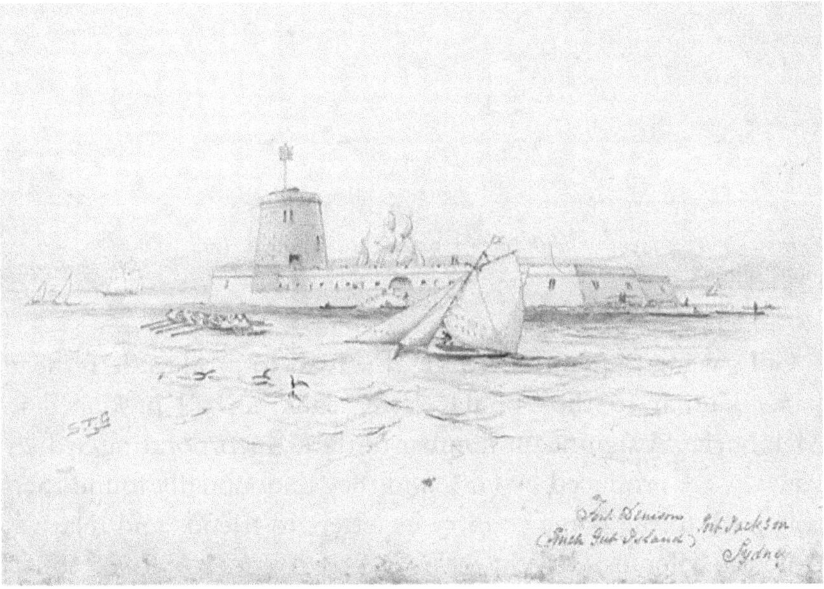

Fort Denison, Pinch Gut Island, Port Jackson, Sydney (State Library of Victoria)

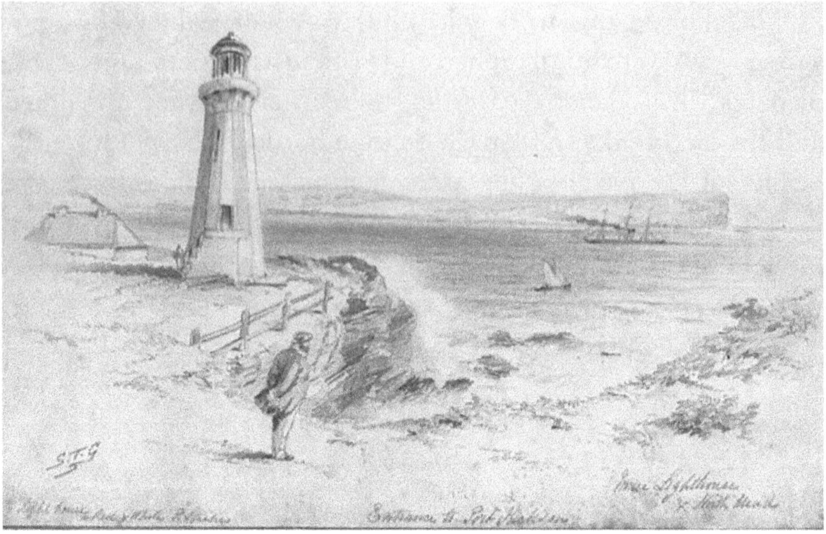

Entrance to Port Jackson, with Inner Lighthouse and North Head
(State Library of Victoria)

Gill's vignette paintings were also used to produce letterhead paper similar to the popular letterheads he had produced in Melbourne. A significant number of these, incorporating Sydney views, were produced by Gill, and they undoubtedly found their way back to the home country as letters to friends and relatives from the colonies.

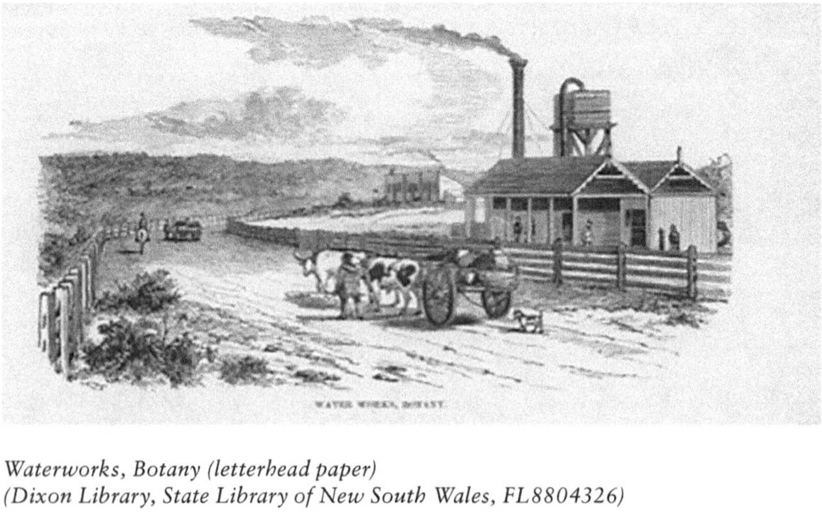

Waterworks, Botany (letterhead paper)
(Dixon Library, State Library of New South Wales, FL8804326)

During the 1850s and 1860s, the mechanisation of industry was well underway. However, the scale of industrialisation was much smaller than experienced during the industrial revolution in Britain and many European countries. Distance from export markets and a small domestic market limited development to small factories which tended to emerge on the western side of the city around Sussex, York, and Kent streets, and later at Pyrmont. All these areas were close to Darling Harbour, the centre of the coal-shipping industry.

Jevons' social survey was extensive and included an assessment of industry and business in 1858:

As regards industry and business, it will be seen that the trade in food is the most widely diffused, extending through all residentiary districts...The banking and monetary centre, comprising banks, chief mercantile houses, stockbrokers, etc., is very well defined, and forms, of course, the principle centre of town... Manufacturers are but little developed in Sydney. The carriage of goods into the interior is chiefly by means of drays, and the accommodation of carriers and their horses and cattle, the sale of food, the manufacture of harnesses, drays, carts, etc., form a pretty distinct business district centring at the Haymarket.[105]

Gill's paintings in and around Sydney included such subjects as Circular Quay, the Botanic Gardens, Saint Mary's Cathedral, the University of Sydney, the School of Arts, Botany Bay, Manly Beach, North Head, South Head, Port Jackson, Mosman Bay, and Coogee Bay. Beyond Sydney, he painted the Hawkesbury River, Newcastle, the Nepean River, and the Blue Mountains. Gill's choice of Lapstone Hill to paint (below) is particularly interesting, as it lies on the eastern escarpment of the Blue Mountains and was climbed by explorers Gregory Blaxland, William Lawson

105 William Jevons, *A Social Survey of Sydney in 1858*, reproduced in the Sydney Morning Herald, Saturday, November 9, 1929, p. 13.

and William Charles Wentworth when they became the first Europeans to successfully cross the Blue Mountains in 1813. This made it possible for the establishment of the first inland settlement at Bathurst.

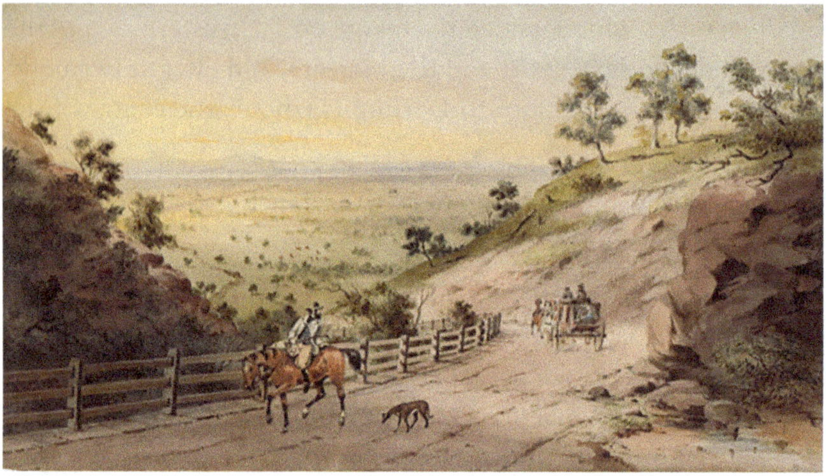

Lapstone Hill, Blue Mountains, NSW
(Dixon Galleries, State Library of New South Wales, FL3266243)

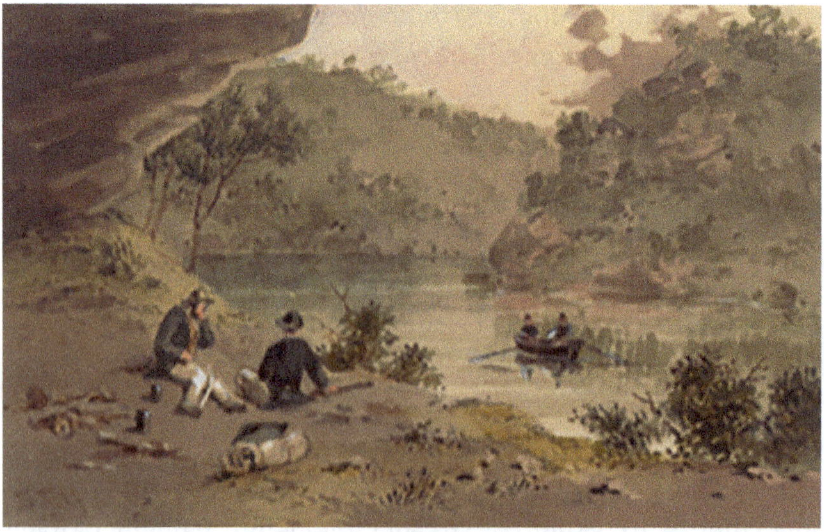

Fisherman's Camp, Upper Hawkesbury, N.S.W.
(Dixon Library, State Library of New South Wales, FL8783285)

Not long after arriving in Sydney, Gill was approached by publisher and entrepreneur, J. R. Clarke, to undertake design work for him. At that time, Clarke specialised in illustrated publications and he felt that someone with Gill's talent would be very useful to his business. One line of his publications was in decorated sheet music. Gill became involved in this area of Clark's business and executed a number of covers with some flair. As an example, in August 1859, J. R. Clark published a piece of music by composer Marmaduke Wilson, entitled *The Irish Emigrant*. The cover was produced by Gill.

Clarke commissioned Gill to do other work, including the design of covers for the first novels in the colony by a woman, journalist and writer Louisa Atkinson. Atkinson had produced work for the *Illustrated Sydney News*, including a series on natural history that she illustrated. She moved into novel writing and approached J. R. Clarke in 1857 to publish her work entitled *Gertrude the Emigrant*. Atkinson apparently produced most of the illustrations for her book, but Gill produced at least two or three of the images. His style, technique and character are different to Atkinson's, which makes his contribution stand out. As I briefly mentioned in Chapter 4 (Native Australians) Gill was also asked to collaborate in assisting with Atkinson's second novel, *Cowanda, the Veteran's Grant*, to be published in 1859. Gill prepared several illustrations for the book, which included the story of a hero living on a lonely station, a shepherd speared to death by Aboriginals and an evil station hand intent on revenge. Clarke subsequently changed his mind and decided to publish the book without illustrations, and hence Gill's commission was changed to providing only the cover illustration. The illustration shows a number of Aboriginal people around a campfire, including a woman holding an infant with four armed men approaching under dark, hidden by dense foliage. Gill had previously produced a few versions of this scene, which he called *Avengers* (see my discussion about this in Chapter 4).

Gill also received several commissions to draw houses. In 1857, a French wool merchant and art collector, Monsieur H. Noufflard, commissioned Gill to paint eight watercolours of his house in Bligh Street, Sydney. Produced with the artist's usual eye for intimate detail, they are the earliest full set of illustrations of the exterior and interior of an Australian residence. The paintings are very important for the information they convey about domestic life at the time, including our understanding of the furnishing and decorations of a house of the period. Few such records of an unpretentious middle-class residence were produced in Australia before the advent of dry plate photography in the 1880s. Noufflard was a temporary resident of Sydney, who rented the house for the decade he spent there (when he returned to France he took the paintings with him). Jones et al. commented that Gill's approach to art was exactly what was required to record the interior and exterior details of the house and garden:

> *Much of Gill's work is characterised by these seemingly trivial details, rare in the work of other professional artists of the period...Gill was a visual reporter who...recorded exactly what he saw... This approach is superbly suited to the depiction of a domestic environment, and it was a happy coincidence that brought Noufflard and Gill together in Sydney at the same time...*[106]

The set of watercolours of Noufflard's House were sold at auction in March 1983 and returned to Australia in the possession of a private collector. S. T. Gill's only other domestic interior was possibly a scene in Melbourne, he titled T*he Lucky digger who returned*, showing a relaxed digger sitting on a sofa with a child and an adoring wife (Gill painted several versions of this scene). Other interior drawings were of dance halls, restaurants, churches and theatres.

106 Shar Jones, & Michael Reymond, *Monsieur Noufflard's House: Watercolours by S. T. Gill, 1857*, Historic Houses Trust of New South Wales, 1983, p. 3.

At about the same time as he recorded the Noufflard house, Gill did several sketches of the interior and exterior of St. Mark's church, Darling Point. Also in 1857, Gill painted a very different subject - the first cricket match between New South Wales and Victoria, played in the Domain. In 1862, he also painted a match between an all-England eleven and a New South Wales team, which took place in the Outer Domain on January 29, 30, and 31, and 1 February 1862.

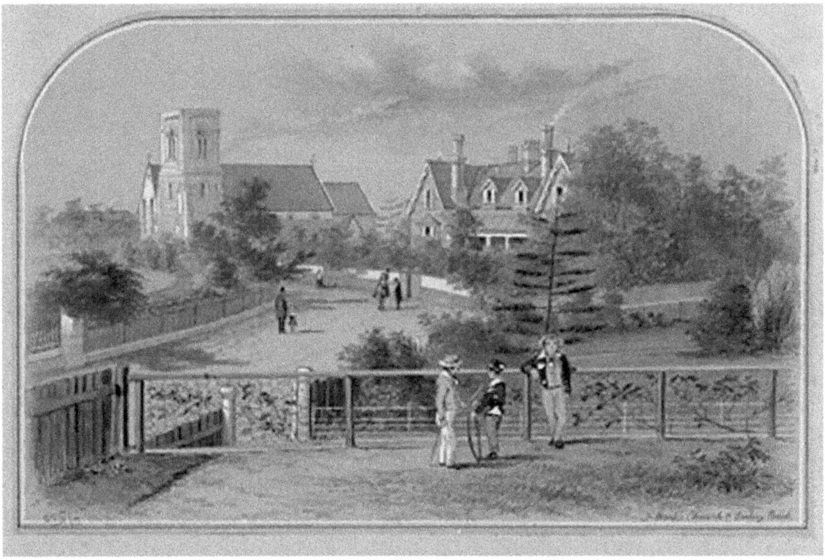

St. Mark's Church, Darling Point
(Dixon Library, State Library of New South Wales, FL183065)

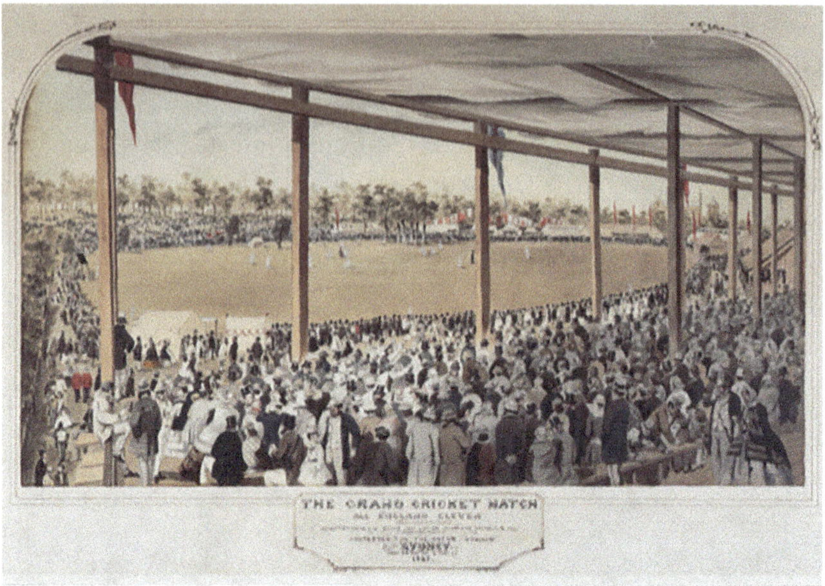

The Grand Cricket Match: all England eleven versus twenty-two of New South Wales (Mitchell Library, State Library of New South Wales, FL3140337)

Since his early days in South Australia, Gill had developed an interest in capturing kangaroo hunting on paper, and had, over time, produced a number of studies on the subject. While in Sydney, in 1858, he produced three larger scale tinted lithographs. The first of the lithographs was announced in the *Sydney Morning Herald* on 30 October 1858:

Mr. S. T. Gill, whose reputation in every branch of his art is now so thoroughly established, has cleverly drawn on stone lithograph, 'No. 1, The Meet', representing a bush party preparing to go out kangaroo hunting in the interior of Australia. This picture, which is of tolerably large size, is carefully printed on good paper, by Messrs. Allan and Wigley, of this city. The rude wooden hut in the wilderness, slim dogs, and strong, swift horses, with the colonial Nimrods and their attendants, form altogether a very pleasing and lively group.

I have not been able to locate a copy of the lithograph described by the newspaper, but I have included a copy of another of Gill's kangaroo hunt images depicting the scene after the kill, rather than the scene at the start of the hunt. In this sepia style image, Gill has included two Aborigines in the background.

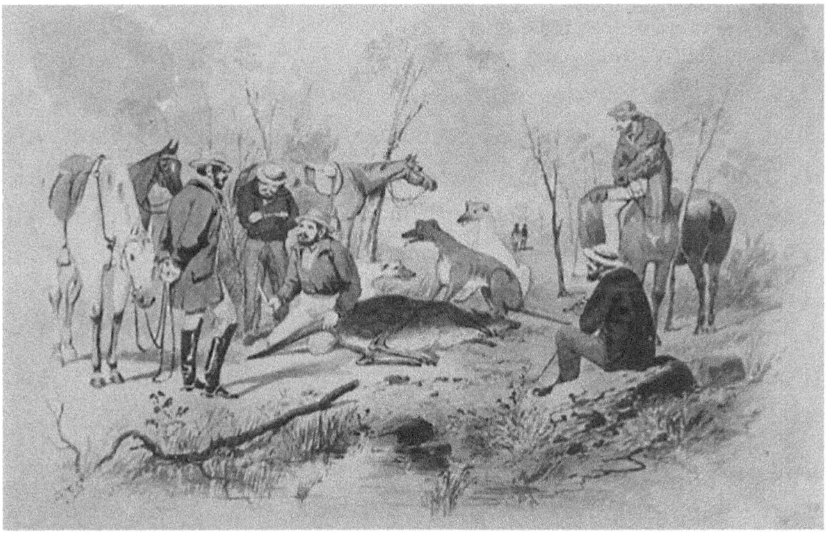

Kangaroo Hunting
(Dixon Library, State Library of New South Wales, FL8803666)

The long-established English practice of hunting on horses with hounds for sport found its way to the colonies, but with a colonial twist. The quarry was kangaroos, and it seems the dogs used were usually greyhounds. Gill's early paintings of kangaroo hunting in South Australia were clearly depicting an English style sporting activity, with the hunters dressed like those participating in the fox hunts in the home country. Geoffrey Mundy, a visitor to the antipodes, commented on his experience of participating in a colonial kangaroo hunt in 1846:

On the whole, taking into consideration the hardness of the ground, the stump-holes, sun-cracks and deep fissures caused by water, the stiffness of the underwood and frequency of the trees, living, dying, and dead, burnt and burning, the riding in a kangaroo hunt may be considered tolerably dangerous. It affords in short, to English manhood that quantum of risk called sport.[107]

Gill's work was regularly seen exhibited in the large plate glass window of Mader's stationery shop. It's interesting that a Sydney photographer, W. Blackwood, who was experimenting with the daguerreotype process, was receiving some favourable comments about his Sydney scenes in the press, and his work was available for inspection at F. Mader's stationery shop. There is no record of any interaction between the artist and photographer, although Gill had purchased daguerreotype equipment when in Adelaide and would have been familiar with the process (see further discussion about this in Chapter 13). Commenting on Blackwood's work, on 26 March1858, the *Sydney Morning Herald* reported:

The other day we had the opportunity of inspecting some very excellent photographs, by Mr. W. Blackwood, of Rushcutter's Bay, who has recently opened a photographic institution there. The most noteworthy were the premises of the Commercial and the New South Wales Banks, in George-street.

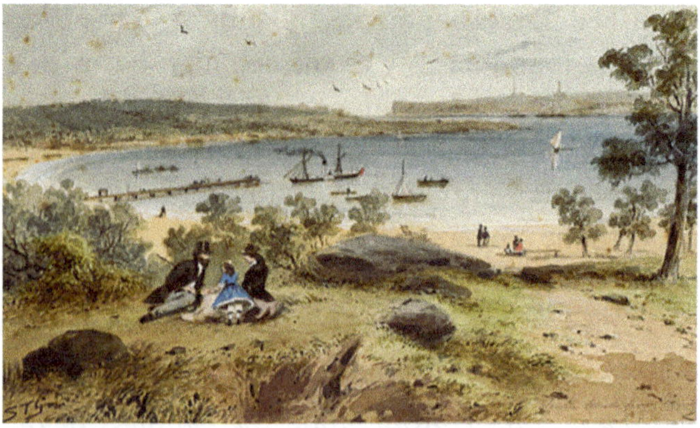

South Head from Manly Beach
(Dixon Galleries, State Library of New South Wales, FL3266612)

107 Geoffrey C. Mundy, *Our Antipodes, or, Residence and Rambles in the Australian Colonies*, Richard Bentley, London, 1852, p. 337.

With regard to Gill's newspaper work, he did, at times, produce items done from his imagination. On one such occasion in 1858, his reputation suffered because he produced an illustration of a horse race between a Melbourne champion (*Alice Hawthorne*) and a Sydney champion (*Veno*). The matter ended up in court and was dubbed the 'Veno' case. A newspaper, *Bell's Life*, claimed Gill's illustration of the finish of the horse race published in the *Era,* had not been drawn from life. The proprietors of the *Era* sued and were embarrassed when Gill admitted under cross-examination that he had drawn the horse and the mare from description and he was not sure he had ever seen Veno. The local horse was regarded as a champion by the people of Sydney and there was apparently a song written about him. Publisher J. R. Clarke rushed dance music into print, entitled *The Veno Galop,* the cover of which had been created by Gill.

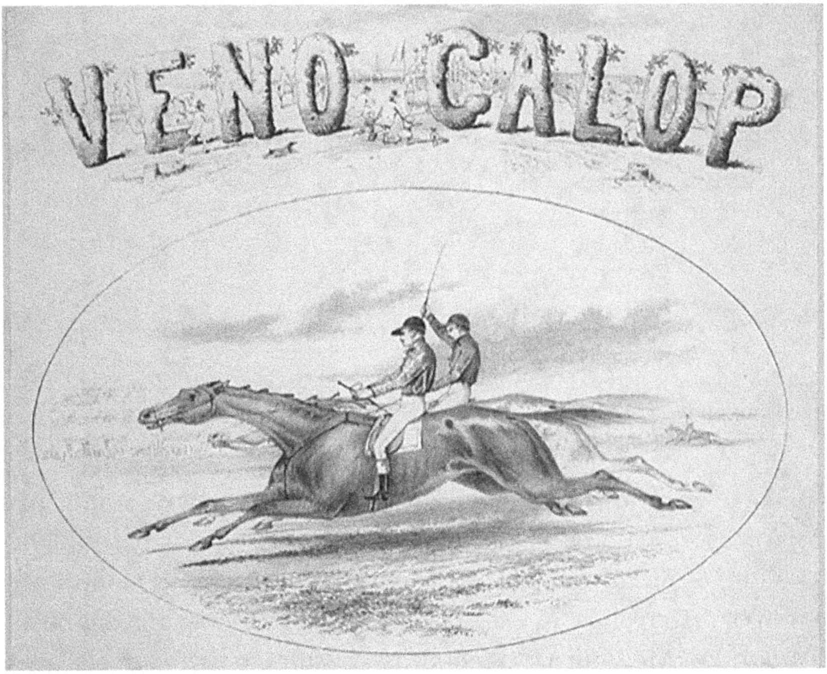

The Veno Galop (cover for a piece of dance music)
(Dixon Library, State Library of New South Wales, FL3245622)

During his time in Sydney, Gill produced a large body of work, including the illustrations for Edward Wilson's *Rambles in the Antipodes* (London, 1859). Wilson acknowledged and praised the work Gill produced for him. Gill also produced a series of satirical watercolours while in Sydney, which some claim are some of his most brilliant paintings, incorporating subjects ranging from light comedy to black humour. The men in the image below, although armed and presumably intent on robbing the mail, are depicted in a rather casual, slightly humorous, almost disinterested manner.

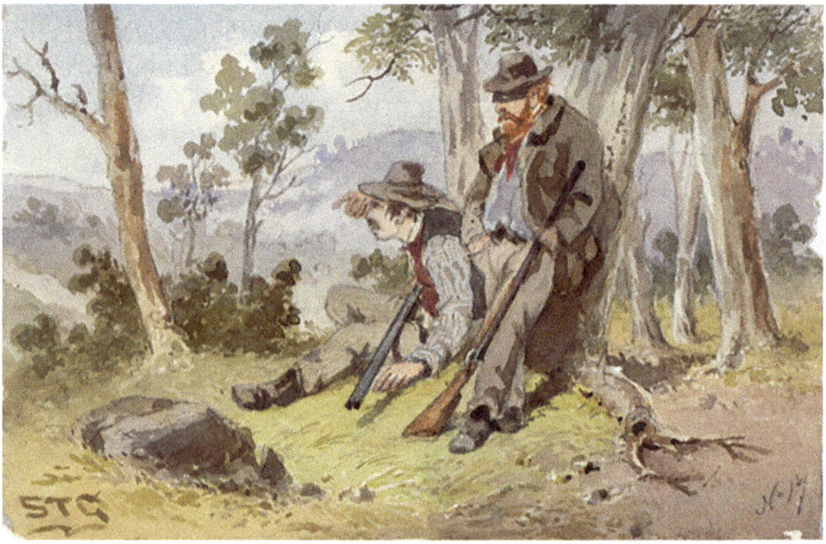

Road to Wagga Wagga, Waiting for the Mail (Dixon Library, State Library of New South Wales, FL8802404)

I have mentioned previously that Gill's work was at times copied by others and used commercially without his permission. In about 1860, a number of his paintings were used to produce a novelty souvenir, *Roseate*, featuring 28 miniature engraved vignettes of Melbourne, Geelong, and Williamstown streetscapes and buildings. It was printed by C. Adler of Hamburg and folded into quarters to form a small bouquet of pink roses printed in colour. The images were largely taken from *Victoria Illustrated* (1857). The Roseate opens to form a circle, revealing the 28 separate miniature engraved vignettes. A copy is held by the State Museums of Victoria. I have not been able to ascertain if Gill was involved in this project (possibly to help financially) or if it was an example of his work being used without his permission.

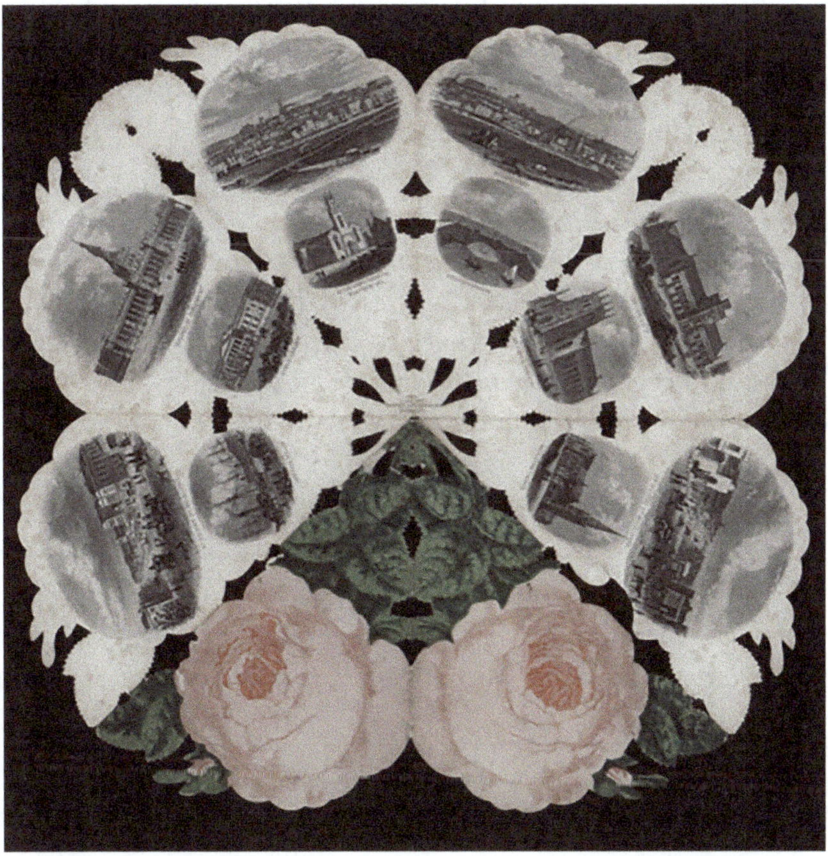

Roseate c. 1860 (Museums Victoria Collections https://collections.museumsvictoria.com.au/items/1397977)

By this time of Gill's stay in Sydney, he was again struggling financially. In May 1860, he was once more declared insolvent. Despite this, he was still busy preparing ten impressive watercolour drawings dealing with the Burke and Wills expedition (they can be found in the Mitchell Library). There was an enormous amount of interest in the expedition and their attempt to cross the continent south to north in 1860-61. The illustrated newspapers contained images relating to the expedition, including the disastrous outcome. As a result of the considerable public interest, many commemorative drawings and prints were produced for sale.

Gill's work was included in an exhibition of paintings held in Sydney in October 1861. As a consequence, some very favourable comments on Gill appeared in the *Sydney Morning Herald* on Saturday, 26 October 1861:

Regarding him as our great national artist, more from the happy manner in which he catches our colonial peculiarities, whether of figure or of scene, than from any mere reference to his skill as a colourist, the present Exhibition would have been incomplete had not some work from his pencil appeared amongst the gathered contributions; and it is therefore with considerable satisfaction that we find two illustrations of colonial life forwarded for exhibition by Mr. Gill...

... The two pictures are carefully as well as artistically coloured, showing evidently that a large amount of time and labour has been bestowed upon them, in order to make them worthy of the occasion that has called them into being, and of the high reputation that Mr. Gill has secured to himself.

Gill's contributions to the exhibition were: *The Flight of the Bushranger* and *The Overlanders*. These were two of his favourite subjects and appeared many times in different versions of his work. Many of the colony's newspapers tended to glamourise the deeds of bushrangers, sometimes giving the perception that they robbed from the rich and helped the poor and became outlaws as a result of oppression and unjust treatment. Some historians have proffered the view that they were symbols of an emergent Australian national feeling. While there would be differing views on this, it is clear bushrangers became part of both Australian history and folklore. It's possible Gill produced many bushranger images because, like many others in the colonies, he felt they embodied a spirit of defiance and protest, a symbolic striking back of the poor and dispossessed against those perceived as their oppressors. In many of his bushranger paintings, the subjects are being chased by the law, leaving the viewer with the impression they were never caught. Gill had little empathy for the wealthy and powerful and often depicted them in an unsympathetic manner.

Regarding the overlanders theme, he first painted this subject when he was in South Australia, and observed cattlemen bringing cattle overland from Sydney to parts of the southern state. In these works, Gill displays his interpretation of the harsh Australian environment together with the resilience and toughness of the new breed of authentic Australians who were different from the English. They were frequently painted in the outback surrounded by the 'irregular' or 'disorderly' Australian bush which was very different to the more 'formal' English countryside. It's clear that Gill identified with the bushman and was inclined to make fun of the squatter.

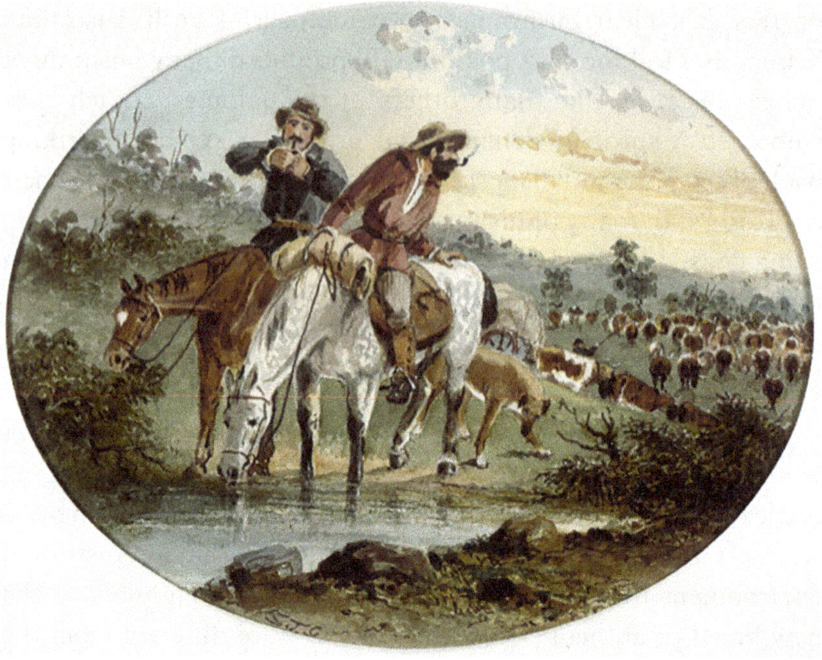

The Overlanders (State Library of Victoria)

While in Sydney, Gill met Doctor John Thomas Doyle. Doyle had a flair for public lecturing and performing. During his time in Australia, he had performed in Melbourne, Sydney and Maitland (where he lived for a short time). In 1863, he announced he intended to move back to Ireland, where he had plans to lecture about his time in Australia. Doyle wanted to take a sketchbook of his experiences in Australia with him to complement his lectures and performances. While Doyle was capable of making simple sketches, his artwork was rather basic. He therefore needed an artist who could convey humour and life and bring out that which was quintessentially Australian—Gill was perfect for the task. Hence, in the period 1862-63 Gill entered into a collaborative arrangement with Doyle to provide sketches for themes chosen by the doctor. The arrangement was unusual, as S. T. Gill was not to be acknowledged in the sketchbook for his artwork (implying to the viewer that Doyle was the artist). Gill had some previous experience in working as a 'ghost artist' but this was a much larger and more complex project. While agreeing to provide the images for Doyle's sketchbook, Gill was not entirely happy with not being acknowledged as the artist. As a protest, he cleverly inserted his initials into much of the artwork, and the inscriptions describing the subject on several pieces of the artwork are clearly in Gill's handwriting. He also included himself in the frontispiece he designed for the collection, and his dog as a mark of his work in some of the images. In addition to this, Gill also left some clues for the viewer, such as incorporating a 'G' on the shoulder of horses in several of the paintings that involved native stockmen. The 45 images include a number of life on the goldfields, Indigenous people, and life in outback Australia. He used some of his drawings from his general stock which incorporated the usual STG marking. It appears Doyle, intent on taking credit for these images, crudely changed the 'S' into a 'J' and the 'G' into a 'D' with ink. Although not all artwork was provided by Gill, his work is clearly evident throughout the sketchbook. While Doyle's artistic abilities were limited, some of the sketches, clearly not Gill's, were probably made by the doctor. In fact, the sketchbook was incomplete when Doyle left Australia, and it seems that further drawings were executed by an unknown artist in either England or Ireland. I have the feeling this was not a project that excited Gill and he was pleased when he was able to part company with Doyle. It's highly likely he only agreed to participate and stayed with the project because of his financial situation (for a reconstruction of the *J. T. Doyle Australian Sketchbook* together with extensive commentary see the work of Sasha Grishin).[108]

Although Gill's rate of production hadn't declined, the buoyant market he had found for his work in Melbourne was absent in Sydney, and thus he was forced to supplement his income by

108 Sasha Grishin, *Dr. Doyle's Sketches in Australia: a Collection of Prints from the Original Watercolour Drawings in the Mitchell Library*, Mitchell Library Press & Centaur Press, 1993.

taking students, producing images for publisher J. R. Clarke, and working for the illustrated newspapers. One of Gill's pupils was William Garling, son of artist Frederick Garling. William apparently had a particular interest in painting horses, possibly influenced by Gill's interest in horses. He later commented that STG frequently wore a top hat, cut-away coat, and carried a racing crop. Garling later produced several sketches of Gill dressed as he remembered him. This form of dress is not how I imagine Gill as he wandered about rural South Australia and the Victorian goldfields on horseback, and certainly wasn't how he was depicted in his latter years, when he moved about Melbourne looking more like a homeless person.

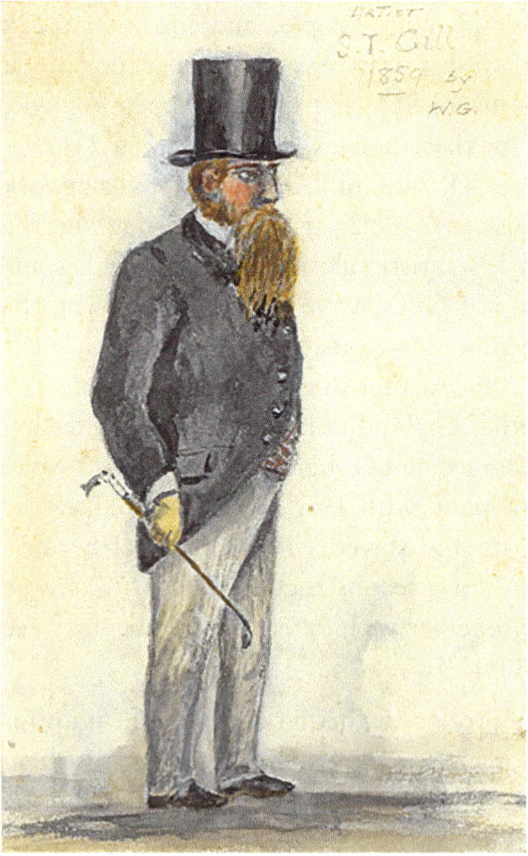

S. T. Gill, 1859 (Mitchell Library, State Library of New South Wales, FL1069524)

As mentioned above, Gill had a fascination with bushrangers; he produced a number of images of carriages being bailed up, of suspicious looking characters waiting for their prey to arrive, and of bushrangers escaping from mounted police. The image below is fairly typical of what looks like a dramatic hold-up of the Royal Mail. This watercolour was possibly one of the last paintings Gill made before leaving Sydney, either in the latter part of 1863 or early 1864. It was reproduced in 1864 by Hamel and Ferguson, Melbourne as a colour chromolithograph.

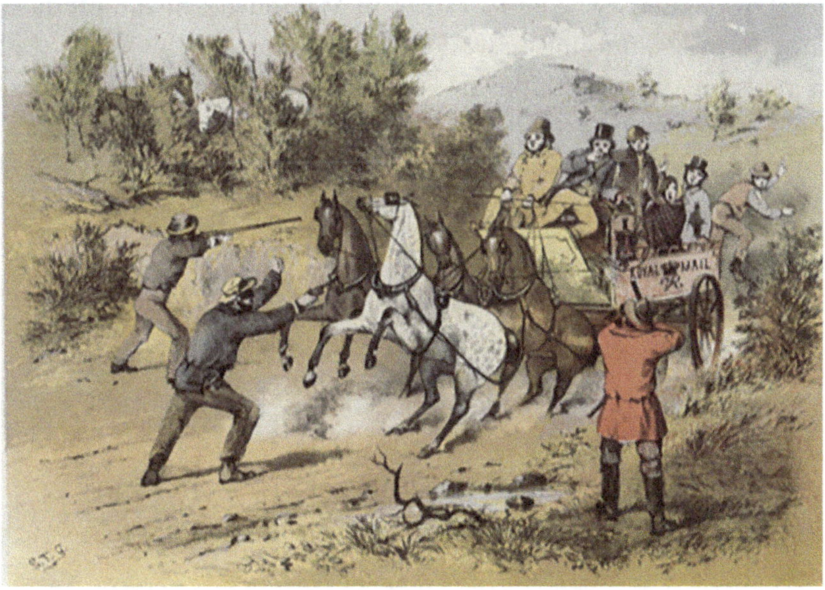

Attacking the Mail, Bushranging, New South Wales (State Library of Victoria)

The fallout from the Veno case of 1858 may have contributed to Gill's decision to leave Sydney. Artwork was an important part of newspaper production and editors required factual and accurate work. Clearly, the work for illustrated newspapers was an important source of income for many artists, including Gill. He may have lost the confidence of Sydney editors and an important, even if small source of income. Gill was having health problems, including recurrent nightmares relating to the

Horrocks expedition, possibly drinking too much, again having financial difficulties, and he was nostalgic for Victorian country life, particularly the goldfields. It was probably a combination of these factors that influenced STG to return to Melbourne. Hence, after eight years in Sydney, S.T. Gill moved back south in 1864. He travelled alone (Sydney directories in 1864 listed a Mrs Gill living in Stanley Street, Woolloomooloo).

Although the eight years in Sydney may not have been a financial success for Gill and he may never have achieved the level of popularity he had attained in Melbourne, he did produce an enormous amount of work. Clearly, some of this work was a revision or redevelopment of previous themes (overlanders, bushrangers, kangaroo hunting); he nevertheless left a wonderful collection of images of Sydney and parts of rural New South Wales.

Chapter 11—Back in Melbourne

...Melbourne, young as she is,
is without doubt, the overtopping
wonder of the world.

—William Kelly, 1859[109]

When S. T. Gill returned to Melbourne from Sydney in 1864, he found he had been largely forgotten in a rapidly changing city of over 100,000 inhabitants. The public art market showed little interest in his work at that time. Michael Cannon felt the realism in Gill's work was no longer interesting or acceptable:

> *Members of the bourgeoisie, which included many families owing their establishment to gold and its multiplier effects on the economy, were engaging in the process of drawing a veil over their raw colonial beginnings, and instituting an outward system of strictly moral respectability in which truths about convicts and gold-digging were best forgotten.*[110]

While Gill never regained his previous level of popularity in Melbourne, he nevertheless produced many fine works after his

109 William Kelly, *Life in Victoria*, Chapman & Hall, London, 1859, p. 42.
110 Michael Cannon, (ed.), *The Victorian Gold Fields: an Original Album by S. T. Gill*, Melbourne, Library Council of Victoria, 1982, p.15.

return. His first project was to publish a sketchbook illustrated with lithographs. He thus set to work at a frenetic pace, and some of the lithographs for the project were available by the end of the year; by early 1865, the work was complete and the sketchbook, entitled *The Australian Sketchbook*, was on sale. It contained chromolithographs (a process that produced multi-coloured prints), a cover, title page and 24 colour plates. There was some similarity between this sketchbook and the Doyle sketchbook. He incorporated a number of themes in common with the Doyle sketchbook, but added new themes on bushrangers, finding lost children, a bush funeral, kangaroo hunting, the life of the rural workers and the hardships of the overlanders. The focus was on rural rather than urban life (the majority of scenes are of Aboriginal life and outback Australia) and are based largely on his work over the preceding 25 years. It was published by Hamel and Ferguson in Melbourne and was the creation of one of the great lexicons of nineteenth-century Australian art.

Dutton felt Gill's work in the sketchbook was:

... cruder and more sentimental than his earlier water-colours and drawings, he has become less of an artist and more of an illustrator.[111]

On the other hand Sasha Grishin felt that by this time in Gill's life, he:

... had to some extent established a repertoire of themes which stemmed from prolonged immersion in Australian life in South Australia, Victoria and New South Wales, to create a powerful statement on life in the Australian colonies.

'The Australian Sketchbook' is also in some ways Gill's most considered expression of the Australian character.[112]

111 Geoffrey Dutton, *Paintings of S. T. Gill*, Rigby, 1962, p.8.
112 Sasha Grishin, *S. T. Gill and His Audiences*, National Library of Australia, State Library of Victoria, 2015, p.164.

On the frontispiece and title page for the *Australian Sketchbook,* Gill produced a satirical illustration showing himself barefooted, with a bushy, unkempt beard, a worn hat, well-used clothes, and standing in a stream with his sketchbook under his arm; he is watched by two Aboriginal men in a rather bemused manner and a snake is looking warily at him. This was similar to the frontispiece that Gill produced for the *J.T. Doyle Sketches in Australia,* except in the Doyle work, the natives look rather threatening, the snake is about to strike, and Gill had to disguise his initials as a clue to his authorship.

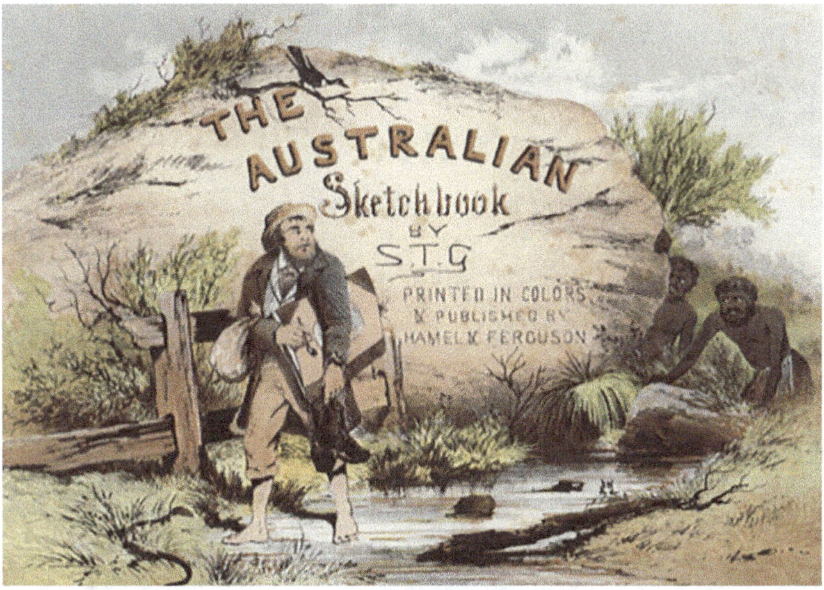

The Australian Sketchbook Frontispiece (State Library of Victoria)

Gill clearly loved the country, and his emphasis on country scenes in the *Australian Sketchbook* was as much about his saying he felt comfortable in that environment, even though it may at times be hostile, as it was about displaying the many country themes he had painted over a long period. Six of the images focus exclusively on the life of Indigenous Australians and a further eight include an Aboriginal presence.

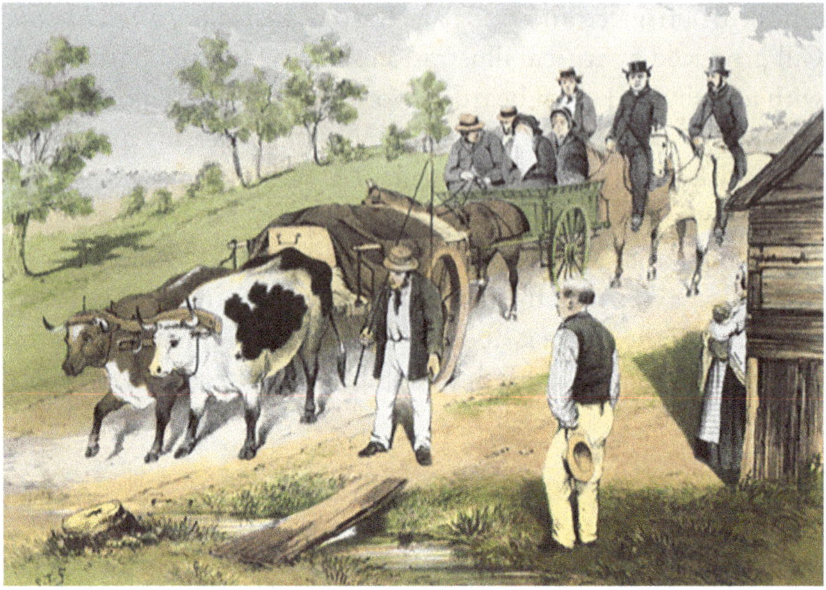

Bush Funeral (State Library of Victoria)

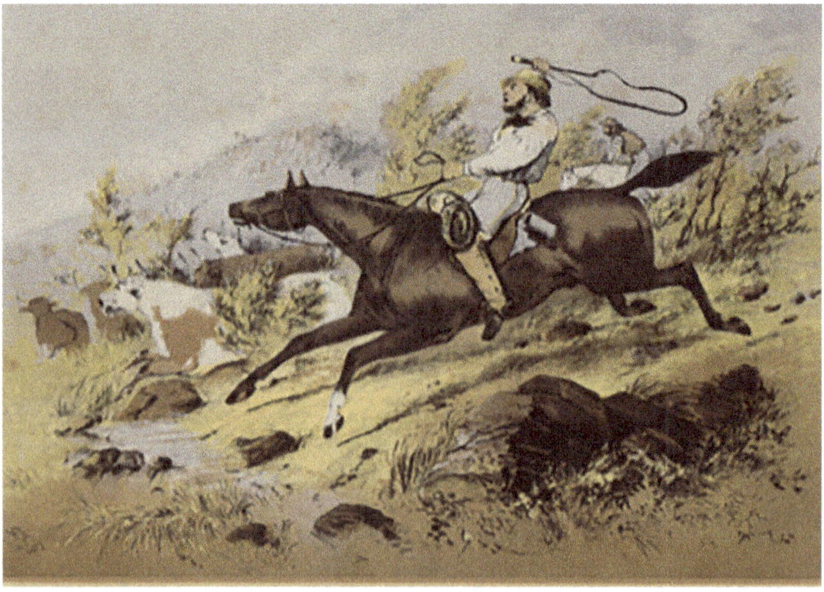

Stockman (State Library of Victoria)

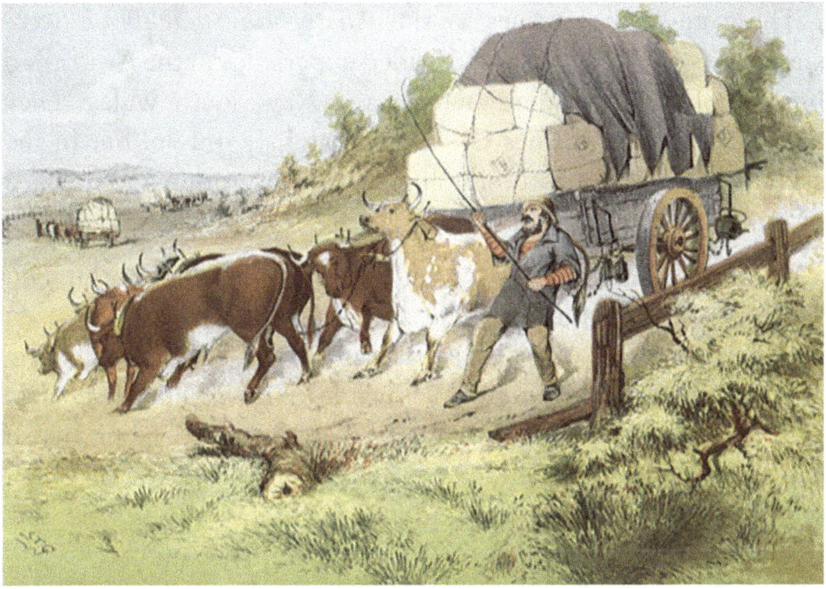

Wool Drays (State Library of Victoria)

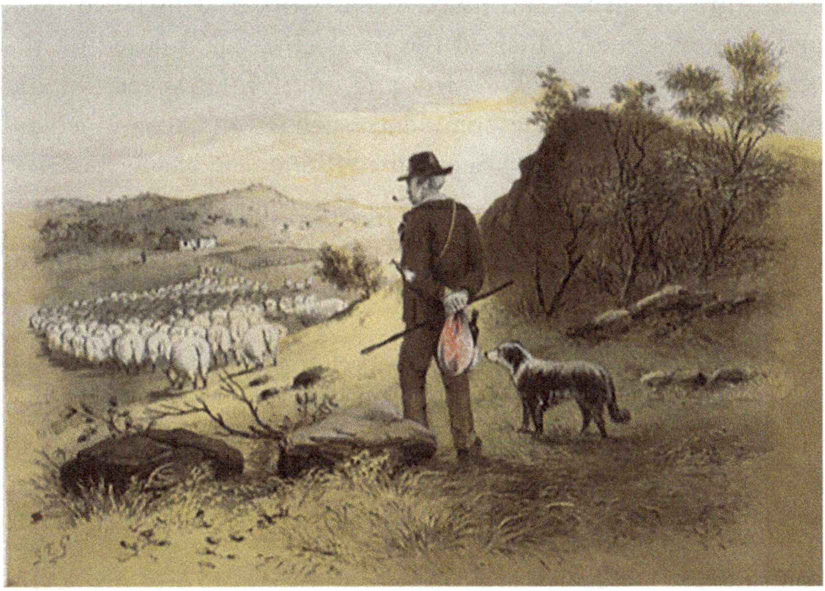

Homeward Bound (State Library of Victoria)

These and other scenes in the *Australian Sketchbook* were statements of Gill's long and distilled experience in the Australian bush in South Australia, Victoria and New South Wales. They often represented themes Gill had previously drawn, but in the sketchbook he frequently simplified the composition and focused more on the main details.

Work in Melbourne was not as readily available as it had previously been, and so Gill travelled around areas close to Melbourne to take views at a number of places, including Queenscliff and Mornington Peninsula. He was no longer able to travel long distances on horse back and in 1865 he produced a typical, full-of-life-Gill style watercolour of seaside Brighton with people on the promenade and a holiday atmosphere. He painted further scenes of Brighton Beach into the mid-1870s.

Twelve of his watercolour drawings were hung in the Intercolonial Exhibition in Melbourne in 1866. His work was a mixture of earlier and more recent work and included bush and Sydney scenes. Much of the press coverage focused on the work of Chevalier, von Guerard, and Buvelot. However, Gill did receive some favourable comments such as that contained on page 4 of *The Argus* on 1 September 1866:

... a quantity of colonial sketches, drawn with much vigour and fidelity, by Mr. S. T. Gill, of Melbourne.

One notable work in that period was that of a Cobb & Co coach in Bourke Street, about to depart for Beechworth (the Albion Hotel is in the background). Gill included Cobb & Co coaches in many of his sketches and drawings.

Gill did work for the *Melbourne Herald* at that time and continued to send sketches to them up to the time of his death. One of his last sketches for the paper depicted a dust storm in Elizabeth street. He also produced occasional illustrations that appeared in the *Illustrated Melbourne Post* and *The Australian News for Home Readers*.

One of his newspaper images featured as a large black-and-white print on page 4 of the March 24, 1864 edition of *The Australian News for Home Readers*, entitled *Bourke Street West in the Forenoon*. A copy of the illustration in the newspaper article produced from Gill's sketch is reproduced below.

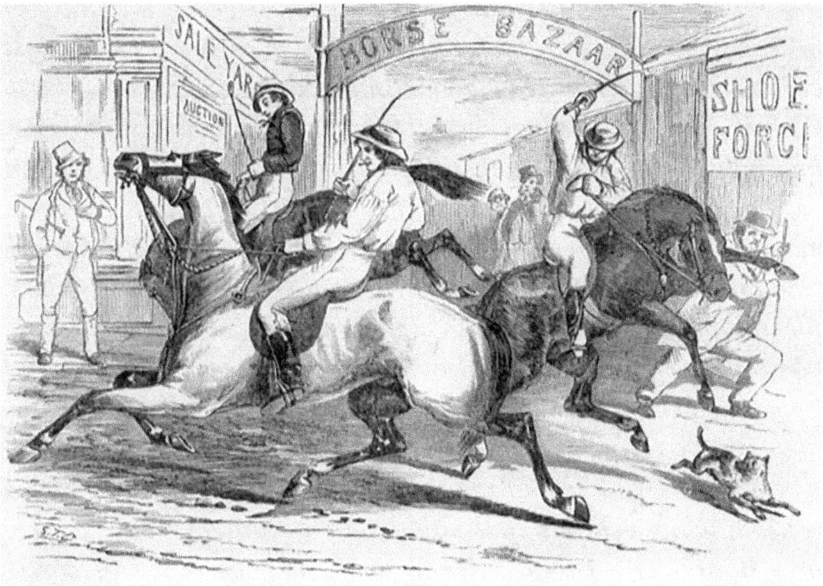

Bourke Street West in the Forenoon (State Library of Victoria)

The drawing was made by Gill to illustrate a story about the auctioning of horses, and it was then made into a wood engraving by well-known engraver, Frederick Grosse. The article was a rather dramatic story of the arrival in town of wild horses for an auction at a horse bazaar in Bourke Street (that part of Melbourne was traditionally home to horse bazaars, most famously Kirk's, and allied trades including saddlers, ironmongers and coach builders in the nineteenth century):

Bourke Street West in the Forenoon

The new country or city seldom presents a more attractive object of contemplation to the inquiring eyes of that philosophic personage, the travelling Englishman, than the bazaar, where horses most do congregate for the pleasure or profit of mankind. We Anglo-Saxons are pre-eminently a horsey race, and a little discourse about the universal favourite is never out of season. The adjacent lively view of Bourke street west, taken between the hours of ten and twelve a.m. ... The arrival of a "mob" of horses from the country for sale in town, is one of the most curious nocturnal sights and sounds that strikes the "New Chum". These arrivals generally take place an hour or two after midnight. In the nocturnal stillness the approaching quick tread of hoofs grows louder and louder in the distance till it comes on us with the sound of a legion of cavalry, the clank of sabres being supplanted by the loud cracks of the advanced and rear riders' formidable stock whips. It is a gallant sight to see the dashing picturesque figure of the first horsemen leading a squadron of wild long tailed colts up Elizabeth street at a canter, each covering his file with the regularity of a well drilled cavalry troop. A splendid wheel up the rise of Bourke street west—furious cracks of the terrible whip—shouts that could only permit Rip van Winkle or a Bourke street westender to sleep, and the mob is securely penned ready for the auctioneer's hammer, and tho rough riders' persuasions to equine civilisation, ere the rising sun has attained his meridian.

There is no attribution in the article to Gill as the artist or Grosse as the engraver of the large picture of a rather wild scene of horses arriving in Bourke Street west. However, the initials STG are very clear in the lower left-hand corner of the picture. It's very fortunate that the engraved printer's wood block prepared by Grosse has been preserved and is held by the National Museum of Australia, Canberra. This wood block is rare, and an important part of the history of how images were created for illustrated newspapers and other printed matter in colonial Australia.

In woodblock printing, an image is carved in reverse on a piece of wood (like an image on negative film), leaving the image's outline. The block is then inked and printed on material, such as paper or fabric. It's a very time-consuming process and was developed in China between the mid sixth to late ninth centuries. Nineteenth century illustrated newspapers used the process to publish and republish thousands of illustrations, from the sensational to the mundane, the portrait to the panorama, and enabled the reading public to be saturated with visual experiences. This technique effectively made the illustrated newspaper the progenitor of mass media. One of the first periodicals in the United Kingdom to effectively use this technique was *The Penny Magazine* (1832), whose proprietor, Charles Knight, emphasised his magazine's ability to bring useful knowledge and high-quality illustrations inexpensively to the masses.

Perhaps the most famous nineteenth-century periodical to adopt wood-engraved illustrations was *The Illustrated London News* (ILN—1842). In its first issue, the paper loudly trumpeted the technique as offering 'the very form and presence of events as they transpire, in all their substantial reality,' embodying 'whatever the broad and palpable delineations of wood engraving can be taught to achieve'. The ILN became a huge success, spurring competition from other illustrated periodicals, each of which sought to capture or expand the market.

The Illustrated Australian News, *Illustrated Sydney News* and *Australasian Sketcher* were the best-known illustrated papers in colonial Australia. However, a number of illustrated newspapers and newsletters emerged in the 1850s and 1860s, with many having a very short life. The defining feature of these papers was their illustrations produced as wood engravings, this being the only printing technique available for the mass production of imagery in combination with the letterpress. It wasn't until the late 1880s, following the development of the photomechanical half-tone process in the United States, that photographs could be reproduced in the press. Before this date, the only means by which sketches for illustrations, photographs, and paintings could be reproduced in the press was as wood engravings. Start-up capital was important in launching illustrated papers, as they were expensive to produce, since the engraving of wood blocks was a highly skilled, labour-intensive and time-consuming process.

The wood block prepared by Frederick Grosse to illustrate S. T. Gill's illustration of the horses arriving in Bourke Street for the auction, which appeared in *The Australian News for Home Readers,* is a very important and, I suspect, rare artefact in the history of newspaper illustrations in colonial Australia. It's in two sections joined by internal screws to form a complete block and Gill's initials are clear on the wood block. It was fairly common to engrave an image on more than one block and then lock them together for printing.

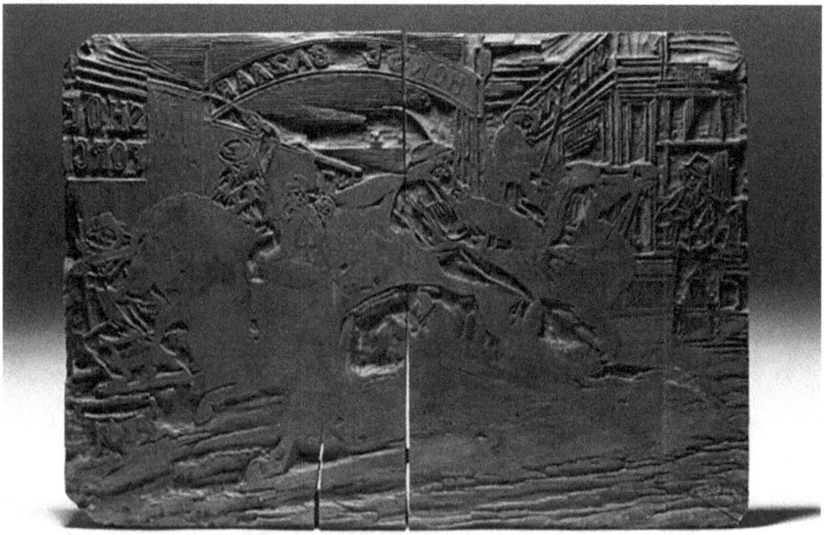

Engraved Printer's Woodblock (artist S. T. Gill, engraver F. Grosse) (Photo: George Serras, National Museum of Australia)

In 1869, the trustees of the Melbourne Public Library commissioned Gill, for a fee of £53.10s, to produce a set of forty watercolours based on his earliest goldfields sketches. The resulting collection, *The Victorian Goldfields*, is a superb depiction of all aspects of gold mining and goldfields life. It's interesting that the paintings in the collection follow similar themes to Gill's earlier paintings and sketches of the goldfields; however, there are some differences in his 1872 versions, which appear more orderly. Grishin believes the library may have stated that Gill's commission was to produce a set of images that played down the gritty realism of the goldfields and showed that the:

Gold rushes were not at all dirty, violent and chaotic, as Gill's earlier images recorded, but now they appear as quite an orderly occurrence, where the gentle folk from England acquired new wealth for the new colony and for themselves, despite a few disruptive souls of 'low degree'.[113]

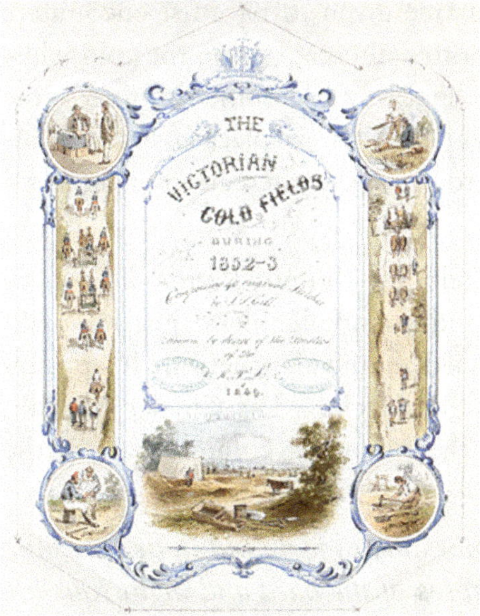

Cover for the Melbourne Public Library Series entitled: The Victorian Goldfields (State Library of Victoria)

113 Sasha Grishin, *S. T. Gill and His Audiences*, National Library of Australia, State Library of Victoria, 2015, p. 200.

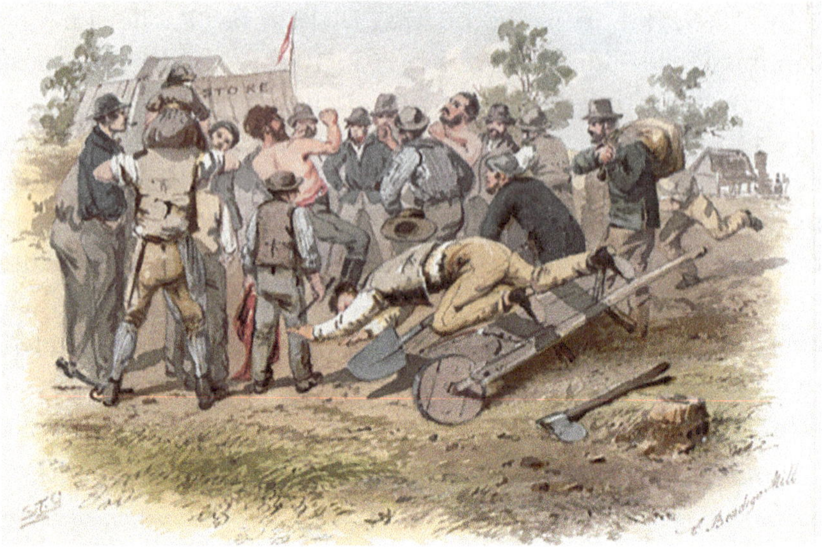

A Bendigo Mill (State Library of Victoria)

The above painting, *A Bendigo Mill,* was a theme that Gill had painted previously. It was a name given to bare fist encounters between two men; there were often altercations on the goldfields. As soon as a dispute started, diggers would come running; some came to see the outcome, while others to place a bet. In this image, Gill portrays the rush to get to the altercation by having a digger trip over a barrow.

This undertaking for the Melbourne Public Library may have been Gill's last commission and possibly came at just the right time to help with his distressed financial situation. It appears the library was pleased with his sketches. The Chief Librarian, Mr. C.A. McCallum, made the following comment about the watercolours:

Each sketch, is a vignette, not only in form but in its revealing and sometimes sardonic glimpses of the hard and inglorious life actually led by the diggers.[114]

114 C. A. McCallum, in Barnett, Charles (ed), Gold in Australia, Cassell, London, 1951, p. 98.

The library also acquired Gill's *The Australian Sketchbook* and Wilson's *Rambles at the Antipodes,* illustrated by Gill.

In 1872, he painted another series of 50 coloured sketches of the goldfields as they were in 1852-3. They closely resemble those painted for the library trustees. It would seem he had plans to produce a new series of lithographs with the title, *The Gold-Fields of Victoria during 1852-3 Comprising Fifty Sketches of Life and Character, Primative [sic] Operations &c. &c. By S. T. Gill Melbourne 1872* (the title page which Gill designed contains these words together with a very elaborate set of eight small scenes of life on the diggings).

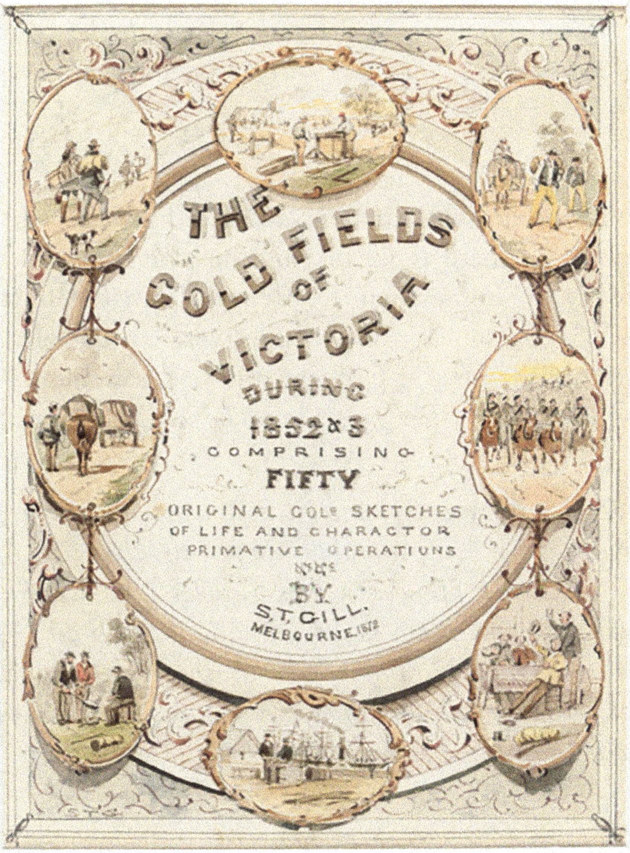

Cover Page for the 1872 Gold Fields Series (State Library of Victoria)

The set was not published in his lifetime, and it seems there was no exposure of this work in the press. It's possible that goldfields images were no longer popular, that people had moved on from the rough and tumble of that era and that 'serious' art was increasingly associated with oil paintings. It's also possible that from the 1860s, the people of Melbourne were interested in pursuing more 'sophisticated' activities. Clara Aspinall was certainly impressed by the social life of Melbourne at that time:

Melbourne is one of the gayest places in the world and the ladies and gentlemen...are the most indefatigable, and I believe the most accomplished dancers in the world... For the gay, then there are balls and small dances... for the more quiet and conversational, dinners parties; and for the musical, there are most agreeable 'soirees musicales'... Picnics, too, are greatly the fashion in summer...[115]

Gill had an eye for humorous situations and often painted with a sense of humour. In these types of paintings, he provided a visual commentary on human nature, frequently in the form of characterisations. A set of six of these were produced as lithographs and published by De Grouchy and Leigh in 1866. A comment on the set appeared on page 13 of *The Australasian* on April 28, 1866:

Mr. S. T. Gill is a humourist as well as an artist, and has contributed sketches of considerable merit to the list of those which colonial art possesses. His subjects are usually Australian and local, and there is an individuality about the touch of his pencil, a freedom, and a spirit of fun, which makes his contributions to the album always agreeable. His latest productions are perhaps the best he has yet produced.

115 Clara Aspinall, *Three Years in Melbourne*, L. Booth, London, 1862, p. 37.

The set of six included: *Native Dignity, A City of Melbourne Solicitor, Ease without Opulence, and Spirits in Bond.* Gill had intended to publish a much larger set of these drawings as *Colonial Comicalities.* Although the publication did not materialise, a number of lithographs produced after his death survive in public collections. It seems Gill had egalitarian views and values and in these paintings and drawings, he was attacking the social structures that prevailed in the colonies at that time.

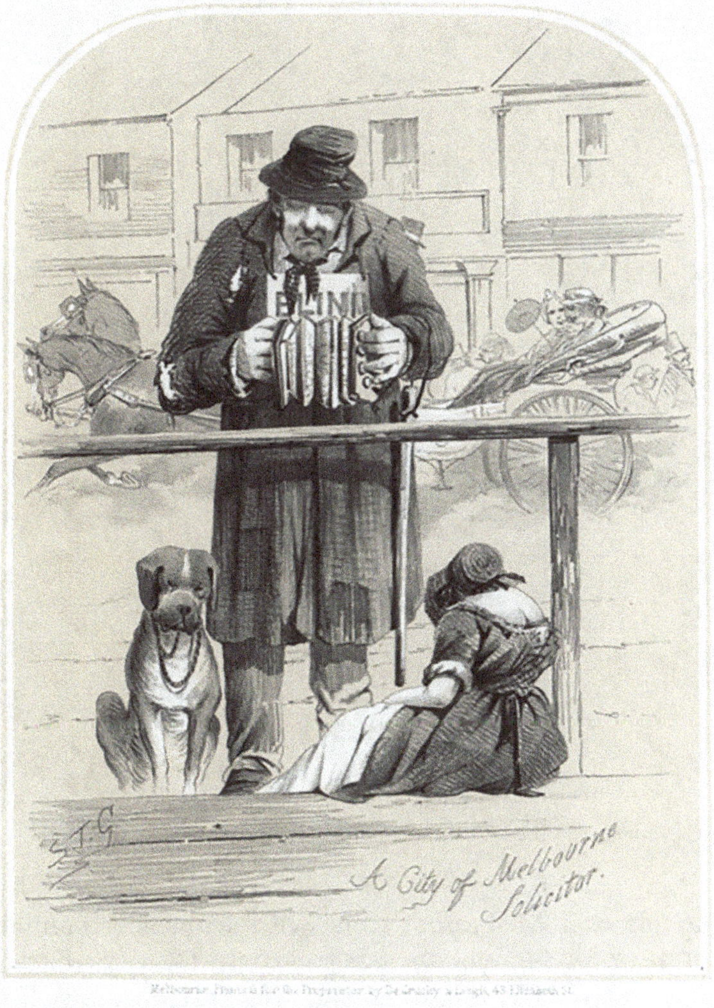

A City of Melbourne Solicitor (State Library of Victoria)

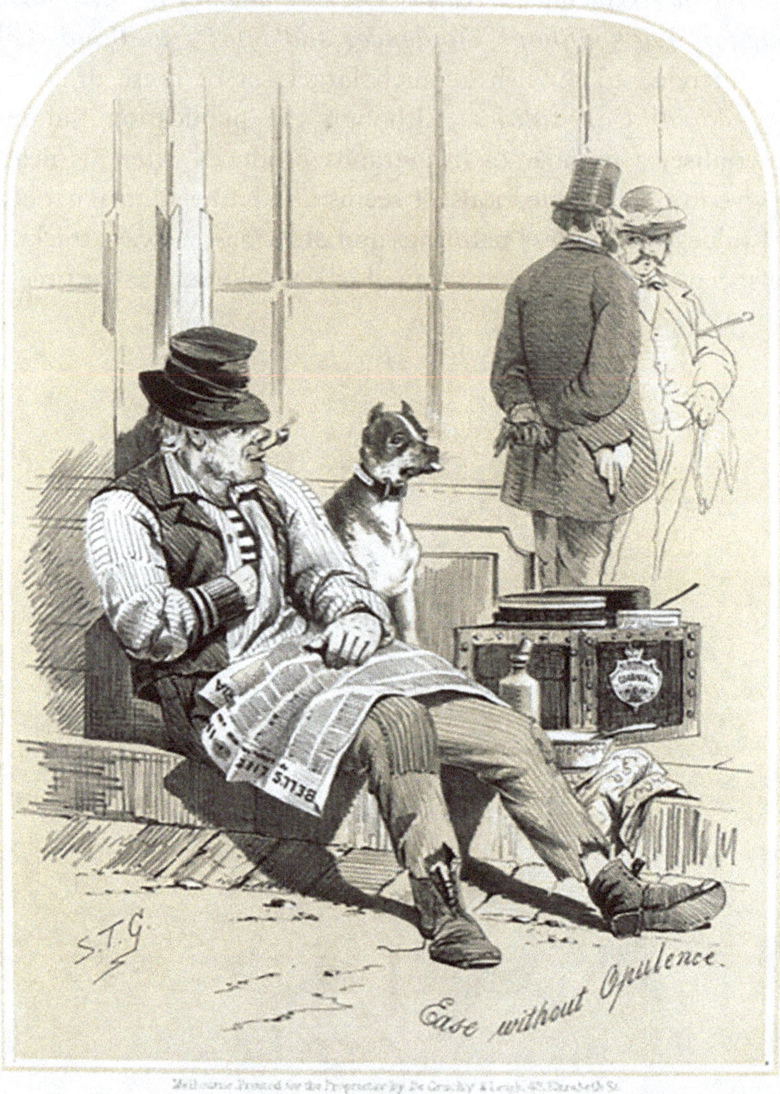

Ease Without Opulence (State Library of Victoria)

An example of a Melbourne scene with a touch of humour was his *Transitory Enjoyment*. It depicts two lovers sitting on the back of a water cart, blissfully ignorant of the water that is soon to pour on them from the water tap above their heads. He created many humorous situations like this one while observing daily life.

There were negative comments and assessments made of Gill towards the end of his life; these appear to reflect his physical state and demeanour. Unfortunately, these comments have been interpreted by some as a judgement that his work was of poor quality at that time. While the quantity of Gill's work may have diminished, I don't believe the quality was poor, considering the work he produced in the last few months of his life. For example, he produced two very significant watercolour paintings in July 1880. The first was of a scene in Collins Street (*Doing the Block, Gt Collins St),* a delicate watercolour showing fashionable Melbourne at its best (it was apparently trendy for some Melbourne folk to dress elaborately and parade in leisurely fashion in the afternoon; Gill found this to be a fascinating and possibly amusing spectacle). The second painting (*Grand Locomotive Race*) is a characterisation of the subjects, painted with a sense of boldness and humour. The painting contains much detail, with many clues as to what message Gill is portraying to the viewer. It has been interpreted by some as a comment on race relations in America, with a prompt for the viewer to see a parallel to what was occurring in Australia.

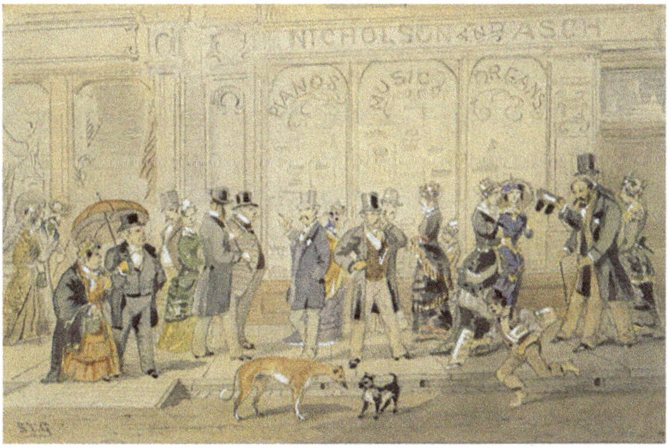

Doing the Block, Collins Street (State Library of Victoria)

Clara Aspinall, who keenly observed social behaviour in Melbourne during her three-year stay, commented on the activity that Gill called *Doing the Block*:

> *… the most elegant description may be seen from two to four o'clock in the afternoon marching up and down in good step, two or three abreast; and occasionally standing in most formidable groups, around the fashionable lamppost at the corner of Swanston Street and Collins Street, from whence they contemplate the fair promenaders.*[116]

In the latter years of his life, Gill spent time with a group who had some literary interests, including Marcus Clarke and Adam Lindsay Gordon. Like Gill, Clarke undertook work for newspapers and magazines. All three men had difficulty with alcohol, had health problems, and couldn't manage their financial affairs. Clarke and Gordon suffered from depression, and it's possible Gill was also afflicted. For Gordon, life became too difficult and he committed suicide on 24 June 1870. By that stage, Gill was moving accommodation fairly frequently, and at times his lodgings may have been provided by friends. He had no regular income and no reserves to draw upon. Commissions were rare by this time, although architect friend, Arthur Peck, engaged him to provide sketches periodically.

One of Gill's haunts was the Mitre Tavern in Bank Place, which he incorporated into one of his last watercolour paintings of a street scene in Melbourne. It was signed S.T.G., dated 1880, and was typical Gill, full of detail and activity. In these last years, Gill often sold sketches in the Mitre Tavern for two shillings and sixpence. Clearly, he was desperate and had no source of regular income. His two and sixpence sketches are now highly valued by collectors of S. T. Gill paintings and drawings.

116 Clara Aspinall, *Three Years in Melbourne*, L. Booth, London, 1862, p. 12.

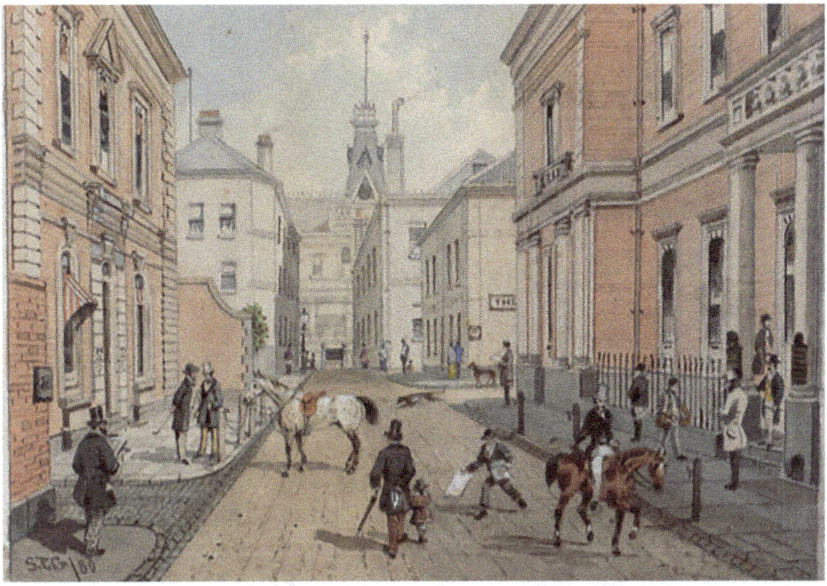

Bank Place, Melbourne 1880
(Dixon Library, State Library of New South Wales, FL3263788)

S. T. Gill struggled personally and as an artist when he returned to Melbourne from Sydney. Melbourne had changed, and it seems he had difficulty getting into the countryside and riding around the colony on horseback, which he had previously enjoyed. Nevertheless, he did produce a number of wonderful images of Melbourne and its environs, giving us a window into the growth and development that had taken place in his absence. Although we can see the progress with building and streetscape from his work, it was always the people and the activity Gill was most interested in recording.

Chapter 12—
S. T. Gill and Colonial History

... his work contains the hugeness of the land and the bounce of its inhabitants.

—Geoffrey Dutton[117]

Samuel Thomas Gill is possibly the best known of the colonial artists, and his work is often viewed with great affection. This wasn't always the case, and clearly, he ended his life in obscurity. During his forty-year career in Australia from 1839 to 1880, several writers indicated that Gill probably produced over 1500 works of art, making his output the largest of any Australian artist. However, Sasha Grishin sees this as a substantial undercount. As the result of a grant from the Australian Research Council, he has been able to develop a database which contains close to 4,000 items of Gill's work.[118] This is an enormous output, and these images greatly enrich our understanding of nineteenth-century Australia.

Gill's work is frequently assessed on its quality or merit as works of art, and in this context, is often compared to his

117 Geoffrey Dutton, *Paintings of S. T. Gill*, Rigby, Adelaide, 1962, p.11.
118 Sasha Grishin, *S. T. Gill and His Audiences*, National Library of Australia, State Library of Victoria, 2015, p.13, for information on the data base plus an email to me of February 25, 2021 which updated the published figure. See also Appendix I.

contemporaries; for example, his landscapes are often singled out for comparison with other nineteenth-century landscape artists. During his period the two outstanding landscape artists were John Glover and Eugene von Guerard. Glover, influenced by seventeenth-century European landscape masters, produced some great Australian landscape paintings in the 1830s. Von Guerard, trained in a German romantic tradition, produced possibly the best nineteenth-century Australian landscapes. While Glover and von Guerard were outstanding nineteenth-century colonial artists, there are some art historians who believe Gill's work compares favourably with them and other contemporary artists. The consensus is that Gill's work has substantial artistic merit; some say that his best works were probably his rural landscape paintings, the exploration landscapes of the Horrocks expedition, and his scenes of Adelaide and the Port. Art teacher and 'realist' painter, Herbert Badham, believed Gill was somewhat unorthodox and went on to paint in a manner that was not particularly influenced by the principles and traditions of the masters:

His drawings... are strong in detail and instinct with topical anecdote... It must be remembered, however, that Gill's art was truely (sic) his own according to the general taste in English anecdotal painting of the day... The artist-colonist was thrown on his native resources and he drew his world untroubled by theory and fashion.[119]

Geoffrey Dutton, in writing about the quality of Gill's work, believes that *Gill is underrated as an artist.*[120]He contends that because Gill painted smaller watercolours rather than grander oils, and because some of his art was classified as satirical in style, it was not taken seriously by some art historians. Dutton also feels Gill was judged negatively by some because of his

119 Herbert E. Badham, *A Study of Australian Art*, Currawong Publishing, 1949, p.28.
120 Geoffrey Dutton, *S. T. Gill's Australia*, Macmillan, 1981 p. 7.

drunken lifestyle. Dutton further contends that Gill was the first artist to understand Australia and record Australian life:

Gill was by temperament the observer and by his gifts the recorder of Australian life in the 1840s and 1850s. But as his landscapes show, he was more: for all his unevenness and the deterioration of his talent, he was a true artist who accepted and understood Australia long before any other major painter.[121]

Sasha Grishin is somewhat scathing of those who, while admiring Gill, are reluctant to describe him as a great painter. He says of his art:

It was art as information, it was art as entertainment, it was art which disseminated 'knowledge' to a very broad audience.[122]

Some critics of Gill have at least partly based their assessment on his private life, particularly in the latter part. This has resulted in some derogatory comments, similar to the way poet and writer, Henry Lawson, was patronised until more recent times.

While I have appreciated the depth of assessment and the considerable amount of work undertaken by those with a greater knowledge of art than myself, and the conclusions they have formed about the artistic value of Gill's work, I have been much more interested in looking at his work from the viewpoint of a historian, appreciating his contribution to our understanding of nineteenth-century colonial Australia.

Hence, my focus and interest has been on the 'snapshots' that Gill provided of everyday colonial life and the value of his contribution to our understanding of what nineteenth-century Australia and early Australians were like. Bernard Smith, in his *Australian Paintings 1788-1960,* comments on Gill and his art as forming:

121 Ibid. p.50.
122 Sasha Grishin, *S. T. Gill and His Audience*, National Library of Australia, State Library of Victoria, 2015, p.12.

...a most valuable commentary upon life of the times, a commentary which is expressed with much gusto and great humour. Gill is the first artist whose work expresses a distinctly Australian attitude to life: sardonic humour, the nonchalance of the irreverent attitude to all forms of authority, so frequently remarked upon by the students of Australian behaviour, are all present in his work.[123]

There have been a number of art historians and commentators who have agreed with the tenor of Smith's comments. For example, Allan McCulloch, in *Artists of the Goldfields* (1976) states:

What Mark Twain was to the American short story, S. T. Gill was to Australian drawing and painting.[124]

As someone who has been passionate about photography from an early age, I have particularly appreciated Gill's work, because most of his paintings and drawings are relatively small and in watercolour or pencil; they resemble, for me, a large collection of black and white and colour photographs of everyday life. In fact, art historian Daniel Thomas speaks of Gill as follows:

Nobody in Australian art has captured the cheerful animation of the city crowds, of miners or bush workers so well... He is a very democratic pictorial journalist, who might have taken up photography at a later age and exploited its immediacy and speed.[125]

It's interesting that Thomas suggested photography may have been something that Gill might have been drawn to at a later time. In fact, it appears Gill briefly experimented with photography while

123 Bernard Smith, *Australian Paintings 1788-1900*, Oxford University Press, 1962, p.50.
124 Alan McCulloch, *Artists of the Australian Gold Rush*, Lansdowne Editions, 1977, p.68.
125 Daniel Thomas, *Outlines of Australian Art: The Joseph Brown Collection*, Third Edition. Macmillan Australia,1973, p.14.

in South Australia in the 1840s. He was possibly the first person to import daguerreotype equipment to the colony. On November 8, 1845, the *South Australian Register* announced:

A daguerreotype has been sent to the colony, and is in the hands of Mr Gill, the artist. It appears to take likenesses as if by magic... The portrait is, in fact, a preserved looking-glass. We understand Mr Gill will soon be prepared to show us as we are.

However, Gill did not persevere with the process. He sold the equipment early in 1846 to Adelaide publican Robert Hall, and there is no record of existing daguerreotypes images that can be attributed to STG. It also appears he made limited use of the equipment (the *South Australian Register* reported briefly on December 24, 1845, that *a few portrait images had been viewed*). It's possible the process didn't deliver the images in either quality or timelines that he was seeking, which he was able to produce with his paintings and drawings in a much more timely manner. Also, Gill's use of colour and inclusion of movement and activity wasn't possible with photography at that time. For example, Gill's images of the goldfields differ markedly from those created in the carefully posed compositions of goldfields photographs. The process developed by Louis Daguerre, which had been made public on 19 August 1839 (known as the Daguerreotype) involved making an image on a metal plate and developing it using mercury vapour. To prepare, expose and process a Daguerreotype plate required a considerable amount of apparatus and manipulation. Reactions to the invention varied widely. On one hand, there was wide-eyed astonishment and enthusiasm, such as the report in the *Perth Gazette*, which exclaimed on 4 April 1840:

An invention has recently been made public in Paris that seems more like some marvel of a fairy tale or delusion of necromancy than a practical reality: It amounts to nothing less than making light produce permanent pictures and engrave them at the same time in the course of a few minutes. The thing seems incredible.

However, some in the art world were also astonished but somewhat disturbed by this invention. It was reported that painter Paul Delaroche exclaimed:

From today, painting is dead![126]

Although the Daguerreotype process had many disadvantages, including the amount of equipment and time required, the quality of the image was astounding, with brilliant clarity and detail. The process of photography may have appealed more to Gill later in the century when it had been further developed and simplified. During the nineteenth century, most photography was done by professionals using bulky equipment, with many of the images being taken in a studio. In 1851, there was an improvement with the development of a wet-plate process, and although it simplified photography and permitted the reproduction of multiple copies on albumen paper, the cost of the equipment and the knowledge required restricted its use to a small group of professionals and wealthy hobbyists. Photography didn't really become popular until the beginning of the twentieth century with the development of roll film, which made it cheaper, easier and available to the amateur.

Even with the emergence of photography and its progressive expansion during the nineteenth century, Gill's paintings and drawings of everyday life were extremely important. They were snapshots of people and places that would later be produced on film, but contained much more life, colour, and movement than early photographs.

Robert Hughes referred to Gill as:

The most robust and "Australian" of all Colonial artists... The eye of a journalist[127]

126 Bryan Coe, *The Birth of Photography*, Hutchinson Publishing Group Ltd. 1977, p. 17.
127 Robert Hughes, *The Art of Australia*, Penguin Books, 1970, p. 20

McCulloch believed Gill's work revealed Australia in a new light:

He opened up the heart of an Australian psyche and revealed its possibilities, and he opened up the country and showed its beauty.[128]

Gill's hundreds of images produced during his some forty years in Australia constitute an enormous contribution to Australian colonial history. Some commentators have been critical of the quality of some of his work, on the basis that some mass production occurred, particularly as an endeavour to live on the sale of his work. This is not something that particularly concerns me as a historian, as I think all the images are important to our understanding of nineteenth-century Australia. Even his duplicates of various pet subjects contained some subtle and interesting differences that I believe added to the viewers' appreciation of the subject. I have examined an enormous number of Gill's sketches and paintings, and I have found abundant life and detail in even his most rudimentary sketches.

We are indebted to Gill, not only for our knowledge of what the buildings and streets looked like, but also for what the people from all walks of life and all ages wore, what they carried, what dogs and horses they owned, how they stood, and how they moved.

As Michael Cannon put it so precisely:

Few artists before or since have devoted themselves to the social history of ordinary Australians acting out their daily lives. He was a born reporter - and much more than that, a creative interpreter of human existence.[129]

128 Alan McCulloch, *Artists of the Australian Gold Rush*, Lansdowne Editions, 1977, p.191.
129 Michael Cannon, *The Victorian Gold Fields 1852-3*. An Original Album by S.T. Gill, O'Neil Publishers, 1982, p.15.

It would be nice to know more about Gill the man. Had he been a writer as well as an artist, we would clearly have known much more about his thoughts, feelings and views. However, he was too absorbed in his artwork and his subjects, and probably an introvert by nature, to have time to write about himself. His diary, however, kept during the Horrocks expedition, does provide some very useful information about his thoughts and feelings, as well as what he painted. But the facts about Gill during his some forty years of artwork in Australia are relatively meagre and we are forced to carefully study his work, to look carefully at the layers and study the content, in order to glean some understanding of Samuel Thomas Gill, the man.

By the 1870s, Gill's health was failing. It seems that he had been receiving outpatient treatment from the Melbourne Hospital, probably for heart problems (his father had died from a heart attack). His health problems were most likely aggravated by his heavy drinking and an unhealthy lifestyle. Naturally reticent, he became a forgotten man, moving restlessly around hotels, exchanging quick sketches for the price of a drink. Occasionally, a drawing was commissioned, and he was able to produce it with something of his former brilliance. The accumulation of wealth had never interested S. T. Gill. A more ambitious person would certainly have made capital of his opportunities, but Gill was absorbed in his art and roving life, and repeatedly displayed little interest in the business side of his affairs. In fact, his work was often shamelessly plundered and plagiarised by lithographers and engravers and even by some artists. Once Gill's lithographs became available, piracy of his designs became widespread, particularly his gold rush imagery.

On 27 October 1880, at the age of 62, he collapsed and died, destitute, on the steps of the Melbourne Post Office. An autopsy revealed he died from a ruptured aorta. He was buried in a pauper's grave in the Melbourne General Cemetery. The people of Melbourne were not particularly interested in the death of a painter when there was so much publicity being given to Ned

Kelly's trial, which commenced the following day. There was also excitement in the city because a great international exhibition had opened in the Carlton Gardens, and internationally famous pianist, Henri Ketten, was entertaining and enthralling audiences at the Town Hall. The Melbourne Daily Telegraph on October 28 briefly mentioned the death of an unknown man on the steps of the Melbourne Post Office. About a week later, on 6 November 1880, the Adelaide people were given more information about Gill's death in the *Adelaide Observer*, although the notice was buried in a very lengthy column containing information about a very wide range of mostly mundane matters:

The Late Mr. S. T. Gill. —Our Victorian telegrams on Friday contained the announcement of the sudden death of Mr. S. T. Gill. The deceased gentleman, who formerly lived in South Australia, where his parents also resided, was an artist of some considerable ability, his best efforts being in the direction of water-colour painting. Several of his water-colour sketches of colonial scenery have been sent over to this colony at various times, and were much admired for the softness of the colouring and the boldness of execution. Much of Mr. Gill's talent lay in the direction of original sketches, and he was a contributor to several illustrated periodicals. He had a taste for marine views, in which he succeeded, but in portrait-painting; to which he gave some attention, he was not so much at home.

There are very few images of S. T. Gill made by artists or photographers. As mentioned in Chapter 10, one of Gill's Sydney pupils, William Garling, painted him from memory—wearing a top hat, cut-away coat and carrying a riding crop, which Garling said was his normal dress; this was clearly not Gill's attire in the last few years of his life and probably not how he dressed when wandering around country South Australia, Victoria and New South Wales on horseback. There is also the photographic image of Gill by an unknown photographer at the front of this book, taken around 1870, probably in a studio. However, it's clear that

Gill was a bit like Alfred Hitchcock, who frequently made brief cameo appearances in many of his movies. Starting early in his painting career, he included himself and possibly his dogs in a number of his paintings. This was a practice that commenced while he was in England developing his sketch book. The last entry in the sketch book shows him at the age of 20 dressed as a hunter, returning from the kill with his dogs. Gill continued this practice in Australia; one of the best examples of this is on the cover piece and title page of his *Australian Sketchbook*. Gill is seen clutching his sketch book, cooling his feet in a stream, wearing a worn hat and clothes and sporting a rough red beard, which is showing some grey around the edges. From these images, it appears Gill was a large-framed man with red hair and beard, and of a convivial, though solitary, nature.

After Gill's death, there were no obituaries in the papers. It was more than a decade before an acknowledgement of his work appeared in the press, and it was a personal reflection written by one of Gill's contemporaries, journalist Maurice Brodzky:

Perhaps his humour was, at times, a little coarse, but it was true humour for all that. He seized upon the broadly grotesque, and, without exaggerating it, made it palpable, patent and easily comprehensible. It was not subtle humour, but it was living, active and incisive... They never looked laboured, and yet they were never carelessly done. Every line had its meaning, and every detail, however minute, had a distinct purpose. Indeed, it is astonishing what an extraordinary amount of material he was able to put into bits no bigger than an ordinary visiting card... His latter days were clouded. Perhaps all his life was more or less clouded. He always seemed a solitary man, about whom nobody knew very much. He was never talked about in the newspapers. His goings and comings were unnoticed, and when he died there was no long biographies of him... although his name is not high upon the scroll of artist-fame, his work, wonderful, abundant, and in its way, perfect, is intimately associated with the social history of this colony[130].

130 Maurice Brodzky, *S. T. Gill: A Reminiscence. Table Talk*, May 1, 1891, p.5.

Gill's body was eventually moved to a private grave in 1913, thanks to a subscription raised by the Historical Society of Victoria, which also arranged for a headstone to be placed there (his grave is, interestingly, not far from the graves of Burke and Wills). Gill's unmarked resting place had been drawn to the notice of the Melbourne public in a lengthy piece on page 7 of *The Argus*, Saturday 14 September 1912, by A. W. Grieg, entitled *An Australian Cruikshank*. Grieg finished with the following plea:

Are there any Victorian's alive to-day who, for the sake of his art and the sake of the days that are gone, would rescue the last resting place of poor "S.T.G" from the oblivion to which it has fallen?

Grieg presented a paper to the Royal Historical Society on Gill's life and work in 1913.

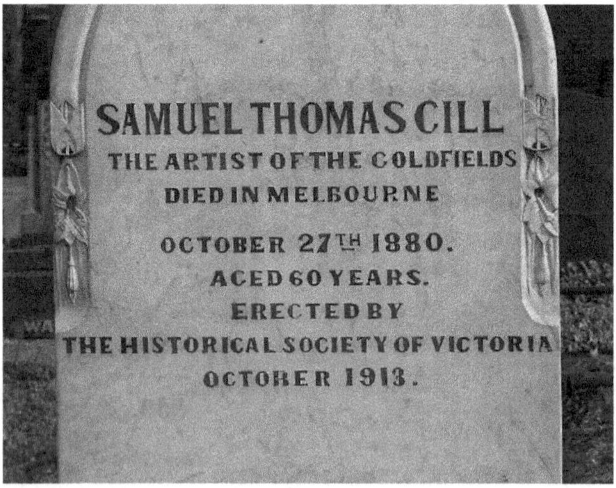

Headstone from S. T. Gill's grave[131]

131 The age on the headstone is incorrect, S. T. Gill was 62 when he died. Note that the grave was restored by Lodge Bros. in 1997 as the first project of the National Trust Cemetery Restoration Appeal. Project funding was provided by public donations and tours of the cemetery. There was an earlier restoration arranged about 1939 by C.J. Thompson of Adelaide, S. T. Gill's niece. Gill's work is acknowledged in South Australia with a brass plate in the footpath in North Terrace. There is also a street named after Gill in the suburb of Lyneham, Canberra (the streets of Lyneham are named after artists and people associated with the development of early Canberra).

Despite that his life was undoubtedly, at times, very difficult, and his circumstances trying and tragic, it was S. T. Gill who, so brilliantly, often conveyed in a light-hearted, comic, or sad way, the lifestyles of those he met and the landscapes they inhabited.

The appeal of his art lies in the ability to document the past in its tiniest details, to give us today a picture of that time, which is as fresh now as it was then when he wielded his paintbrush.

I believe S. T. Gill's considerable body of artwork has made an enormous contribution to our understanding of Australia's colonial history. We know so much, in such great detail, from his paintings, drawings and lithographs about the people, places and events of the nineteenth century. The scale of his contribution was acknowledged and nicely summarised by Robert Campbell, a former Director of the State Gallery of South Australia:

...there's no doubt that Gill has left us a complete - the most complete - pictorial record of the manners and customs, as well as the setting, whether in town or country, of the pioneering days...[132]

132 Robert Campbell, Early South Australian Artists, lecture (undated), p. 13, State Library of South Australia, Call No. 759.99423C189.

Appendix I—Location of Gill's Work

Paintings, drawings, prints, and lithographs by Gill are held in many Australian galleries, museums and libraries, including the Art Gallery of New South Wales, the Queensland Art Gallery & Gallery of Modern Art, the Art Gallery of South Australia, the National Gallery of Victoria, the Art Gallery of Western Australia, the Art Gallery of Ballarat, the Castlemaine Art Museum, the National Museum of Australia, the Tasmanian Museum and Art Gallery, the National Library of Australia, the La Trobe Library (State Library of Victoria), the Mitchell Library (State Library of New South Wales), the State Library of Western Australia and the State Library of South Australia.

Library Holdings

National Library of Australia

The National Library of Australia (NLA) holds 95 watercolours and about 80 wash, sepia wash or pencil drawings of S. T. Gill. In addition, it has a very large number of lithographs and chromolithographs engraved by Gill, as well as wood engravings, and photolithographs of his paintings and sketches.

Some of Gill's books of lithographs, such as *The Australian Sketch Book* (1855), *Sketches of the Gold Diggings* (1855) and *The Gold Fields of Victoria* during 1852 & 3 (1872), are held in the Australian Collection at the NLA. Loose plates from these and other publications are also held in the Pictures Collection.

State Library of Victoria

The library has 633 items attributed to S. T. Gill.

The holdings include 102 watercolour paintings, 50 drawings (pen and ink, pencil, wash), 240 lithographs and chromolithographs, 140 steel engravings and 40 wood engravings.

The library also holds copies of the following:

- Two photographic copies of early illustrations of Adelaide, South Australia plus about 10 other photographic copies of Gill's work.
- A scrapbook containing photographs, newspaper clippings and drawings by S. T. Gill and other artists, from the publishing firm James J. Blundell & Co.
- *The Victorian Gold Fields during 1852-3*: album comprising 40 original sketches by S. T. Gill and *The Goldfields of Victoria 1852-53* (1872) album containing 50 original sketches.
- *Sketches in Victoria* album compiled by James Blundell & Co. containing miscellaneous images including lithographic sketches by S. T. Gill, photographic views of Victoria and newspaper clippings.
- *Sketches of Australian life and scenery* containing seven hand-coloured lithographs.
- *Melbourne Sketches 1854* compiled by Campbell & Ferguson containing seven coloured lithographs.
- *Views of Sydney* containing a large number of prints and drawings.
- Twelve hand-coloured postcards of Melbourne in the 'Fifties" incorporating Gill's work produced in the period 1905-10

- *The Australian Sketchbook (1864)* produced by Hamel & Ferguson, containing 25 chromolithograph prints.

State Library of New South Wales

The library holds an extensive range of Gill's work representing over 700 items of his work in various formats including a number of albums and individual items including:

- *S. T. Gill: Original Sketches, 1844-1866*, comprising 46 watercolours and 17 pencil sketches in three portfolios.
- *Dr. Doyle's Sketchbook* in 3 volumes containing 44 watercolours.
- *Victorian Goldfields 1852-53*, a collection of 6 photolithographs (originals in the State Library of Victoria).
- Original drawings of the Victorian Gold Fields c. 1852 comprising 14 pencil sketches.
- Album part of the David Scott Mitchell Collection comprising 42 lithographs and 2 watercolours (1853-1875).
- Album part of David Scott Mitchell Collection containing 28 ink drawings (1870-72).
- Album of town views, landscapes and natural history, part of David Scott Mitchell Collection comprising 20 watercolours and pencil drawings and two lithographs.
- *Frome Collection*, Royal Empire Societies, containing letters and nine drawings and three watercolours by S. T. Gill.
- Two unnamed collections: one with 22 pencil drawings and watercolours and another with six watercolours and five pencil drawings.

The library also holds many individual items of Gill's work, including 194 lithographs (some coloured), 128 watercolours, 34 photographic prints of watercolours, 31 drawings with wash, 23 pencil drawings, 22 zincographs, 15 wood or copper engravings, 13 coloured transparencies of watercolours, 6 black and white negatives, one charcoal drawing and one oil painting. There are also a number of large family history collections that contain one or two items of Gill's work.

State Library of Western Australia

The library holds the following items:

- *The Australian sketch-book* - 50 pages, 24 plates of lithographs, coloured.
- *Victoria Illustrated* - 46 leaves of plates (46 pages of images). Drawn by S.T. Gill, engraved by J. Tingle. Vignette on t.p.: 'Entrance to Port Phillip' engraved by A. Willmore.
- *Sketches of the diggings* - collection of original 24 pencil sketchings. May also be included in the book *The goldfields illustrated* below.
- *The goldfields illustrated* - 108 pages - Published book, not originals. 48 images included, and features pencil sketches.
- *Rambles at the Antipodes* - includes two maps and twelve tinted lithographs, illustrative of Australian life, by S. T. Gill.

State Library of South Australia

The library holds some collections, a number of individual items and photographs of Gill's work.

- *The Australian Sketchbook 1865* - 24 plates in colour produced by Hamel & Ferguson.
- *The Victorian gold diggings & diggers as they are 1852* -in two parts, each containing 24 colour lithographs.
- *Victoria Illustrated - first series 1856-57,* 44 steel engravings produced by Sands & Kenny.
- Horrocks Expedition collection of 10 sepia watercolours.
- Burra mines collection of four hand-coloured lithographs showing interior of mines, township and surface operations.

The library also holds 30 individual lithographs, approximately 20 black & white photographs, some glass plate negatives, six colour art prints of the Victorian goldfields and two sketches by Gill.

Gallery & Museum Holdings

Note: n/a signifies year not known.

National Gallery of Victoria

The gallery holds 88 items of Gill's works including the following:

- *Native corroboree,* lithograph print, 1850s
- *Bushrangers flight* from '*Sketches in Victoria*', lithographic print, 1856
- *Sunday flag, 'Clydesdale' Fiji,* watercolour over pencil, 1870
- *Landscape with Aborigines,* watercolour, n/a

- *Mount Gambier, South Australia,* oil on cardboard, 1852
- *Forest Creek Mount Alexander Diggings,* hand-coloured lithograph, 1852
- *Botany Bay in 1874,* watercolour, 1874
- *Native sepulchre,* watercolour, c.1864
- *Corroboree at night,* watercolour, 1871
- *Kangaroo stalking* (TAS), colour lithograph, 1864
- *Night camp* (TAS), colour lithograph, 1864
- *Native sepulchre* (TAS), colour lithograph, 1864
- *Surveyors* (TAS), colour lithograph, 1864
- *Prospection* (TAS), colour lithograph, 1864
- *Grim evidence,* watercolour over pencil & gum, n/a
- *The avengers,* watercolour gum arabic over pencil, c.1869
- *Mother's pride,* watercolour & pen & ink, 1860s
- *Frontispiece of TAS,* colour lithograph, 1864
- *Homeward bound* (TAS), colour lithograph, 1864
- *The new rush* (TAS), colour lithograph, 1864
- *Wool drays* (TAS), colour lithograph, 1864
- *Emu sneaking* (TAS), colour lithograph, 1864
- *Attacking the mail,* colour lithograph, 1864
- *Father's hope,* watercolour & pen & ink, 1860s
- *Attack on store dray* (TAS), colour lithograph, 1864
- *The Duff children* (TAS), colour lithograph, 1864
- *Corroboree* (TAS), colour lithograph, 1864
- *Bush mailman* (TAS), colour lithograph, 1864
- *The inquiry,* watercolour with gum arabic, 1870s
- *Stockman* (TAS), colour lithograph, 1864

- *Ballarat Flay from Black Hill*, lithograph, 1855
- *Native police* (TAS), colour lithograph, 1864
- *Cattle branding* (TAS), colour lithograph, 1864
- *Squatters' tiger* (TAS), colour lithograph, 1864
- *Native Miami* (TAS), colour lithograph, 1864
- *Bush funeral* (TAS), colour lithograph, 1864
- *Bushman's hut* (TAS), colour lithograph, 1864
- *Splitters* (TAS), colour lithograph, 1864
- *Overlanders* (TAS), colour lithograph, 1864
- *Night fishing* (TAS), colour lithograph, 1864
- *Flemington Hill,* watercolour, gum arabic/pencil, c.1865
- *The waterfall,* watercolour & pencil, n/a
- *Attacking the mail* (TAS), colour lithograph, 1864
- *Ballarat Flat,* from the Black Hill+, lithograph, 1855
- *Quartz crushing, base of Black Hill Ballarat+,* lithograph, 1855
- *Store drays camped on road to Ballarat+,* lithograph, 1855
- *Horse puddling machine, Forest Creek+,* lithograph, 1855
- *Interior of John Alloo's Restaurant Ballarat+,* lithograph, 1855
- *John Alloo's Chinese Restaurant, main road+,* lithograph, 1855
- *Govt camp from across the creek, Creswick+,* lithograph, 1855
- *Cover for series+,* lithograph, 1855
- *Ballarat from Mount Burrangong+,* lithograph, 1855
- *Market Square from Little Maple St, Geelong+,* lithograph, 1855

- *Township of Ballarat from Bath's Hotel+*, lithograph, 1855
- *Govt camp, Castlemain+*, lithograph, 1855
- *Mount Macedon from the Black Forest+*, lithograph, 1855
- *Arrival of Geelong Mail, main road Ballarat+*, lithograph, 1855
- *Geelong from the bay+*, lithograph, 1855
- *Market Square, Castlemaine, Forest Creek+*, lithograph, 1855
- *Township of Kyneton (main street north)+*, lithograph, 1855
- *Deep creek, mail & passengers to Melbourne+, l*ithograph, 1855
- *Creswick Creek from Spring Hill+*, lithograph, 1855
- *Williamstown Lighthouse+*, lithograph, 1855
- *Township of Keilor looking south+*, lithograph, 1855
- *Deep sinking, Ballarat+*, lithograph, 1855
- *On the Barwon near Fyans Ford, Geelong+*, lithograph, 1855
- *On the Barwon above Fyans Ford, Geelong+*, lithograph, 1855
- *Eureka near insurgent's stockade+*, lithograph, 1855
- *The Flinders Range*, watercolour on paper on cardboard, c.1865-70
- *The Bendigo mill 1852*, watercolour over pencil, c.1865
- *Approach to Richmond north bank of Yarra*, engraving & relief painting, 1886
- *Yarra Street south to bay of Geelong*, engraving & relief painting, 1857
- *Spring Hill, road to govt camp, Creswick's Creek*, engraving & relief painting, 1857

- *City Police Station & Town Hall, Melbourne,* engraving & relief painting, 1857
- *Post Office, Melbourne,* engraving & relief painting, 1856
- *Prince's Bridge & City Terminus,* engraving & relief painting, 1856
- *Government offices, Melbourne,* engraving & relief painting, 1856
- *Great Bourke Street, looking east,* engraving & relief painting, 1856
- *Queen's Wharf, Melbourne, West End,* engraving & relief painting, 1856
- *St Francis Cathedral, Melbourne,* engraving & relief painting, 1857
- *Creswick's Creek from Spring Hill,* engraving & relief painting, 1857
- *National model & training school, Melbourne,* engraving & relief painting, 1857
- *Post Office, Melbourne,* engraving & relief painting, 1856
- *Belfast, Port Fairy,* engraving & relief painting, 1857
- *Mother's pride & Father's hope,* watercolour & pen & ink, 1860s

TAS is *The Australian Sketchbook*

+From a series published by James J. Blundell & Co. Melbourne in 1855 entitled: T*he diggers and diggings of Victoria as they are in 1855,* comprising a set of 24 lithographs.

Art Gallery of New South Wales:

The gallery holds 14 items of Gill's work, including the following:

- *Nuggetting,* lithograph, printed on paper, 1854
- *Bush Funeral,* colour lithograph, printed on paper, 1864
- *Squatter's tiger,* colour lithograph, printed on paper, 1864
- *Land auction, Ballarat,* pencil, grey wash on buff paper, 1854
- *Title page,* lithograph, 1856
- *General Post Office,* lithograph, 1856
- *Australian Club House,* lithograph, 1856
- *City Railway Terminus,* lithograph, 1856
- *Avenue approach Botanic Gardens,* lithograph, 1856
- *Circular Quay, Sydney,* tinted lithograph on white wove paper, 1856
- *Dry Dock, Balmain,* lithograph, 1856
- *The stockman,* watercolour, opaque white, scraping out, 1854
- *Overlanders,* pencil, watercolour, white gouache, c.1865
- *Landscape with crater & cone,* pencil, watercolour, gum, white gouache, c.1870
- *Toorak House,* pencil, gouache on pink pastelboard, 1857

Queensland Art Gallery & Gallery of Modern Art

The gallery holds over 40 items of Gill's work including the following:

- *Emu hunt,* watercolour & gouache over pencil, n/a
- *Digger's wedding Melbourne,* watercolour over pencil, cream wove paper, c.1862
- *Landscape with Aborigines,* watercolour on wove paper, 1866

- *Beach scene,* watercolour & gouache over pencil, n/a
- *Mt. Nicholson & Mt. Aldis, Qld,* pencil, brush & ink with gum arabic, c.1850
- *Bushman's hut* (TAS), colour lithograph on smooth wove paper, 1865
- *Surveyors* (TAS), colour lithograph on smooth wove paper, 1865
- *Kangaroo stalking* (TAS), colour lithograph on smooth wove paper, 1865
- *Stockman* (TAS), colour lithograph on smooth wove paper, 1865
- *Homeward bound* (TAS), colour lithograph on smooth wove paper, 1865
- *Emu sneaking* (TAS), colour lithograph on smooth wove paper, 1865
- *Native Miami* (TAS), colour lithograph on smooth wove paper, 1865
- *Attack on store dray* (TAS), colour lithograph on smooth wove paper, 1865
- *Native police* (TAS), colour lithograph on smooth wove paper, 1865
- *Squatter's tiger* (TAS), colour lithograph on smooth wove paper, 1865
- *Night fishing* (TAS), colour lithograph on smooth wove paper, 1865
- *Native sepulchre* (TAS), colour lithograph on smooth wove paper, 1865
- *Wool drays* (TAS), colour lithograph on smooth wove paper, 1865

- *Bush funeral* (TAS), colour lithograph on smooth wove paper, 1865
- *The Duff children* (TAS), colour lithograph on smooth wove paper, 1865
- *Attacking the mail, NSW* (TAS), colour lithograph on smooth wove paper, 1865
- *Overlanders* (TAS), colour lithograph on smooth wove paper, 1865
- *Night camp* (TAS), colour lithograph on smooth wove paper, 1865
- *Bush mailman* (TAS), colour lithograph on smooth wove paper, 1865
- *Prospecting* (TAS), colour lithograph on smooth wove paper, 1865
- *Splitters* (TAS), colour lithograph on smooth wove paper, 1865
- *The new rush* (TAS), colour lithograph on smooth wove paper, 1865
- *Corroboree* (TAS), colour lithograph on smooth wove paper, 1865
- *Cattle branding* (TAS), colour lithograph on smooth wove paper, 1865
- *Frontispiece* (TAS), colour lithograph on smooth wove paper, 1865
- *Cover* (TAS), lithograph on cardboard, 1865
- *Untitled* (beach scene/fishermen), wash & pen, brown ink over pencil, c.1850
- *Untitled* (ruined castle), wash & pen, brown ink over pencil, c.1839

- *Untitled* (cook's River, Sydney), pencil highlighted with chalk brown wove paper, c.1850-60
- *Untitled* (two Aborigines), pencil on wove paper, n/a
- *Landscape* (cows & fence), wash & pen, brown ink over pencil, c.1839-80
- *Untitled* (river landscape), wash & pen, brown ink over pencil, n/a
- *Untitled* (lower Murray), pencil on brown paper, c.1842
- *Untitled* (Aboriginal woman), pencil on brown paper, n/a
- *Mt. Gambier, SA,* pencil on wove paper, n/a
- *Flinders Ranges,* pencil on brown paper, c.1846
- *Untitled* (near Port Albert), wash & pen, brown ink over pencil, n/a
- *Untitled* (Portland Bay), wash, pen, brown ink over pencil, c.1850
- *Untitled* (Lower Barwon), wash, pen, brown ink over pencil with chalk, n/a

TAS is *The Australian Sketchbook.*

Art Gallery of South Australia

The gallery holds some 322 items, including a large number of watercolours, lithographs, some pencil drawings and steel engravings:

- *View of Lake Torrens, August 22,* watercolour, 1846
- *Looking SW from Table Land August 22,* watercolour, 1846
- *Halt on stony ground August 31,* watercolour, 1846
- *Sketch from Sunni, Flinders Ranges,* watercolour, 1846

- *Spencer's Gulf from camp,* watercolour, 1846
- *Camp in creek bed Flinders Ranges,* watercolour, 1846
- *First camping ground after leaving Campbell's Station August 9,* watercolour, 1846
- *Rhodes' Cattle Station on Gawler Section 471, November, 1844,* watercolour, 1844
- *Flinders Ranges, near Mt Brown, South Australia, looking east-south-east,* wash on paper, c.1846-8
- *Near Mt Arden, Flinders Ranges,* brush & ink, wash on paper, 1846
- *Flinders Ranges, north of Mt Brown,* watercolour, c.1846-50
- *The Vice,* lithograph, 1852
- *The Gawler River,* watercolour, 1844
- *Forest Creek Mt Alexander Diggings from base of Red Hill,* lithograph, 1852
- *Captain Davidson's house, "Blakiston" near Mt Barker* watercolour, 1848
- *MacLarens, main road Ballarat,* watercolour, 1855
- *Adelaide Hindley Street, lithograph printed in colour,* 1844
- *Known by his deeds,* lithographic crayon on stone, 1849
- *The Response Sweethearts & Wives,* lithographic crayon on stone, 1849
- *Todling after Commission,* lithographic crayon on stone, 1849
- *Wanted a Directory,* lithographic crayon on stone, 1849
- *Stocks At Par,* lithographic crayon on stone, 1849
- *Gentleman in the Bush,* lithographic crayon on stone, 1849

- *True Blue,* lithographic crayon on stone, 1849
- *Nothing Like O.G.,* lithographic crayon on stone, 1849
- *Father Matthew after a pledge,* lithographic crayon on stone, 1849
- *Throw physic to the dogs,* lithographic crayon on stone, 1849
- *Without reserve (Nathaniel Hailes),* lithographic crayon on stone, 1849
- *Poor exile of Erin (Campbell),* lithographic crayon on stone, 1849
- *Acting Purveyor General/G. Coppin,* lithographic crayon on stone, 1849
- *This comes hopping,* lithographic crayon on paper, 1849
- *Montague Featherstonhaugh,* lithographic crayon on stone, 1849
- *The noun Legislator nominative case,* lithographic crayon on stone, 1849
- *Stony Creek My Remarkable Survey,* watercolour, 1846-7
- *Approach to Mt Crawford,* watercolour, c.1842-3
- *Dares Hut, McVitties Flat,* watercolour pen, brush & brown ink, 1851
- *Government camp Castlemaine,* lithograph hand-coloured, 1855
- *Mt Macedon from Black Forest,* lithograph hand-coloured, 1855
- *Deep Creek, mail passengers,* lithograph hand-coloured, 1855
- *Township of Keilor looking south,* lithograph hand-coloured, 1855

- *Township of Kyneton looking north,* lithograph hand-coloured, 1855
- *Quartz crushing Black Hill Ballarat,* lithograph hand-coloured, 1855
- *Deep sinking Ballarat,* lithograph hand-coloured, 1855
- *Store drays camp road to Ballarat,* lithograph hand-coloured, 1855
- *Ballarat Flat from Black Hill,* lithograph hand-coloured, 1855
- *Township of Ballarat from Bath's H.,* lithograph hand-coloured, 1855
- *Kapunda copper mine sketch 2,* pencil black & grey watercolour wash, 1849
- *Kapunda copper mine engine house,* pencil black & grey watercolour wash, 1849
- *Kapunda copper mine sketch 6,* pencil black & grey watercolour wash, 1849
- *Kapunda copper mine sketch 55,* pencil black & grey watercolour wash, 1849
- *Kapunda copper mine sketch 4,* pencil black & grey watercolour wash, 1849
- *Kapunda copper mine sketch 3,* pencil black & grey watercolour wash, 1849
- *Rankin's Station Mt Crawford,* pencil, c.1842-3
- *Crater of extinct volcano, pencil,* c.1845
- *Depot Creek, SA, looking west,* pencil, 1846
- *Looking towards Spencer Gulf,* pencil, 1846
- *Old Police Station, Moorundie,* pencil, 1843
- *Cradling Forest Creek,* lithograph, 1852

- *Mustering Cattle,* lithograph, n/a
- *The Claim Disputed,* lithograph, n/a
- *The Bush Ranger pursued,* lithograph, n/a
- *Native Sneaking Emus,* lithograph, n/a
- *Old Watermill S.A.,* watercolour, pencil & gouache, c.1844
- *Old Watermill,* watercolour, pencil, pen & brown ink, 1844
- *Adelaide 2,* Hindley St looking east, lithograph, 1851
- *Adelaide 1,* Hindley St from KW St, lithograph, 1851
- *Mt Arden from NW Bluff,* watercolour, c.1846
- *Departure of Captain Sturt,* lithograph, hand-coloured, 1846-7
- *Hindley St from corner KW St,* lithograph (colour), n/a
- *Sketchbook,* pen & brown ink, watercolour, n/a
- *Adelaide 3, Rundle St looking east,* lithograph, 1851
- *Stockman,* lithograph, 1865
- *Native Sepulchre,* lithograph, n/a
- *The newly arrived enquiring,* lithograph, n/a
- *Puddling,* lithograph, n/a
- *Provident diggers in Melbourne,* lithograph, n/a
- *Pensioners Forest Creek,* lithograph, n/a
- *Zealous gold diggers Bendigo,* lithograph, 1852
- *Fossicking,* lithograph, n/a
- *Lucky digger that returned,* lithograph, n/a
- *Diggers shipping from Melbourne,* lithograph, n/a
- *Tin dish washing,* lithograph, n/a

- *Unlucky digger that never returned,* lithograph, n/a
- *Nuggeting,* lithograph, n/a
- *Making the claim,* lithograph, n/a
- *Improvident diggers in Melbourne,* lithograph, n/a
- *Butcher's shamble,* lithograph, n/a
- *Fryers Creek Mt Alexander diggings,* lithograph, n/a
- *Road to Bendigo from Forest Creek,* lithograph, n/a
- *Diggers licensing Forest Creek,* lithograph, n/a
- *Sunday camp meeting Forest C,* lithograph, n/a
- *Little Bendigo Forest Creek,* lithograph, n/a
- *Coffee tent,* lithograph, n/a
- *The claim disputed,* lithograph, n/a
- *Diggers wedding Melbourne,* lithograph, n/a
- *Surfacing,* lithograph, n/a
- *Convivial diggers Melbourne,* lithograph, n/a
- *Road in Black Forest,* lithograph, n/a
- *Mounted police escort Mt Alexander,* lithograph, n/a
- *On Bendigo creek,* lithograph, n/a
- *Iron Bark Gully,* lithograph, n/a
- *Cradling Forest Creek,* lithograph, n/a
- *Diggers Hill Forest Creek,* lithograph, n/a
- *Mt Alexander escort to Melbourne,* lithograph, n/a
- *Approach to Eagle Hawk Gully,* lithograph, n/a
- *Successful diggers to Bendigo,* lithograph, n/a
- *Diggers auction Eagle Hawk,* lithograph, n/a
- *Gold buyer Eagle Hawk,* lithograph, n/a

- *Diggers on route to deposit gold,* lithograph, n/a
- *Diggers of low degree,* lithograph, n/a
- *Diggers of high degree,* lithograph, n/a
- *Diggers on way to Bendigo,* lithograph, n/a
- *Ah Phil my hearty are that you,* lithograph, n/a
- *A Bendigo mill June 20,* lithograph, 1852
- *The invalid digger,* lithograph, n/a
- *Wayfaring diggers,* lithograph, n/a
- *Recovery of stray horses,* lithograph, n/a
- *Investing statement,* lithograph, n/a
- *Gold taken via Bendigo,* lithograph, n/a
- *Iron Bark,* lithograph, n/a
- *License inspected Forest Creek,* lithograph, 1852
- *Metcalfe's Station River Murray,* black & grey watercolour wash, 1844
- *Shepherd & sheep near Burra,* black & brown watercolour wash, c.1847
- *Heads of people,* lithograph crayon on stone, 1849
- *Heads of people 2,* lithograph, 1849
- *Hindley Street Adelaide,* hand coloured lithograph,n/a
- *Approach to Geelong from bay,* black & brown watercolour wash, c.1855
- *Near Mt Remarkable SA,* black & grey watercolour wash, 1846
- *Title page Australian Sketchbook,* colour lithograph, 1865
- *Kangaroo Hunting 3,* hand coloured lithograph, n/a
- *Gt Bourke St. looking east,* steel engraving, n/a

- *Gt Collins St looking west,* steel engraving, n/a
- *Gt Collins St looking east,* steel engraving, n/a
- *St Paul's Church from Swanston St,* steel engraving, n/a
- *Post office Melbourne,* steel engraving, n/a
- *City Police Station & Town Hall,* steel engraving, n/a
- *National model Training School,* steel engraving, n/a
- *Hobson's Bay from Signal Stn,* steel engraving, n/a
- *Government Office Melbourne,* steel engraving, n/a
- *View on Yarra near Dight's Mill,* steel engraving, n/a
- *Kangaroo Hunting 2 the chase,* hand coloured lithograph, n/a
- *Dight's Mill Yarra Yarra,* steel engraving, n/a
- *St Francis Cathedral Melbourne,* steel engraving, n/a
- *The University of Melbourne,* steel engraving, n/a
- *Queen's Wharf Melbourne,* steel engraving, n/a
- *Prince's Bridge Melbourne,* steel engraving, n/a
- *Approach to Melbourne,* steel engraving, n/a
- *Sandridge Williams Town,* steel engraving, n/a
- *Railway Terminus Geelong,* steel engraving, n/a
- *Fyan's Ford Barwon River Geelong,* steel engraving, n/a
- *On the Barwon River, Fyan's Ford,* steel engraving, n/a
- *Kangaroo hunting 1, the meet,* hand coloured lithograph, n/a
- *Geelong, near Windsor Castle,* steel engraving, n/a
- *Moorabool St, Geelong,* steel engraving, n/a
- *Market Square, Geelong,* steel engraving, n/a
- *Market Square from Matop St,* steel engraving, n/a

- *Yarra Street Geelong,* steel engraving, n/a
- *Steam packet wharf Geelong,* steel engraving, n/a
- *Approach to Geelong from the Bay,* steel engraving, n/a
- *Approach to Richmond from Yarra,* steel engraving, n/a
- *Portland from the Bay,* steel engraving, n/a
- *Belfast, Port Fairy,* steel engraving, n/a
- *Port of Warrnambool,* steel engraving, n/a
- *Sandhurst,* steel engraving, n/a
- *Township of Keilor,* steel engraving, n/a
- *Mt Macedon from Lagoon,* steel engraving, n/a
- *Govt Camp Creswick's Creek,* steel engraving, n/a
- *Spring Hill from Creswick's Creek,* steel engraving, n/a
- *Creswick's Creek from Spring Hill,* steel engraving, n/a
- *Market Square Castlemaine,* steel engraving, n/a
- *Attacking the mail 24,* colour lithograph, n/a
- *The Duff children,* colour lithograph, 1865
- *Prospecting 22,* colour lithograph, n/a
- *Native police 21,* colour lithograph, n/a
- *Ballarat Post Office & township,* colour lithograph, n/a
- *Ballarat from Black Hill,* colour lithograph, n/a
- *Ballarat looking NW,* colour lithograph, n/a
- *Entrance to Port Phillip,* colour lithograph, n/a
- *Forest Creek from Castlemaine Rd,* steel engraving, n/a
- *Bendigo from Eagle Hawk Rd,* steel engraving, n/a
- *Kyneton, towards bridge,* steel engraving, n/a
- *Lydiart St from Bath's Hotel,* steel engraving, n/a

- *Cattle branding 20,* colour lithograph, n/a
- *Night fishing 19,* colour lithograph, n/a
- *Attack on store dray 18,* colour lithograph, n/a
- *Bush mailman 17,* colour lithograph, n/a
- *Native sepulchre 16,* colour lithograph, n/a
- *Splitters 15,* colour lithograph, n/a
- *Bush funeral 14,* colour lithograph, n/a
- *Bushman's hut 13,* colour lithograph, n/a
- *Overlanders 12,* colour lithograph, n/a
- *Corroboree 11,* colour lithograph, n/a
- *Surveyors,* colour lithograph, 1865
- *Wool drays 9,* colour lithograph, n/a
- *Night camp 8,* colour lithograph, n/a
- *Native Miami 7,* colour lithograph, n/a
- *Squatters tiger 6,* colour lithograph, n/a
- *Homeward bound,* colour lithograph, n/a
- *Emu sneaking 4,* colour lithograph, n/a
- *The new rush 3,* colour lithograph, n/a
- *Kangaroo stalking 2,* colour lithograph, n/a
- *Stockman,* colour lithograph, n/a
- *Trinity church,* lithograph, n/a
- *Old Colonists' Festival Dinner,* lithograph, 1851
- *Port Adelaide,* steel engraving, n/a
- *King William Street,* steel engraving, n/a
- *View from Stanley Range,* engraving, n/a
- *The Adelaide plains,* engraving, n/a

- *Hindley Street Adelaide,* lithograph hand-coloured, n/a
- *Port Adelaide,* lithograph hand-coloured, n/a
- *The departure of Capt. Sturt,* lithograph hand-coloured, 1844
- *Knocked up,* brown watercolour wash, white gouache, c.1846
- *The departure of Capt. Sturt,* lithograph hand-coloured, 1844
- *Hindley Street from KW Street,* lithograph hand-coloured, 1845
- *Merry Monarch,* lithograph, 1851
- *Portrait of a man,* lithograph, n/a
- *Old Colonist festival dinner,* lithograph, 1851
- *Queen's Wharf Melbourne,* steel engraving, n/a
- *Creswick's Hill from Spring Hill,* steel engraving, n/a
- *Market Square north Geelong,* steel engraving, n/a
- *National model & training school,* steel engraving, n/a
- *Lydiart St from Bath's Hotel,* steel engraving, n/a
- *Prince's bridge & city terminus,* steel engraving, n/a
- *Christ Church, North Adelaide,* brown watercolour wash, white gouache, 1849
- *Hindley St from King William,* lithograph (colour), 1844
- *Trinity Church Adelaide,* black & brown watercolour wash, white gouache, 1849
- *Old colonists festival dinner,* lithograph, 1851
- *St James Anglican Church Blakiston,* watercolour, 1848
- *Squatter of P. Phillips,* watercolour & ink, c.1870
- *Kooringa, Burra Burra township,* watercolour, 1847

- *Kooringa from quarry,* watercolour, 1850
- *General view of Burra Burra mine,* watercolour, 1847
- *Thomas Harding of Kapunda,* watercolour, 1850
- *The Flinders Ranges,* pencil & watercolour, c.1865-70
- *Agricultural & Horticultural Society,* watercolour, 1843
- *Adelaide plains from Sleep's Hill,* watercolour, gouache & pencil, c.1870
- *Big Manly Beach Sydney,* black & grey watercolour wash, white gouache, c.1857
- *Emu Plains Lapstone Hill NSW,* black & brown watercolour wash, c.1856-64
- *New Wesleyan Chapel Adelaide,* lithograph, n/a
- *Looking Nth from Depot Creek,* watercolour, pen brush & brown ink, 1846
- *Landscape,* watercolour, pen brush & brown ink, c.1868
- *R.F. Macgeorge,* watercolour, 1850
- *Camp Site River Murray,* watercolour, n/a
- *River Murray scene,* watercolour, n/a
- *Burra Burra Mine,* watercolour, 1847
- *Grand Locomotive race,* watercolour, brush & brown ink, 1880
- *A call from the Ministry,* watercolour, n/a
- *A call to the Ministry,* watercolour, n/a
- *Tanunda Creek,* Angas Survey, watercolour, brush & brown ink, n/a
- *Floraville near Gawler,* watercolour, 1847
- *South Australian landscape,* watercolour, brush & brown ink, 1845

- *Diggers,* watercolour & brown ink wash, n/a
- *In the scrub,* watercolour, n/a
- *Burra Burra Mine Surface Operation,* watercolour, 1847
- *Promenade,* watercolour, n/a
- *Rivoli Bay,* watercolour, brush & brown ink, n/a
- *Sturt's overland expedition,* watercolour, 1845
- *The Gorge Mt Remarkable Survey,* watercolour, brush & brown ink, n/a
- *Landscape with stream,* watercolour, 1847
- *Great fall, Stony Creek,* watercolour, pencil, gouache, c.1846-7
- *Spencer Gulf from Flinders R,* watercolour, pencil, 1846-7
- *Stony Creek from waterfall top,* watercolour, 1846-7
- *Kooringa from quarry,* watercolour, 1850
- *Kooringa Burra Burra township,* watercolour , 1847
- *Burra Burra surface operation,* watercolour, 1850
- *General view of Burra Burra,* watercolour, 1847
- *Burra Burra smelting works,* watercolour, 1850
- *View leads of Prospect House NW,* watercolour, gouache pen & black ink, 1850
- *Prospect House,* watercolour & gouache, 1850
- *View leads of Prospect House E,* watercolour, gouache, pen & black ink, 1850
- *View Prospect House to Hindmarsh,* watercolour, gouache, pen & black ink, 1850
- *Prospect House SA,* watercolour, pen & black ink, 1850
- *Horrocks' Party in North,* watercolour, pencil gouache, c.1865-70

- *Near Mt Crawford SA,* watercolour, c.1865-70
- *Horrocks return to Depot Camp,* watercolour, 1846
- *Native attack Horrocks Nth west,* watercolour, brush & brown ink, gouache, c.1865-70
- *Invalid's tent on salt lagoon,* watercolour, pencil, gouache, 1846
- *Flinders Ranges from tableland,* watercolour, brown ink, gouache, 1846
- *Invalid's tent salt lake NW Mt Arden,* watercolour, 1846
- *Horrocks & Gill Pioneer Party Camp,* watercolour, brush & brown ink, gouache, 1846
- *Interview with Blacks,* watercolour, brush & brown ink, gouache, c.1865-70
- *Port Adelaide east to Nth Parade,* watercolour, 1846
- *Sturt's overland expedition leaving,* watercolour, 1844-5
- *Return of invalid,* watercolour, 1846
- *Travelling through the bush,* watercolour, 1846
- *Hindley Street looking east,* watercolour, 1845
- *Glen Osmond Mine,* watercolour, 1845
- *Kapunda Mine,* watercolour, 1845
- *Burra Burra Mine,* watercolour, 1845
- *Rundle Street Adelaide,* watercolour, 1845
- *Nth Terrace looking SE,* watercolour, 1845
- *Bank of SA & Legislative Council,* watercolour, 1845
- *From Verandah Vale Farm,* watercolour, c.1850
- *Vale Farm,* watercolour, c.1850
- *Macclesfield Township,* watercolour, pen & brown ink, n/a

- *Port Adelaide east along Nth Parade,* watercolour, 1847
- *Port Adelaide looking north,* watercolour, 1847
- *Port Adelaide across Gawler Reach,* watercolour, 1847
- *Monument to Colonel Light,* watercolour, 1848
- *Copper Co. Smelting Works,* watercolour, 1850
- *Kooringa Township,* watercolour, 1847
- *General View Burra Burra Mine,* watercolour, 1847
- *Neales' Stopes Burra Burra Mine,* watercolour, 1847
- *Penny's Stopes Burra Burra Mine,* watercolour, 1847
- *Trinity Church Adelaide,* watercolour, 1845
- *Rundle Street Adelaide,* watercolour, 1845
- *Port Adelaide across Gawler Reach,* watercolour, 1848
- *Kermode Street Nth Adelaide,* watercolour, 1845
- *Sturt's Expedition leaving Adelaide,* watercolour, 1844-5
- *King William St. looking north,* watercolour, 1845
- *Hindley Street looking west,* watercolour, 1845
- *Agricultural & Horticultural Show,* watercolour, 1845
- *Tanunda Creek,* pen & brush with sepia & black ink, 1839
- *Entrance to a Gorge,* pen & brush with sepia & black ink, 1839
- *In Flinders Range SA,* pen & brush with sepia & black ink, 1839
- *Adelaide Plains from Sleep's Hill,* pen & brush with sepia & black ink, 1839
- *North Terrace Adelaide,* watercolour, 1844
- *Extinct Crater Nth Spencer Gulf,* watercolour, 1845

- *Portrait of a man,* watercolour, black & sepia ink, 1868
- *Agricultural & horticultural Show,* watercolour, 1846
- *Old Police Station Moorundie,* watercolour, 1844
- *Government House North Terrace,* watercolour, 1845

Art Gallery of Western Australia

The Gallery holds fourteen items of Gill's work plus a copy of the *Australian Sketchbook* (25 chrome lithographs) and a copy of *Victoria Illustrated:* (? lithographs)

- *On Cook's river, NSW,* watercolour, brown wash, n/a
- *Wild Dog Creek, near Creswick,* watercolour, n/a
- *Splitters,* coloured lithograph, 1865
- *Surveyors,* coloured lithograph, 1865
- *Smith, Jones & Robinson,* pencil & wash, 1852
- *Adelaide, Hindley Street,* coloured lithograph, n/a
- *Entrance to Port Phillip* (Vic Illust.), lithograph, 1857
- *St Paul's Church Melbourne,* lithograph, 1857
- *Market Square, Geelong,* lithograph, 1857
- *Lydiart St from Bath Hotel Geelong,* lithograph, 1857
- *Market Square from Malop St,* lithograph, 1857
- *St Francis Cathedral, Melbourne,* lithograph, 1867
- *Police Stn & Town Hall Melbourne,* lithograph, 1856
- *Landscape,* watercolour & pencil, n/a

Tasmanian Museum and Art Gallery

- *Native bee hunting,* watercolour, n/a

Art Gallery of Ballarat

The gallery holds a significant number of items of Gill's work including 22 watercolours, 17 lithographs (some hand coloured), 3 engravings, 2 chromolithographs and one ink & pencil drawing. The gallery also holds a copy of *Victoria Illustrated* printed by Sands & Kenny in 1857 (containing 50 engravings), a photographic facsimile of *Victoria Illustrated* and *The Australian Sketchbook* produced by Hamel & Ferguson in 1865 (containing 24 chromolithographs plus a title page). The individual items are as follows:

- *Subscription Ball, Ballarat,* watercolour, 1854
- *Lucky Digger that returned,* watercolour, 1852
- *Unlucky Digger that never returned,* watercolour, c.1852
- *Making the claim,* watercolour, 1852-56
- *Fair prospects,* watercolour, c.1852
- *Rural landscape,* watercolour, 1852-56
- *Dangerously suspicious,* watercolour, c.1852
- *The invalid digger,* watercolour, c.1852
- *Surveyors,* watercolour, 1865
- *Mountain muster,* watercolour, c.1852-6
- *Refreshment shanty,* Ballarat, watercolour, 1854
- *Bad results,* watercolour, c.1852
- *Convivial diggers in Melbourne,* watercolour, c.1852
- *Improvident diggers in Melbourne,* watercolour, c.1854
- *Melbourne wants & supplies,* watercolour, c.1852
- *The newly arrived inquiring,* watercolour, c.1852
- *Diggers hut Forest Creek,* watercolour, c.1852
- *Pensioners on guard Forest Creek,* watercolour, c.1854
- *Diggers on route to deposit gold,* watercolour, c.1852

- *Recovery of stray horses,* watercolour, c.1852
- *Shepherd by his hut,* watercolour, c.1852
- *Arrival of Geelong Mail, Main Road, Ballarat, May 2nd, 1855,* watercolour, 1855
- *On the road from Forest Creek to Ballarat, May 2nd, 1855,* watercolour, c.1852-6
- *Diggers on the way to Bendigo,* lithograph, hand-coloured, 1855
- *Arrival of Geelong Mail, Main Road, Ballarat,* lithograph, 1855
- *Wayfaring diggers,* lithograph, 1852
- *Diggers hut, Forest Creek,* lithograph, 1854
- *Ballarat flat from Black Hill,* lithographed, coloured, 1855
- *John Alloo's Restaurant, Main Road, Ballarat,* lithograph, coloured, 1853
- *Deep sinking, Ballarat,* lithograph, c.1853
- *Store drays, road to Ballarat,* lithograph, 1853
- *Township of Ballarat from Bath's Hotel,* lithograph, 1855
- *Eureka in the neighbourhood of Insurgent's Stockade,* lithograph, 1855
- *Site of Bentley's Hotel, Eureka,* lithograph, 1855
- *Ballarat in 1852 (looking north-west from Mt. Buninyong),* lithograph, 1852
- *Creswick Creek (near Ballarat) from Spring Hill,* lithograph, 1855
- *Township of Kyneton, main street looking north,* lithograph, 1855

- *Site of the Eureka Stockade shortly after the fight 3rd Dec.*, lithograph, 1854
- *First quarts crushing battery, base,* lithograph, coloured, 1855
- *Black Hill, Ballarat Ballarat in 1852 (looking north-west from Mt. Buninyong),* lithograph, hand-coloured, 1852
- *First quarts crushing battery Hill, Ballarat,* Black engraving, 1855
- *Lydiart Street from Bath's Hotel,* engraving, 1857
- *Ballarat Post Office & township from Government enclosure,* engraving, 1857
- *Splitters,* chromolithograph, 1865
- *Native sepulchre,* chromolithograph, 1865
- *Sketches, Melbourne to Castlemaine,* ink & pencil sketch, c.1852-6

Castlemaine Art Museum

The art museum holds a copy of the album: *Victorian Goldfields 1852-3* containing 41 colour plates, ten framed prints of the Victorian goldfields, a copy of *Victoria gold diggings & diggers as they are in 1852* (from the original held by the State Library of Victoria) and a number of individual items as follows;

- *Approach to Eagle Hawke Gully,* black & white lithograph, c.1852
- *Cradling Forest Creek,* black & white lithograph, 1852
- *Diggers auction, Eaglehawk,* black & white lithograph, c.1852
- *Diggers licensing Castlemaine Camp* reproduction of original, watercolour, c.1852-3
- *Diggers of high degree,* black & white lithograph, c.1852

- *Diggers of low degree,* black & white lithograph, c.1852
- *Diggers on route to deposit gold,* black & white lithograph, c.1852
- *Forest Creek from Castlemaine Rd,* black & white engraving, 1857
- *Fossicking,* black & white lithographs, 1852
- *Fryers Creek near Castlemaine* reproduction of original watercolour, c.1852-3
- *Interesting statement washing stuff,* black & white lithograph, c.1852
- *Invalid digger,* black & white lithograph, c.1852
- *Iron Bark Gully,* black & white lithograph, c.1852
- *Iron Bark,* black & white lithograph, c.1852
- *Iron Bark,* black & white lithograph, 1854
- *Little Bendigo Forest Creek,* hand coloured lithograph, c.1852
- *Mounted Police escort Mt Alexander,* black & white lithograph, c.1852
- *Mt Alexander gold escort* coloured lithograph, c.1852-3
- *Prospecting for gold,* hand-coloured lithograph, 1850s
- *Recovery of stray horses,* black & white lithograph, c.1852
- *Road from Forest Creek to Bendigo,* reproduction of original watercolour, c.1852-3
- *Successful diggers from Bendigo,* black & white lithograph, c.1852
- *The newly arrived inquiring,* black & white lithograph, c.1852
- *Tin dish washing,* reproduction of original watercolour, c.1852-3

- *Wayfaring diggers,* black & white lithograph, c.1852
- *Eaglehawk Gully,* print c.1852-3
- *Coach & horses* black & white engraving, 1856
- *Forest Creek from Castlemaine Rd,* engraving, c.1856
- *Forest Creek Mt Alexander diggings,* hand-coloured lithograph, 1852
- *Government Camp Castlemaine,* hand-coloured lithograph, 1855
- *Two diggers,* black & white lithograph, c.1852
- *Digger's Hut,* black & white lithograph, c.1852
- *Gold buyers Forest Creek,* coloured lithograph, 1850s
- *Cradling,* coloured lithograph, 1850s
- *Market Square Castlemaine,* steel engraving, 1857
- *Bullock driver,* black & white engraving, 1857
- *Two men standing,* black & white lithograph , c.1852
- *Sly grog shanty,* reproduction of original watercolour, n/a

Burra Regional Art Gallery

The gallery has four watercolours from the twelve that S. T. Gill's produced of mining activities in South Australia.

- *Panorama of Burra mine,* watercolour, 1847
- *Panorama of Kooringa,* watercolour, 1847
- *Burra mine panorama,* watercolour, 1847
- *Burra Mine portion of surface op.,* watercolour, 1850

All four of these watercolours were donated or purchased and were, at one time, displayed in the Burra Town Hall before being placed in storage. They were discovered in the 1960s and were in a poor condition. The Burra District Council had them restored in 1995. At the opening of the Burra Regional Art Gallery for the Mid North in October 1996, they were hung in a special place in the gallery.

National Museum of Australia

- *Native Miami**+, colour lithograph, n/a
- *Night fishing**+, colour lithograph, n/a
- *Attack on store dray**+, colour lithograph, n/a
- *Corroboree+,* colour lithograph, 1870
- *Deep sinking, Ballarat,* colour lithograph, 1853
- *The Australian Sketchbook**, chromolithographs, 1865

*These works published by Hamel & Ferguson

These are part of the Museum's Christensen Fund Collection

Note that the Museum also holds a printer's woodblock with a Gill engraving on it entitled 'Bourke Street West in the Forenoon', engraved by Frederick Grosse and published in the *Australian News for Home Readers*, 24 March 1864 (see Chapter 11 for more details).

Many of the holdings of the libraries and galleries have been digitised and can be viewed online.

It's clear that a substantial number of Gill's works are held by private collectors in Australia and abroad; the number possibly being in excess of 3,000 items.

Emeritus Professor Sasha Grishin, Australian National University, has developed a database listing Gill's work and as of February 2021 has a record of almost 4,000 individual pieces.[133] However, Gill was a prolific chronicler of colonial life in its many permutations and Grishin feels his output would likely be about 10,000 images during his lifetime.

133 Email Grishin, personal communication to author, February 24, 2021.

Appendix II—
List of Images Reproduced in this Book

Frontispiece

S. T. Gill, artist, c. 1870 (unknown photographer).

Chapter 1 - Adelaide and the Port

2. *King William Street, looking north 1845* (black & white photograph from watercolour by S. T. Gill).

3. *North Terrace, Adelaide* (colour lithograph from a watercolour by S. T. Gill published in the *Chronicle Annual* 4 October 1847).

4. *Rundle Street, looking east from King William Street,* c. 1845 (photograph of sketch by S. T. Gill).

5. *Hindley Street from corner of King William Street* c. 1847 (hand-coloured lithograph from a watercolour by S.T. Gill).

6. *Bank of South Australia & Legislative Council Room, North Terrace, Adelaide,* 1845 (colour photograph of watercolour by S. T. Gill).

7. *North Terrace, showing Trinity Church* (black & white photograph of sketch by S. T. Gill).

8. *Customs House Wharf, Collectors Office, East View, Port Adelaide* 184? (sepia wash of sketch by S. T. Gill).

9. *Port Adelaide (*watercolour by S. T. Gill).

10. *Port Adelaide 1848* (black & white photograph of sketch by S. T. Gill).

11. *Agricultural & Horticultural Show* 1845 (black & white photograph of sketch by S. T. Gill).

12. *Agricultural & Horticultural Show, Adelaide* (black & white photograph of sketch by S. T. Gill).

13. *Heads of People - Sheet 3* (lithograph by S. T. Gill).

14. *Capt. John Finnis, True Blue* (from *'Heads of People'* lithograph by S. T. Gill).

15. *From Verandah of Vale Farm* (colour photograph of watercolour by S. T. Gill)

16. *Prospect House, the seat of J.B. Graham, Esqr., near Adelaide* (colour photograph of watercolour by S. T. Gill).

17. *Old Colonists' Festival Dinner* (lithograph by S. T. Gill).

Chapter 2 - Gill's Seasons and Months

18. *Spring* (watercolour by S. T. Gill).

19. *Summer* (watercolour by S. T. Gill).

20. *Autumn* (watercolour by S. T. Gill).

21. *Winter* (watercolour by S. T. Gill).

22. *February* (watercolour by S. T. Gill).

23. *April* (watercolour by S. T. Gill).

24. *June* (watercolour by S. T. Gill).

25. *November* (watercolour by S. T. Gill).

Chapter 3 - Rural South Australia

26. *Buttunga, Echunga, South Australia* (black & white photograph of watercolour by S. T. Gill).

27. *Captain Davidson's House, Blakiston near Mount Barker* (colour photograph of watercolour by S. T. Gill).

28. *St. James Anglican Church, Blakiston* 1848 (colour photograph of watercolour by S. T. Gill).

29. *An Outback District Police Station, Mount Gambier* (drawing with colour wash by S. T. Gill).

30. *Stockmen in the Morning* (watercolour by S. T. Gill).

31. *The Gorge, Flinders Ranges, South Australia* (watercolour by S. T. Gill).

32. *Flinders Ranges North of Mount Brown* (watercolour by S. T. Gill).

33. *Grass Tree, South Australia, a view* (watercolour by S. T. Gill).

Chapter 4 - Native Australians

34. *Australian Aborigines, spear and net fishing from a canoe and the riverbank,* 1848 (watercolour by S. T. Gill).

35. *Encounter between Gill & Horrocks and two Aboriginal Men,* 1846 (black & white photograph of watercolour by S. T. Gill).

36. *Native Worley* 1846 (sepia watercolour sketch by S.T. Gill).

37. *Squatter's Tiger* (chromolithograph colour image from watercolour by S. T. Gill).

38. *A Native Corroboree at Night* (watercolour by S. T. Gill).

39. *Native Dignity* 1860 (watercolour S. T. Gill).

Chapter 5 - Mining in South Australia 1840-51

40. *Kapunda Mine* 1845 (colour photograph of watercolour by S. T. Gill).

41. *Kapunda Mine* Works (sketch by S. T. Gill).

42. *Glen Osmond Mine* 1845 (colour photograph of watercolour by S. T. Gill).

43. *The Burra Burra Mine* 1847 (watercolour by S. T. Gill).

44. *Burra Burra Mine - Surface Operations (*hand-coloured engraving made from an 1847 watercolour by S. T. Gill for use in the *Illustrated London News*, December 2, 1848).

45. *Kooringa - the Burra Burra Township* (hand coloured engraving made from an 1847 watercolour by S. T. Gill for use in the *Illustrated London News*, December 2,1848).

46. *Leading from Stokes to Paxton's Lode, Burra Burra,* 1847 (watercolour by S. T. Gill).

47. *The opening of lode in Stokes' air-hole,* 1847 (watercolour by S. T. Gill).

48. *Burra Burra Mine, South Australia, showing chief portion of surface operation* 1850 (colour photograph of watercolour by S. T. Gill).

Chapter 6 - Charles Sturt's Final Exploration 1843

49. *Overlanders (*watercolour by S. T. Gill)

50. *Sturt's Overland Expedition Departing South Corner of Currie and King William Streets* (colour lithograph from a watercolour by S. T. Gill).

51. *Sturt's Overland Expedition Departing North Along King William Street* (colour lithograph from a watercolour by S. T. Gill).

52. *Anna—branch of the Darling* (watercolour by S. T. Gill based on a sketch by Charles Sturt).

53. *Aboriginal Village Northern Interior* (black & white photograph of watercolour by S. T. Gill based on a sketch by Charles Sturt).

54. *Sandy Ridges of Central Australia - Chaining Over the Sand Hills to Lake Torrens* (watercolour by S. T. Gill based on a sketch by Charles Sturt).

55. *Monument to Charles Sturt, Victoria Square, Adelaide* (photograph by author).

Chapter 7 - The Horrocks Expedition 1846

56. *Horrocks Expedition Map* (drawing National Library of Australia).

57. *Mount Brown at the Head of Spencer Gulf - 10 August* (black & white photograph of a sketch by S. T. Gill).

58. *Creek Bed Camp, Flinders Ranges* (colour photograph of watercolour by S. T. Gill).

59. *Extinct Crater, North of Spencer Gulf* (sepia watercolour by S. T. Gill).

60. *Encounter with two Barnggarla Men, Uro Bluff* (watercolour by S. T. Gill).

61. *Looking South West from Table Land - 22 August* (colour photograph of watercolour by S. T. Gill).

62. *Country N.W. of Point Encounter,* 1846 (sepia watercolour by S. T. Gill).

63. *Desert Interior* (black & white photograph of a sketch by S. T. Gill).

64. *Halt on Stony Ground - 31 August* (colour photograph of watercolour by S. T. Gill).

65. *Salt Lake North West of Mount Arden* (sepia watercolour by S. T. Gill).

66. *Invalids Tent on Salt Lake* (black & white photograph of watercolour by S. T. Gill).

67. *Transporting the Wounded Horrocks,* 1846 (black & white photograph of a sketch by S. T. Gill).

68. *Memorial to Horrocks, Penwortham, South Australia* (colour photograph).

Chapter 8 - The Gold Rush

69. *Diggers on the way to Bendigo,* 1852 (watercolour by S. T. Gill).

70. *Gold Buyer Forest Creek* (watercolour by S. T. Gill).

71. *Sunday Camp Meeting Forest Creek* (watercolour by S. T. Gill).

72. *Butchers Shamble Forest Creek* (watercolour by S. T. Gill).

73. *Eagle Hawke Gully, Bendigo,* 1852 (watercolour by S. T. Gill).

74. *Sly Grog Shanty* (watercolour by S. T. Gill).

75. *Zealous Gold Diggers, Castlemaine* (watercolour by S. T. Gill).

76. *John Alloo's Chinese Restaurant Main Road Ballarat* (lithograph by S. T. Gill).).

77. *Interior of John Alloo's Restaurant Ballarat* (lithograph by S. T. Gill).

78. *Mt. Alexander Gold Escort en Route to Melbourne* (lithograph by Macartney and Galbraith from sketch by S. T. Gill).

79. *Puddling* (lithograph by Macartney and Galbraith from sketch by S. T. Gill).

80. *Diggers Licensing Forest Creek* (lithograph by Macartney and Galbraith from sketch by S. T. Gill).

81. *Concert Room, Charles Napier Hotel, Ballarat, June 1855, Thatcher's Popular Songs* (watercolour by S. T. Gill).

82. *Fryer's Creek, Near Castlemaine* (watercolour by S. T. Gill).

83. *Cradling* (watercolour by S. T. Gill).

84. *View of Kyneton Looking Towards the Bridge* (steel engraving by Arthur Willmore from artwork by S. T. Gill).

85. *On Bendigo Creek* (pen and ink and sepia wash by S. T. Gill).

86. *Road to Black Forest - letter head series* (engraving from artwork by S. T. Gill).

Chapter 9 - Melbourne 1852-56

87. *Provident Diggers* (watercolour by S. T. Gill).

88. *Improvident Diggers* (watercolour by S. T. Gill).

89. *Forest Creek, Mount Alexander Diggings* 1852 (watercolour by S. T. Gill).

90. *Collins Street, looking west from Russell Street* (lithograph with tint stone by S. T. Gill).

91. *Dress Circle Boxes, Queen's Theatre* (watercolour by S. T. Gill).

92. *Subscription Ball, Main Road Ballarat* (watercolour by S. T. Gill).

93. *The Digger's Wedding* (watercolour by S. T. Gill).

94. *Diggers Celebrating (Convivial Diggers) in Melbourne* (watercolour by S. T. Gill).

95. *The Melbourne Exhibition Building* (sepia-toned lithograph by S. T. Gill).

96. *Approach to Richmond from North Bank of Yarra Yarra in the 'Fifties'* (colour photograph of postcard produced from watercolour by S. T. Gill).

97. *Victoria Illustrated - cover* (steel engraving by Arthur Willmore from sketch by S. T. Gill).

98. *Johnston Street Bridge South Yarra* (engraving by Arthur Willmore from sketch by S. T. Gill).

99. *Steam Packet Wharf Geelong* (engraving by J. Tingle from sketch by S. T. Gill).

100. *Government Offices Melbourne* (engraving by J. Tingle from sketch by S. T. Gill).

101. *Miscellaneous Sketches by S. T. G. 1856* (colour lithograph by S. T. Gill).

102. *Portland from the Bay* (steel engraving by J. Tingle from sketch by S. T. Gill).

103. *Belfast Port Fairy* (steel engraving by J. Tingle from sketch by S. T. Gill).

Chapter 10 - Sydney and Beyond

104. *The Squatters Exchange: a view of the corner of George and Margaret Streets* (watercolour by S. T. Gill).

105. *Watsons Bay, Port Jackson* (watercolour by S. T. Gill).

106. *Part the First, Cover Containing Six Lithographic Sketches of Scenery in and Around Sydney* (lithographs by Allen & Wigley of drawings by S. T. Gill).

107. *Sketch of Lower Pitt Street Sydney* (pen and ink drawing by S. T. Gill).

108. *View of Cockatoo Island* (watercolour by S.T. Gill).

109. *Fort Denison, Pinch Gut Island, Port Jackson, Sydney* (pencil drawing by S. T. Gill).

110. *Entrance to Port Jackson, with Inner Lighthouse and North Head* (pencil drawing by S. T. Gill).

111. *Waterworks, Botany - letterhead paper* (wood engraving from sketch by S. T. Gill).

112. *Lapstone Hill, Blue Mountains, N.S.W.* (watercolour by S. T. Gill).

113. *Fisherman's Camp, Upper Hawkesbury, N.S.W.* (watercolour by S. T. Gill).

114. *St. Mark's Church, Darling Point* (pencil drawing with some touches of Indian ink by S. T. Gill).

115. *The Grand Cricket Match: all England eleven versus twenty-two of New South Wales* (watercolour by S. T. Gill).

116. *Kangaroo Hunting* (photograph of drawing by S. T. Gill).

117. *South Head from Manly Beach* (watercolour by S. T. Gill).

118. *Veno Galop - cover for a piece of music* (lithograph of drawing by S. T. Gill).

119. *Road to Wagga Wagga, Waiting for the Mail* (watercolour by S. T. Gill).

120. *Roseate* c.1860

121. *The Overlanders* (watercolour by S. T. Gill).

122. *S. T. Gill* 1859 (watercolour by William Garling).

123. *Attacking the Mail, Bushranging, New South Wales* (chromolithograph from watercolour by S. T. Gill).

Chapter 11 - Back in Melbourne

124. *The Australian Sketchbook Frontispiece* (chromolithograph by S. T. Gill).

125. *Bush Funeral* (chromolithograph by S. T. Gill).

126. *Stockman* (chromolithograph by S. T. Gill).

127. *Wool Drays* (chromolithograph by S. T. Gill).

128. *Homeward Bound* (chromolithograph by S.T. Gill).

129. *Bourke Street West in the Forenoon* (engraving by Frederick Grosse from drawing by S. T. Gill).

130. *Engraved Printer's Woodblock* (photograph by George Serras of engraved woodblock by Frederick Grosse).

131. *Cover for the Melbourne Public Library Series entitled: The Victorian Goldfields* (watercolour by S. T. Gill).

132. *A Bendigo Mill* (watercolour by S. T. Gill).

133. *Cover Page for the 1872 Gold Fields Series* (watercolour by S. T. Gill).

134. *A City of Melbourne Solicitor* (lithograph on tint stone by S. T. Gill).

135. *Ease Without Opulence* (lithograph on tint stone by S. T. Gill).

136. *Doing the Block, Collins Street* (watercolour by S. T. Gill).

137. *Bank Place, Melbourne 1880* (watercolour by S. T. Gill).

Chapter 12 - The Gill Contribution to Colonial History

138. *Headstone from S. T. Gill's grave* (photograph).

Appendix III—
S.T. Gill's Horrocks Expedition Diary

South Australian Gazette and Colonial Register, Saturday 10 October 1846, page 4.

PROGRESS OF DISCOVERY.—EXPEDITION TO THE NORTH-WEST.

We have been favoured by Mr Gill the Artist, who accompanied Mr Horrocks on his recent ill-fated expedition to the north-west, with the following notes of the journey, commencing on the 8th August last, the day on which they left Mr S. White's, being the most distant station in that direction:—

Saturday, 8th August.—Loaded the firearms with ball-cartridge, each carrying his own piece. Started at 10 o'clock, after sending back the native, Kelly, to Mr White's for a bag of clothes left behind. Mr Campbell and I went on to look for a pass through the range. We found the plains very swampy to the foot of the hills, and scarcely knew what to think of the best passage we could find through the range. Mr Horrocks must go himself and examine it particularly; returned to camp about half-past 8, wet, and rather tired. Killed an emu on our route to the range.

Sunday, 9th.—Moved on about 10 o'clock with five horses in the provision dray, and reached the foot of the range. Native

Jimmy and I went to the place where the emu lay with dogs; horses returned and took on the second dray; camped together at 4 o'clock; dined on the emu.

Monday, 10th.—Messrs Horrocks and Campbell went together to examine the pass. I took two sketches from Stoney Point behind the camp. Messrs H. and C. returned at 4 o'clock. They think it is possible to cross.

Tuesday, 11th.—Left Stoney Point, and proceeded to the range. Broke rear-arm of axle before crossing the first creek; bothered a good deal; at last sent a man with dray and horses back to Mr White's to procure another axle, if possible. Pitched the tents and will wait the man's return. Messrs Horrocks and Theakston walked to the ranges to see if anything could be done to facilitate our progress when passing over them. They returned after dark, not thinking it necessary to work on the hills before attempting to pass through the creek. Mr Horrocks entertained an idea of riding with me to the head of the Gulf to examine the crossing there, but now thinks it better to rest the cattle, and defer it until after they have crossed over the ranges.

Wednesday, 12th.—I was engaged in rectifying some sketches. Mr T. arranging his instruments for taking a sight. In the afternoon Mr H. walked to some of the adjacent hills, from which he reports the view to be very extensive.

Thursday, 13th.—I took native Jimmy and went out on the hills sketching; found the country exceedingly rough and stoney, as well as steep and difficult to travel over; returned to the camp about 4 o'clock, very tired and foot-sore.

Friday, 14th.—We are expecting Kilroy to return today, should he have succeeded with Mr White in obtaining an axle. Mr Theakston and Jimmy went out to hunt in the scrub, and returned in the afternoon with a kangaroo, Jimmy right glad to get eased of his load after bearing it near two miles across his shoulders.

Saturday, 15th.—Hobbled the white leading goat, which has been and still is exceedingly troublesome and wild. In the afternoon Kilroy arrived from Mr White's with a pair of arms for the dray, bringing Kelly, the black, and lubra to take back some tools kindly lent by Mr Campbell. I finished a drawing of his station to send back as something in return for his favours. Mr Horrocks and Mr Theakston succeeded in driving out the box of the wheel and fitted another for one of the new arms. All the party quite well, and looking forward to a move early on Monday morning, on which day we hope to get quite over this fearful range.

Sunday, 16th.—Messrs H. and T. superintended the fitting up and loading of the provision dray. We hope to get Kelly, the native, to go to the head of the Gulf with us to take letters back on his return to Mr White's station.

Monday, 17th.—Kelly and lubra bolted from us last evening; we suppose he was afraid to take his wife among the blacks of the tribe he stole her from. Moved on this morning before daylight with heavy dray and four horses, the camel, and goats to the top of the range, which we reached without much difficulty. Sent back the team and brought up the other dray very well. Mr H. loaded the camel with flour from the first dray and went some way down the gully. He had great trouble with Harry (the camel), who bit at his load and wasted some of the flour; yet he managed to take down in three loads all the principal weight of the drays; the horses then took the drays first up the hill, and reached the creek after one capsized; they then rose on the other side of the hill and again upset one dray; righted the carts, and camped late at where the camel had taken the stores; all hands very tired, and glad of their supper and bed.

Tuesday, 18th.—Took the camel to where the drays were left and brought down the remainder of the things. Two horses then took one of the drays to the camp, after we had made the creek as good a passing as we could by working for three hours with pick and spade. In the evening, walked down the bottom of the gulley to the plains, and thought our difficulty near at an end for the present, seeing an hour's work will render it possible to get quite through and bring us to water at the end. **Wednesday, 19th.**—Mr Theakston and Jimmy went to work on the creek. Mr Horrocks, Kilroy, and I went up to bring down the other dray; left the camp at half-past 9, and went down the creek; took out the horses and watered them; filled the water-kegs, and camped about three miles on the plains at the foot of the range.

Thursday, 20th.—Moved on at half-past 9, hoping to make Depot Creek by night; travelled twenty-four miles on the way, and camped on a large creek without any water. In riding up the bottom to search for some, I surprised an old native, who, as well he could, told us to go lower down for water to the other end of the creek; not finding any, I returned to the drays. Mr H. much wished to see the black. I went to look for him, but he had bolted in company with four others, which I saw running across the plains towards Depot Creek. Killed a fine kangaroo in our route across to-day and made a hearty dinner on it to-night.

Friday, 21st.—The horses, being much in want of water, came round the tents in the night, sucking the plugs of the casks, and rambled some way towards the last camping ground; but as we could see them with glass in the morning, we had no trouble in fetching them. Started for Depot Creek, constantly coming on Mr Eyre's old track; we reached it in one hour and a half; I went on to search for the spring, which I easily effected from Mr Eyre's camp-track; returned, when Mr Horrocks, Mr Theakston, and Kilroy took up the cattle. Jimmy brought the camel back with a load for the cook, who killed the troublesome goat, in part for his hide, Mr H. intending to take his supply of water for his trip to the table-land N.W. in goat skins, seeing they are best adapted to ride as a load on the camel. Messrs H. and T. purpose riding to-morrow to look at the crossing at the neck of the Gulf, and see if it is possible to form a Depot on the other side.

Saturday, 22nd.—Mr Horrocks and I left on horseback for the tableland; travelled over the plain to a low scrub, constantly meeting with the track of the kangaroo and emu as well as wallaby; crossed the neck of the Lake dry but found the sand very soft in places. After reaching the other side, crossed many sand ridges covered with dwarfish, dry, dusty scrub; had ridden a considerable way in search of feed and water with no success, when we saw two natives on a large flat of scrub at the foot of the tableland; they got within a quarter of a mile of us unobserved, but on seeing the horsemen they commenced running; cantered up to a woman and child, who were much alarmed; she soon became composed, when we made her understand we wanted water, and induced her to walk with us to show it; we went about two miles, when we overtook three children, which ran off in great terror; the woman much wished to join them, but at last moved onward with us another half-mile, when she hailed two men and another child who stood some time and then boldly advanced, threw down their wallets, and came up with their spears; on which we motioned them to sit down, which they did, spoke to them, and made signs for water. The woman made off on seeing us approach the men, who spoke to us very loud and sulkily, and for a long time declined moving away with us, or showing the water, which was not thirty yards off; with much coaxing, laughing, and patting on the back, we at length succeeded in moving them, the oldest man still very reluctant. On seeing the hole we found that it would only administer to our present want of water for the horses, it being nearly a few gallons of thick, muddy rainwater which had drained from the hills, and was fast drying up. We thought the men spoke of other waters in three other directions, but they would not show. They stood with us some time, but appeared afraid of the horses more than us. Mr H. gave them each a small piece of tobacco, which they appeared to eat; he shewed them how he lit his pipe with the burning-glass; they all the time appeared ill-pleased with us, the old man more particularly; the young one had bound round his head a piece of a red nightcap, unsoiled and unfaded, and knew a knife by name. We showed them the guns and pistols, which they took no notice of; the young man and child drew off, but the old man retreated slowly, and by his antics and loud talk we supposed he was threatening us as he continued to beckon the other man back. Mr H. discharged his gun in the air, which they scarcely appeared to move, the old man still shouting at us. We watered the horses and drank ourselves, mounted, and went on to the south end of the table land; went two miles and tied up the horses. Mr H. and I climbed the hill, which was excessively stoney and steep, taking with us the spy-glass to look over the north-west country, which presented a most desolate aspect—one immense space of dry sandy country, covered with a low, dry, crisp scrub, without the slightest vestige of grass or probability of water. I took a sketch of this un-cheering scene, which shows the distant bit of elevated land. Mr H. did not know what to say about attempting to cross; made our way back to the water-hole, as we could get nothing for the horses to eat there. Having dropped my tinware, it was necessary to follow down on the tracks. On nearing the water, we found the natives had moved round the hill with their fires, and appeared rather restless. We took the liberty of again watering the horses, when we mounted and again jogged on; had not gone many yards when we met a native with a fire-stick, who menaced us, and lit a large fire about 150 yards on a hill to our left; we then saw more natives coming to the top of the hill, shouting to us lustily. On observing them running down towards us with their spears, we halted and fired three balls, which struck the ground very near them, in each case rising the dust in a cloud; this brought them to a stand for a little, but they did not appear to know the use of the arms, as they looked on the ground and moved but little aside. We reloaded and advanced towards them, when they took up their position on the top of the hill, shouting and laughing defiance. We stopped at eighty yards, and gave them three barrels more, when we saw no more of them, and as the night was fast closing in, we did not feel inclined for any further acquaintance with them, but rode six miles towards the neck of the Gulf and stopped the night.

Sunday, 23rd.—Rose at dawn and lit our pipes. Rode across the bed of the creek, and arrived at Depot Creek to the camp about 10 o'clock to breakfast. The horses knocked-up for want of feed in a fifty-mile ride. Had a bathe at the spring, and began to prepare for a fortnight's journey. Mr H. intends, accompanied by me and Kilroy the driver, with the camel, to go in search of water more in a northerly direction before the drays attempt removing.

Monday, 24th.—I was engaged in the morning, with all the rest, in removing the camp higher up the creek, so that time be not so long occupied in fetching water. In the afternoon rectified some recent sketches; and in the evening made some cartridges on an improved principle.

Tuesday, 25th.—Mr Theakston and Jimmy rode out this morning in search of game; they fell in with two fine kangaroos and a couple of emus, all of which they lost after a long run, owing to the inefficiency of the dogs—a result which confirms the opinion I had formed of them long ago—that they were not heavy or strong enough for all purposes. Mr H. and Kilroy preparing for their start, while I am engaged with my sketches.

Wednesday, 26th.—Removed the stores from the dray into the tent, which in our absence will occupy the space we shall not require, and be more secure should the natives visit the camp; not having seen any since I met with those on the creek a little way back, we do not consider them as inclined to be very social; doubtless there are some in the neighbourhood. Jimmy saw an emu on the flat before the camp, which Mr H. and one of the men went out to stalk on, but the bird evaded them. We put but little faith in the dogs until they have redeemed their characters. Hot. Flies troublesome.

Thursday, 27th.—Mr Horrocks and one of the men went to the top of the range, to take the right bearings of the rising land north-west. Returned, and took the sun, when, finding the day too advanced to enable him to prepare in time for leaving the camp, will make the necessary arrangements for a start early in the morning. Have packed my apparatus for the journey contemplated tomorrow. Being very apprehensive that, should we not find water or grass, my pony may be lost, I've made up my mind to walk—an exercise to which I am unaccustomed. It will try my abilities at all events as a bush pedestrian. Hot. Flies very annoying.

Friday, 28th.—Left the Depot at a quarter-past ten. The weather wet and windy. Proceeded until sunset, and camped at the Salt Creek. The night being wet, set no watch.

Saturday, 29th.—Moved on at half-past eight. Travelled 15 miles, and halted that night at the Stony Pass in the Table Ranges. Watched until the moon set. Weather windy and cold, with some rain.

Sunday, 30th.—Left the hills and crossed in our course many red sandy and thickly scrub'd ridges. As yet we have met with no feed or indications of improvement. We saw some fresh tracks of natives crossing our course, but they were few. Met with sufficient water to replenish our kegs, and went on at rather a hurried rate, which tired me much, and made the halt a welcome relief to our sixteen-miles tramp. Having to camp in scrub, set watch through the night. Weather still cool, with some rain through the night.

Monday, 31st.—Moved at a quarter to nine, and crossed more of the same description of country. After some time the timber, or rather scrub appeared to increase in size. Marched on, and at length broke on a sterile stony plain, from which we could distinctly see the rising land we were making for, towering out of dense scrub, which would occur three miles further on. Halted for one hour, to rest and feed the camel, which we did by walking over the plains and collecting salacious plants of such kinds as we had observed him eat before. Went on, and halted about six o'clock. The camel begins to get fagged. Hope to meet with water tomorrow; have dug holes in the sand and laid in the oilskin capes to catch any that may fall through the night. The day has been very warm, but the evening indicates rain.

Tuesday, September 1st.—Moved at half-past eight, and continued walking up to twelve o'clock, when we came on a large lake, with a little water in it, the drainage of the country round. Stopped to test the quality of the water, but found it very salty. I sketched the lake, and we went on intending to round the north end before camping. Had walked about one hour when Kilroy, the man, called Mr H.'s attention to a bird which he saw in some scrub just before us; we stopped for Mr H. to prepare to shoot it. The camel knelt down for me to get at the shotbelt, while Mr H. drew his charge of slugs close by; the beast lurched with his load on the near side on which we stood, when the saddle hove down on the hammers of the gun; on its slipping off, the right-hand barrel, with the ramrod in it, went off, taking off the middle finger of Mr H.'s right hand, and lodging the charge in his left cheek. He instantly fell back, bleeding copiously. We succeeded in staunching the blood with our handkerchiefs, and, after cutting off a part of the finger which hung slightly on, managed to dress it with such stuff as we had brought in case of spear wounds, treating the face in the same way; we laid him down, and fixed the tent; after getting him in, Kilroy started back to the Depot the same evening, leaving me in charge of Mr H. until relief arrived. Soon after Kilroy had left, Mr H. rallied sufficiently to speak, and convinced me that his brain was not affected. We had, of course, a wretched night of it.

Wednesday, 2nd.—Mr H. appears still better. Through the night I kept his lips constantly moistened, and he swallowed a little cold water, which I got into his mouth by squeezing it from the end of a towel; this morning he took some lukewarm tea in the same way. I continue to bathe his forehead and face in warm water, and about eleven o'clock he slept a little. I am cheered by the prospect of his recovery. In the evening he sat up, supported, for a few minutes, but passed a very restless night.

Thursday, 3rd.—Went to where Kilroy had dipped some rain water, but not finding any, fetched some salt-water from the Lake, which may be useful. Mr H. is certainly better and more composed this morning. I feel much fatigued from anxiety and want of rest. Shall expect relief from tomorrow morning. Mr H. expresses great concern lest Kilroy should not reach back—the distance being near seventy miles, and through a scrub, without any likelihood of finding water.

Friday, 4th.—Mr H. slept well towards morning. I got him some tea, and after bathing his face and cheek, left him composed, and went about two miles to the northward to look for water; not finding any, returned, and found him calling me. Soon after, at his urgent request, managed to dress him, and remove him from the tent to walk a little in the open air; was out of bed about half-an-hour, when he again laid down, and I applied the 3rd poultice to his cheek, after which he sat up, supported, for some time. About half-past one in the afternoon, Mr Theakston and Kilroy arrived on horseback, which was a great relief to Mr H. and myself. We prepared some arrowroot, which Mr H. partook of, and in half-an-hour were on our way back. Rode five miles and camped the night, after shaving Mr H. and dressing his wounds.

Saturday, 5th.—Started at seven and walked about 25 miles in three rapid stages, resting half an hour at each halt, to recruit the invalid with arrowroot, arrived to where we expected to find water, and found just sufficient to serve us. Camped at dark, the horses very jaded, not having had water since they passed up on their way to the salt lake, and scarcely any food. Mr H. was very exhausted, but slept at intervals through the night. We were all nearly knocked up for want of water and rest; but a good night's sleep with half a gallon of tea, quite recruited me.

Sunday, 6th.—Rose at daylight and started soon after for the depot; halted at eleven and again at three, and made the depot at eight in the evening, all very tired and sore. Mr H. bore the journey well; Mr K. and myself rode and drove the camel in turns, travelling at the rate of 4 miles an hour over the sand ridges and through the scrub, which made the supper and bed a very desirable termination to our trying tramp.

Monday, 7th.—Mr H. continues to improve but feels anxious on account of his finger—it is possible Dr Brown may arrive tomorrow; he was sent to on Kilroy's return to the depot. I bathed this morning, which has much refreshed me, not having washed for seven days from the scarcity of water.

Tuesday, 8th.—Yesterday it was discovered that one of the horses was missing—Mr Theakston, Jimmy, and I, have been looking for it today, but without success—Kilroy has been shoeing. We expect to leave this on our route back on Thursday.

Wednesday, 9th.—The horse came home this morning. I went to the top of the range sketching. Mr H. gets stronger.

Thursday, 10th.—Left the creek about half-past nine, and reached the large creek, 5 miles north of Mount Brown; walked about 19 miles, camped the night. The weather was very showery through the day.

Friday, 11th.—Mr H. and Kilroy left the camp for Campbell's station; on their way to the village no surgeon having come up it is very important to go to where he can have attendance. We left the creek at eight and went on to Stony Creek, where we got plenty of water and feed. Camped at 5 o'clock. This day we saw a great many kangaroo and emu; I ran the dogs to no purpose, they would not kill.

Saturday, 12th.—Left the camp after filling the barrels. At three o'clock saw numbers of emu and kangaroo; I again tried the dogs without any better effect. Halted at a fine creek one hour; sketched and went on to the next creek, which was very rough to pass over. Camped on the south side; missed the goats which I saw cross when I returned to bring in my pony; all hands searched until dark, but could not find them nor a clue of their route.

Sunday, 13th.—Rose early, and again scoured the county in search of the goats; I shot a kangaroo by the way, and returned without the goats, at twelve o'clock; they had not been seen by any of the rest of the party in the search. I took a horse and fetched home the kangaroo; have since given up hopes of the goats; Jimmy can't get a clue to them. In the evening the cook returned with another kangaroo he had shot. We leave in the morning.

Monday, 14th—Mr T. and Jimmy went out and got on the horses after some little trouble. Left the creek at 8 o'clock, and crossed about 3[?] miles of country; found more water for our horses, and camped in good feed one hour before sunset; a good part of the way was thick brush and rather heavy pulling.

Tuesday, 15th.—Moved at half-past seven, and reached Ferguson's station at half-past five. I am completely knocked up in the left foot this walking. The pony has a very bad back, and not fit to ride, so I shall use the light cart tomorrow.

Wednesday, 16.—Struck the tent at half-past seven; crossed the brook, and met Mr Ferguson about 10 miles from the station; heard of Mr Horrocks through him, and reached Hope's station at sunset; heavy rain this night.

Thursday, 17th.—Weather very wet; stopped the day. I dressed my foot with marshmallow, and rested it the day; felt much ease towards night.

Friday, 18th.—Moved early, and passed Watt's and Hawker's stations, and stopped at our old camp at Magpie Flat.

Saturday, 19th.—Started at eight o'clock; halted at Mr Gleeson's, and reached the village at 12 o'clock; camped at the back of the mill; found Mr H. at Mr Robinson's very ill; Mr T. went up to see him but could not speak to him. Dr Knott arrived in the evening from town with Mr A. Horrocks, who slept at the camp.

Sunday, 20th.— Mr H. much the same. Mr Oakland Robinson and Dr Knott came to the tent and would overhaul my sketches in the afternoon; a favourable night with Mr H., and he slept well; Mr A. Horrocks and Mr Green went to Dr Campbell's at Dr Knott's, request to be present at the operation on Mr H's. finger; Dr C. was not at home; sent a man out to request his attendance early in the morning. Mr H. had a relapse in the early part of the night.

Monday, 21st.— At dawn, Kilroy, the man attending Mr H., came to the tent to arouse Mr A. Horrocks to relieve him in his watch; he was with his brother all day; in the afternoon Mr T. rode to Dr Campbell and brought him over; Mr H. dangerously ill; struck the tent, and collected the stores; slept in the mill.

Tuesday, 22nd.— Mr H. still worse; his life now despaired of; Mr T. and Jimmy were to leave for town today, but will defer it till a change takes place. Mr T. admitted to his room for the first time today. Dr Knott left for Adelaide in the afternoon. Mr H. was not expected to survive till morning.

Wednesday, 23rd.—Mr H. in the same state this morning; ten o'clock Mr H. gets worse, is sinking fast; he died about half-past seven in the evening.

Thursday, 24th.—Mr H. was carried to his grave by the villagers, followed by his bereaved brother, friends, and the party he had command of in the wilds, and with whom he was a general favourite. His funeral took place about half-past five o'clock, in the ground set apart for a burial place, to be connected with the church, which was about to be erected at Penwortham; and which, in all probability, would have been commenced on his return from the expedition, had not this fearful accident occurred.

Appendix IV—
Artists of the Australian Colonial Period

George French Angus (1822-86)

George Angus was born at Newcastle-on-Tyne, England in 1822. Eldest son of George Fife Angus, who, next to Edward Gibbon Wakefield, was the foremost of the founders of South Australia. Took sketching lessons from Waterhouse Hawkins in London. Arrived in Adelaide 1844. Travelled extensively in South Australia, making watercolour sketches for *South Australia Illustrated*, which he published in 1847. Also published *A Ramble in Malta and Sicily*, *The New Zealanders Illustrated*, *Savage Life and Scenes in Australia and New Zealand*, *The Kaffirs Illustrated* and a set of six views of the Ophir goldfields and illustrated other works. Secretary of the Australian Museum, Sydney, 1853-59. He returned to London two years later, where he lived until his death there on October 4, 1886.

Ludwig Becker (1808–1861)

Ludwig Becker, artist, explorer and naturalist, was born at Darmstadt, Germany, on 5 September 1808 of a notable family. He apparently qualified as a doctor of philosophy and for a time served as an officer in a rifle company. In the 1848 revolution he was at Mainz, but left hurriedly for, it is said, political reasons.

After some time in Rio de Janeiro, he arrived at Launceston on 10 March 1851. For many months he wandered in Van Diemen's Land, paying his way by painting miniatures. While gold digging in Bendigo in 1852-54 Becker made meteorological observations and produced enough sketches for an exhibition in Melbourne in April 1854. Becker's scientific knowledge and artistic ability were invaluable qualifications for his selection as a member of the Victorian Exploring Expedition of 1860-61 (Burke and Wills expedition). He died 29 April 1861 and was buried at Bulloo, eight miles (13 km) south of Cooper's Creek on 28 April 1861. He was unmarried. The La Trobe Library holds Becker's sketchbook, diaries and scientific observations made on the Burke and Wills expedition, as well as other paintings.

Henry Burn (c.1807–1884)

The son of Samuel Burn, described as a 'varnish maker' and his wife Hannah (nee Oliver), Henry Burn was born in Birmingham, England, about 1807. There is evidence that at least between 1840 and 1852, he travelled quite extensively about England—as far north as Yorkshire, as far south as Dorset, and particularly about the Midlands—and lithographed on stone a number of topographical 'Views' of English towns. On 16 October 1852, Burn sailed from Liverpool on the barque *Baltimore*, arriving in Melbourne on 30 January 1853. Burn was essentially regarded as a topographical artist whose watercolours of colonial Melbourne and its suburbs are now of significant historical interest. His works reveal an interest in light effects. He died at the Melbourne Benevolent Asylum on 26 October 1884 and was buried in a public grave at the Melbourne General Cemetery.

Abram Louis Buvelot (1814-88)

Abram Buvelot was born in Switzerland in 1814. Studied at Lausanne Academy and at Berne and Paris. At the age of 21, went to Brazil to work on his uncle's plantation and continued to paint in his spare time. Settled in Rio de Janeiro in 1839. There, the Emperor, Dom Pedro II, became interested in his work and conferred upon him the Order of the Rose. After eighteen years in Brazil, he returned to Switzerland. He emigrated to Melbourne in 1865 and remained there until his death in 1888. Within a few years, several of his landscapes were purchased by the Melbourne Gallery. Buvelot was one of the first important artists to arrive in Australia and the first to express in paint something of the strange beauty of the Australian landscape. His work was an inspiration to the next generation of Melbourne painters, like Tom Roberts (1856-1931), Arthur Streeton (1867-1943), Walter Withers (1854-1914), Charles Conder (1868-1909), and Fred McCubbin (1855-1917).

James Howe Carse (c. 1819-1900)

J. H. Carse was born about 1819 in Edinburgh. He was trained at the new Royal Scottish Academy. He painted with oils and specialised in landscapes. Carse was in London in the early 1860s, exhibiting paintings of Scotland and England. In 1866, he won a gold medal at the Intercolonial Exhibition in Chicago. By 1869, Carse had visited both Australia and New Zealand, and an exhibition of his new work was shown at the Melbourne Public Library. He enjoyed commercial success and an engraving of one of his drawings was included on the front cover of the *Illustrated Melbourne Post*. By 1876, he had helped to found Melbourne's Victorian Academy of Art and the New South Wales Academy of Art, and he had been awarded numerous prizes and awards. In that year, he was described in New South Wales as 'perhaps the best painter in the colony'. In 1880, he joined a group who left the Academy of Art to create the Art Society of New South Wales. Carse was creating a large number of paintings, but from this time, they diminished both in quality and originality as he reworked old subjects. Carse died on 9 September 1900 from the effects of alcoholism.

Nicholas Chevalier (1828-1902)

Nicholas Chevalier was born on 9 May 1828 in St Petersburg, Russia, son of Louis Chevalier and his Russian wife. His father left Vaud, Switzerland, to become overseer of the estates of Prince Wittgenstein, aide-de-camp to Nicholas I, and in 1845, returned to Switzerland with his artistically inclined son. For the next six years, Nicholas studied painting in Lausanne and architecture in Munich. He moved to London in 1851 and achieved some success in lithography and watercolour work. His father had speculated in Victoria, and a son, Louis, who later became manager of the vineyard at Bontharambo near Wangaratta, was on the goldfields. When the family fortunes declined, Nicholas was sent to join his brother. He arrived at Melbourne in February 1855, visited the goldfields, attended to his father's business, and planned his return to Europe. But the newly established *Melbourne Punch* and later the *Illustrated Australian News* found his talents invaluable and he decided to stay. Chevalier's wood engraved cartoons became one of the most popular features in *Punch*. He also introduced chromolithography to Victoria, where it became an important and flourishing art. When the Duke of Edinburgh was touring Australia, Chevalier was invited to join the royal suite on its visit to Tasmania in January 1868. When the duke briefly returned to Melbourne in the following year, Chevalier was invited to rejoin the party in H.M.S. *Galatea* and sailed to London. He produced 120 drawings and many watercolours for Queen Victoria. He died in London on 15 March 1902.

Robert Hawker Dowling (1827-86)

Robert Dowling was born in England in 1827, the youngest son of Rev. Henry Dowling. Aged seven, he went to Van Diemen's Land with his parents in the *Janet*. As a youth, he was deeply impressed by the tragedy of the Tasmanian Aboriginals. He was educated at Launceston and became a saddler. He showed an early ability for drawing and took lessons. In August 1850, encouraged by his father, he changed his trade sign 'saddler' to 'portrait painter'. In 1851, he advertised in Wood's *Almanack* as a portrait and miniature painter. He returned to England and entered Leigh's Academy, London. He exhibited at the Royal Academy in the period 1859-82. His work included scenes from Tasmania, including Tasmanian Aborigines. In 1860, Dowling presented the city of Launceston with his 'Group of Natives of Tasmania', one of four historical group-portraits of Victorian and Tasmanian Aboriginals. In 1885, Dowling returned to Australia. In Launceston, he painted a portrait of the late Sir Richard Dry, and in Melbourne a portrait of Governor Sir Henry Loch. He returned to England in the *Tigrisia* in April 1886 and died in London on July 8.

Chester Earles (1821-1905)

Chester Earles was born on 18 August 1821. After some initial training as a miniature portrait painter at the London National Gallery, Earles entered the Royal Academy Schools in 1842, then studied in Paris in 1846. He exhibited with the Royal Academy from 1844 to 1863 and with the Society of British Artists between 1842 and 1863. Most were portraits, but several were narrative and religious paintings. Following his failure to sell portraits, due to the increasing popularity of photography, he joined family members in Victoria in 1864. Earles worked as an inspector at the Bankers 'Clearing House and continued to paint in his spare time. Earles joined the Victorian Academy of Arts after it was formed in 1870, and three years later he became president, a position he held until the Academy merged with the Australian Artists' Association in 1888. Earles continued to exhibit with the VAA until 1884 and contributed to various intercolonial and international exhibitions held throughout the 1870s and 1880s. Throughout his career, Earles's subject matter was either portraiture or subject paintings inspired by Keats, Milton, Spenser, Tennyson, Shakespeare and the Bible. He died on 15 June 1905 in Melbourne, aged 83.

John Eyre (b c.1771)

John Eyre was born at Coventry, England, about 1771, the son of Thomas Eyre, wool-comber and weaver. He was apprenticed to his father in 1784 and became a freeman of the city in August 1792. He is thought to have studied drawing under Joseph Barnes of Coventry. At Coventry Assizes on 23 March 1799 he was sentenced to transportation for seven years for housebreaking, and reached Sydney in the transport *Canada* in December 1801. He was granted a conditional pardon on June 4 1804, and his drawings, which can be dated accurately, were made soon afterwards. He provided the drawings for four engraved views of Sydney, which appeared in John Mann's *The Present Picture of New South Wales* (London, 1811). For some years, Eyre appears to have eked out a fairly precarious living in the colony. In March 1812, brewer Absalom West published two views of Sydney, engraved by Philip Slaeger from originals by Eyre. On 15 August 1812, Eyre advertised his intention of leaving the colony. He apparently left a considerable number of his works with West and the proceeds of these may well have paid for his passage. In January 1813, West issued a set of twelve views of Sydney, Port Jackson, Botany Bay, Parramatta and Newcastle; no fewer than ten were from originals by Eyre. A second series of twelve views was issued in 1814: four were credited to Eyre and two others were probably from his originals. Nothing is known of him after he left Sydney. He was essentially a topographical illustrator and his work was undertaken with precision and much detail.

Joseph Fowles (?-1878)

Joseph Fowles, artist, arrived in Sydney from London in August 1838, accompanied by his wife, as cabin passenger in the *Fortune*. He was noticed in the *Sydney Morning Herald* on July 26, 1847, for his contributions to the first exhibition of the Society for the Promotion of Fine Arts in Australia. Of the seven paintings by his hand, five were of ships and shipping, and it was as a marine painter that Fowles first made his reputation in Sydney. In July 1848, Fowles published the first part of his series, *Sydney in 1848*; his forty illustrations of the 'elegant' streets and buildings were made with painstaking accuracy. By 1855, Fowles was training and examining young art teachers in drawing for the National Board of Education. Fowles died, after a third paralytic stroke, on 25 June 1878.

Edward Charles Frome (1802-90)

Edward Frome, soldier and surveyor, was born on 7 January 1802 at Gibraltar, the son of Rev. J. T. Frome of Woodlands, Dorset, England. He was educated at Bexley and Blackheath, and at 15, entered the Royal Military Academy, Woolwich. In 1839, the South Australian colonisation commissioners appointed him for ten years as the third surveyor-general of South Australia. He arrived in Adelaide in the ***Recovery*** with his wife, their three children and a party of sappers in September 1839. He was also a competent artist and made many sketches and paintings of landscapes on his surveying expeditions. His pictures are of particular value because of their historical content; three are in the South Australian National Gallery, and films of others are in the possession of the South Australian Archives and the Royal Geographical Society of Australasia (South Australian Branch). He died in 1890 at Ewell in Surrey.

Frederick Garling (1806-73)

Frederick Garling was a customs official and marine artist. He was born on 23 February 1806 at King Street, Holborn, London. He arrived in Australia with his parents in the ***Francis and Eliza*** in 1815. In 1827, he was appointed a landing waiter in the Customs Office in Sydney at £250 a year, and in 1847, was promoted acting landing surveyor. He was entirely self-taught as an artist and specialised in marine subjects. His output was prodigious:

it is said he painted a large proportion of the ships that entered Port Jackson during his lifetime. Most of his work, which was generally unsigned, was in watercolour and characterised by a feeling for atmosphere absent from the work of earlier Australian topographical artists. He died on 16 November 1873, in Sydney.

John Glover (1767-1849)

John Glover was born at Houghton-on-the-Hill, Leicestershire in 1767. He was self-taught as an artist. While employed as a writing master at the Free School at Appleby, he devoted his spare time to the study of drawing and painting. He began his professional career as artist and art teacher at Lichfield in 1805, proceeding later to London, where he became a fashionable drawing master. He exhibited in London and Paris and was President of the British Watercolour Society, 1815 and a founder of the Society of British Artists. On 1 April 1831, Glover arrived in Hobart accompanied by his wife and son, John Richardson, in the *Thomas Lawrie*. By August, he was established in a town house and had bought Ring Farm, eighteen miles (29 km) away. In 1832, he was allocated a grant at Mills Plains on the northern slope of Ben Lomond, and built his house on the Nile River, calling his property *Patterdale*. Here, he painted, and with his family developed the property, which eventually comprised more than 7000 acres (2833 ha). By 1835, he was able to send 68 pictures 'descriptive of the Scenery and Customs of Van Diemen's Land' for exhibition in London. In 1847, he exhibited in a collection assembled by the Launceston Mechanics' Institute. In his last years, he devoted himself largely to religious literature and painted little. Glover was highly prolific in watercolour, but later turned increasingly to oil painting. He died at Patterdale on 9 December 1849.

Henry Gritten (1818-1873)

Gritten was born in 1818, the son of a London picture dealer. He studied art and was on friendly terms with leading artists of the period. He began exhibiting at the Royal Academy in 1835, and during the next 10 years, 12 of his pictures were hung at the academy's exhibitions. In 1848, Gritten went to Brooklyn in the United States and exhibited at the American Art Union. In 1853, Gritten arrived in Australia, initially trying prospecting at the Bendigo goldfields, but soon resumed painting in Victoria and Tasmania. Gritten, a founding member of the Victorian Academy of Arts, showed three oils at the first exhibition in 1870. He died suddenly at Melbourne on 14 January 1873, leaving a widow and four children in poor circumstances.

William Buelow Gould (1801-53)

W. B. Gould was born in Liverpool, England in 1801. He is said to have been a porcelain painter. On 7 November 1826, he was charged at Northampton quarter sessions with having stolen a coat and was sentenced to transportation for seven years. He arrived at Hobart Town in the *Asia* in December 1827 and was sent to work at the brickfields. His record in Van Diemen's Land was never good; there were frequent offences for stealing, forgery and drunkenness. Gould was assigned to Dr. James Scott, colonial surgeon. While with Scott, he painted botanical specimens which were perfect in technical detail. In 1832, after more offences, Gould was again sentenced to Macquarie Harbour, where he painted many exquisite watercolours of flowers, birds and fishes. His sketches of Macquarie Harbour provide a unique topographical record of the settlement. He received his certificate of freedom on 25 June 1835. After working briefly for Henry Palmer, coach builder of Launceston, he returned to Hobart. Over the next years he painted many game, fish and flower studies in oils. He died on December 11, 1853.

Eugen von Guerard (1812-1900)

Johann Joseph Eugen von Guerard was born in Vienna in 1812, son of Bernhard von Guerard. His father was a court painter to Francis I of Austria and his mother the daughter of a field marshal in Vienna. Guerard early on showed artistic talent, and his father took him in 1826 to Italy, where he studied old masters before settling at Naples in 1832. For six years, he painted landscapes in southern Italy and Sicily. He then moved to Dusseldorf. In 1852, he sailed from England in the *Windermere*, lured by the gold rush. He arrived at Geelong on December 24, and two weeks later, left for Ballarat. His diary describes his luckless year on the goldfields, but he did make many pencil sketches. For sixteen years, Guerard travelled and sketched in the wilds of Victoria, Tasmania, New South Wales, South Australia, and New Zealand, sometimes in company with such scientific expeditions as those led by Alfred Howitt in 1860 and Georg von Neumayer in 1862. Later, he transferred many of his pen and pencil sketches to canvases commissioned by wealthy patrons. Guerard occupied studios in Collins and Bourke Streets in the 1850s, and then lived for nearly twenty years in Gipps Street, East Melbourne. Guerard's elaborate album of tinted lithographs, *Australian Landscapes* (Melbourne, 1867), was based on the Western District views which he exhibited in 1858, and which Governor Henry Barkley so admired that he commissioned a similar series of pen and ink drawings. Much of his work was engraved for periodicals, and he illustrated Samuel Bird's *On Australasian Climates* (Melbourne, 1863). In 1882, Guerard returned to Europe where his wife died in London on January 12, 1891. When the Australian banks crashed in 1893, he lost all his investments and apparently lived in poverty until he died aged 89 in Chelsea on 17 April 1901.

Colonel William Light (1786-1839)

The founder of Adelaide. Son of an English merchant captain, he served with distinction in both the navy and army and was also an engineer, surveyor, musician, artist, linguist and author. He had an adventurous career in Europe, including service in the Peninsular War, before coming to South Australia in 1836 as surveyor-general. His selection of the site and plans for the layout of the city of Adelaide aroused great opposition at the time, but have been fully vindicated by history. He resigned his position in 1838.

Joseph Lycett (c.1774-1828)

Joseph Lycett was born in Staffordshire, England, about 1774. By profession a portrait and miniature painter, he was convicted of forgery at Salop Assizes on August 10, 1811, and sentenced to transportation for fourteen years. He sailed in the transport *General Hewitt*, reached Sydney in February 1814, and was soon appointed a clerk in the police office. In May 1815, Sydney was flooded by hundreds of skilfully forged 5s. bills drawn on the postmaster. They were traced to Lycett, who was found in possession of a small copper-plate press. He was convicted of forgery and sent to Newcastle. He received a conditional pardon for design work and painting he undertook in Newcastle. In 1819-20, he executed many private commissions. In February 1820, Governor Lachlan Macquarie sent three of his drawings to Lord Bathurst, including a large view of Sydney. It is generally believed that the absolute pardon which the artist received on 28 November 1821 was a reward for these. In June 1822, he advertised that he intended to leave the colony. He sailed in the *Shipley* in September. Lycett had planned to publish a book of Australian views in England. There were to be twelve sets, published monthly, each with two aquatint views of New South Wales and two of Van Diemen's Land, with descriptive letterpress, and a supplement with maps of both colonies.

By permission, the series was dedicated to Bathurst. The parts began to appear in July 1824 at 7s. plain and 10s. 6d. coloured, and when all had appeared, they were bound together and sold as *Views in Australia* (London, 1825). Burial records in the parish of Birmingham, County of Warwick, show that he died in hospital and was buried on 13 February 1828. Lycett was apparently a quick and prolific artist, and a large body of his work survives. Most are landscapes, but the Rex Nan Kivell Collection (Canberra) has a series of thirteen watercolours of Australian flowering shrubs and three of trees.

Conrad Martens (1801-78)

Conrad Martens was born in London in 1801, son of a German merchant, who had settled there. He studied under Copley Fielding and travelled in many countries before arriving in Sydney in 1835 as official artist accompanying Charles Darwin in the H.M.S. *Beagle*. He finally settled in Sydney as a professional artist and teacher. He worked principally in watercolour. As a landscape painter Martens was very much a product of the English watercolour school and picturesque/romantic movements, following on from the pioneering work of fellow artists such as J.M.W. Turner, John Constable, A.V. Copley Fielding, and influenced by the seventeenth-century Italian landscape painters such as Claude Lorrain and Poussin. Martens' most accomplished artworks - namely his distinctly romantic and atmospheric landscapes in watercolour - were produced in New South Wales between his arrival in 1835 and death there 43 years later in 1878.

Frederick Robert Nixon (c.1817-60)

Frederick Nixon arrived in Adelaide from London in the *Trusty* on May 15, 1838. During his time in Adelaide, he worked as a cartoonist, sketcher, etcher, journalist, and surveyor (under Colonel Light). In 1845, he created an album entitled; *Twelve views of Adelaide and its vicinity.* He moved to Mauritius in May 1846, where he remained until his death in 1860.

William Charles Piguenit (1836-1914)

William Piguenit was born on 27 August 1836 at Hobart Town, eldest son of Frederick Le Geyt Piguenit. For receiving government stores, his father had been sentenced to transportation for fourteen years and arrived at Hobart in the *Royal George* on 8 October 1830. In 1836, Frederick was a clerk in the Convict Department and in 1842, he received a free pardon. Educated at Cambridge House Academy, William Charles received some lessons from Frank Dunnett, a Scottish painter, and was commended for his superior drawing, mapping and penmanship. On September 24, 1850, he was appointed a draftsman in the Survey Office. In 1872, he resigned from the Survey Office to devote himself to landscape painting. In 1874, he travelled on foot to the Gordon River and painted the Arthur Range, Lake Pedder, and Hell's Gates. In 1875, Piguenit had moved to Sydney and contributed to exhibitions at the New South Wales Academy of Arts and held a one-man exhibition. An enthusiastic explorer, he travelled widely, looking for natural scenery to paint. In 1898 and 1900, Piguenit visited Europe, and his work was included in the exhibition of Australian Art at the Grafton Galleries in London and the Paris Salon. In 1902, the New South Wales government commissioned him to paint Mount Kosciusko. The first Australian-born artist of note, he delighted in mountain scenery and often chose dramatic subjects for his painting. Piguenit died on July 17, 1914, at Hunter's Hill, unmarried, and was buried in the Field of Mars cemetery.

John Skinner Prout (1805-76)

John Prout was born on 19 December 1805, at Plymouth, England. He was a nephew of the artist, Samuel Prout (1783-1852), whose renderings of medieval architecture were much admired. Prout acquired some knowledge of lithography and was largely self-trained as an artist. He spent much time in the west of England making topographical views of ancient monuments. After two years of continued difficulties, he sailed in the *Royal Sovereign* with his wife and seven children for Sydney, arriving on 14 December 1840. Prout purchased a lithographic plant and had it established by March 1841, when he reproduced drawings of the fire at the Albion Mills and its ruin. He gave lectures and sketched many scenes of Sydney which were used to produce *Sydney Illustrated.* After a visit to Van Diemen's Land, Prout decided to relocate the family to Hobart Town in 1844. He again lectured on art and later produced the first of several volumes of *Tasmania Illustrated.* In 1847, he spent three months at Port Phillip; six of his sketches there were published as *Views of Melbourne and Geelong.* In April 1848, Prout and his family sailed in the *Derwent* for London. In 1850, at the Western Literary and Scientific Institution, Leicester Square, he lectured and exhibited his dioramic views illustrating convict and emigrant life, and the habits of bushrangers and Aboriginals in Australia. In 1852, he published *An Illustrated Handbook of the Voyage to Australia* and in 1853, *A Magical Trip to the Gold Regions.* Prout died at Kentish Town, London, on 29 August 1876.

Thomas Robertson (c.1819-1873)

Thomas Robertson, marine painter and mariner, was born in England about 1819, probably in Manchester, but spent much of his life at sea. By 1853, he had settled in Melbourne and was working professionally as an artist at Alma Place, St Kilda. A committee member of the Victorian Fine Arts Society, founded that year, he exhibited eight oil paintings at the society's sole exhibition in August. Robertson combined his painting career with that of master mariner. As captain of the steamer *Lady Bird*, he made regular crossings between Melbourne and Launceston from January 1854 to July 1855. The *Hobart Town Courier* called him 'one of the best marine painters in the Australian colonies' in October 1856. As master of the barque *Eli Whitney*, Robertson left Melbourne for Otago on 8 January 1862, carrying passengers to the gold diggings in New Zealand. The following year, he held an art union at Otago in conjunction with an exhibition of his paintings. In 1865-66 he was secretary to the Marine Board and inspector of steamers at Port Chalmers. Several of his large oil paintings, chiefly of famous clippers and other ships of the merchant navy in New Zealand ports, were included in the 1865 New Zealand Exhibition, where he was awarded a bronze medal. Robertson died at Yokohama, Japan in about 1873.

George Rowe (1797-1864)

Born at Dartmouth, England in 1797. He published many lithographic views of Devon, Cornwall and Somerset. He came to Australia in 1857 and remained for three years. He painted on the goldfields and his *Old Bendigo* 1857 is in the William Dixon Gallery. Five of his large Australian watercolours were awarded a medal at the London Exhibition, 1862. He died at Exeter in 1864.

Alexander Schramm (1813-64)

Alexander Schramm was born in Berlin, Germany, in 1813. He emigrated to Adelaide, South Australia in 1849. He had an established reputation as an artist in Germany before emigrating. Schramm travelled from Hamburg to Adelaide on the *Prinzessin Luise* in 1849, aged 35. He became the leading oil painter in the colony of South Australia during the mid-nineteenth century. He painted portraits of colonists, but most of his creative energy was devoted to depicting the Indigenous people of South Australia with great sympathy, at a time when Europeans were destroying their tribal life. Schramm was also the first South Australian artist to depict the distinctive red river gum trees. He won prizes at the South Australian Society of Arts exhibitions of the 1850s and 1860s, before he died in 1864, aged 50.

Owen Stanley (1811-50)

Owen Stanley was born on 13 June 1811, the eldest son of Edward Stanley, bishop of Norwich. With his passion for the sea, Stanley joined the Royal Navy, which lead him to produce numerous watercolours of Port Essington, the Swan River settlement, Sydney, New Zealand, and Tasmania. These images provide a comprehensive and personal record of the antipodes and its inhabitants. In December 1846, he was ordered from England to Australia to survey the region of Hervey Bay in a new project for establishing a colony in that part of northern Australia. He later undertook a mission in New Guinea, which lasted throughout 1849. During this time, he contracted an illness of which he died in Sydney in March 1850.

William Strutt (1825-1915)

William Strutt was born on 13 July 1825, at Teignmouth, Devon, England, son of William Thomas Strutt, a noted miniaturist. In the late 1830s, he studied in Paris in the atelier of Michel-Martin Drölling and later at the Ecole des Beaux-Arts. He spent much time at the Louvre, and Raphael remained a lifelong influence. An excellent draftsman, he received many commissions for illustrating books. Following a breakdown in health and fearful of losing his sight, he decided to leave Europe and on 5 July 1850, he arrived in Melbourne in the *Culloden*, feeling much restored after the voyage. He designed, engraved, or lithographed postage stamps, posters, maps, transparencies and seals, and began to learn all he could about the history of the colony. In between sketching and painting important historical occasions, he received commissions for portraits in oil. He also painted many miniature watercolour portraits of Aboriginal troopers, as well as members of the Victorian mounted police. His most dramatic work was 'Black Thursday' commemorating the tragic bush fires in Victoria in February 1851. He went to New Zealand in February 1855 with his wife and daughter, where he bought 105 acres at Mangorei, New Plymouth, and painted mountain landscapes and Maori groups. He left New Zealand for Sydney in July 1856 and subsequently returned to Melbourne to renew friendships with a number of artists. He left Melbourne for London on 29 January 1862 in the *Great Britain.* He continued to paint and exhibit in England. Aged 89, Strutt died at his home at Wadhurst, Sussex, on 3 January 1915.

Frederick Casemero Terry (1825-1869)

Frederick Terry, artist and engraver, was born at Great Marlow, Buckinghamshire, England. He arrived in Sydney in the early 1850s. Soon accepted as a professional watercolour artist, he did some of his own engraving. Some of Terry's engravings were published by Sands and Kenny as the *Australian Keepsake* (1855). The volume contained scenes of 'Port Jackson', 'Pinch Gut', 'The Gap, South Head', Sydney's streets, fruit markets, and churches, as well as country views of Richmond, Windsor, and East and West Maitland. Terry's output was consistent and ample. By 1860, he was recognised as one of the best colonial painters. His paintings were almost entirely views of Sydney and its environs and were painstaking in detail. Aged 44, Terry died on 10 August 1869, of effusion of the brain, and was buried in the Camperdown cemetery.

Thomas Griffiths Wainewright (1796-1847)

Thomas Wainewright was born in London in 1796. As an artist, he moved in London literary and artistic circles, and he knew Charles Lamb, Dr. Burney, Sir David Wilkie, and other writers and artists of the day. He wrote for *Blackwood's Magazine* and exhibited at the Royal Academy 1821-25. Unable to live within his means, he resorted to forgery. He was also suspected of poisoning three of his relatives but was never charged with these crimes. Convicted of forgery in 1837, he was transported to Tasmania. There he was in demand for his portrait art, working under the eye of an armed guard. He died at the age of 53 after being in poor health for several years.

Thomas Watling (1762-1812)

Thomas Watling was a convict who arrived in Sydney in 1791. He probably made sketches for Collins's *'Account of the English Colony in New South Wales';* they were redrawn in London by Edward Dayes and W. Alexander. He also made paintings of natural objects for John White, some of which are now in the British Museum. The earliest known painting of Sydney Cove is by Watling. He appears to have practised miniature painting in Calcutta from 1801 to 1803 before returning to England, where he died in 1812.

Frances Guillemard Simpkinson de Wesselow (1819-1906)

Francis Guillemard Simpkinson de Wesselow was born on 26 May 1819, in London. Son of Sir John Simpkinson, he was named Frances Guillemard Simpkinson, but at the age of 50, assumed the name of de Wesselow after his great-grandfather, who was Ambassador to Peter the Great at the Court of Vienna. A nephew of Sir John Franklin, a Governor of Tasmania, he joined the navy and sailed with Franklin in his earlier commands, and with Admiral Belcher in his voyage round the world in the *Blossom*. He was one of Humboldt's lieutenants, of whom two were appointed by each nation to take synchronous pendulum observations in various parts of the world (Humboldt laid the foundation for modern geomagnetic and meteorological monitoring). Wesselow was sent to Van Diemen's Land. In the 1840s, he was a naval officer in charge of the Hobart Observatory. He lived in Hobart from 1844 to 1849. Simpkinson was an accomplished artist, and in Hobart he painted a number of landscapes, some of which now belong to the Royal Society of Tasmania and are in the Tasmanian Museum and Art Gallery. Some watercolours by Simpkinson were hung among the 276 works displayed at the first public exhibition of paintings in Australia held on 6 January 1845 in the Legislative Council chambers. In his later years he lived at Cannes but died in London on 4 December 1906.

Bibliography

Allan and Wigley. *Scenery in and Around Sydney, Sets 1 & 2. Lithographs of work of S. T. Gill.* Allan and Wigley, Sydney, 1856.

Allen, Christopher. *Art in Australia: From Colonisation to Postmodern.* Thames and Hudson, 1997.

Appleyard, Ron, Fargher, Barbara, Radford, Ron. *S.T.Gill. The South Australian Years 1839-1852.* Art Gallery of South Australia, 1986.

Askew, John. *A Voyage to Australia & New Zealand, including a Visit to Adelaide, Melbourne, Sydney, Hunter's River, Newcastle, Maitland and Auckland: With a Summary of Progress and Discoveries Made in Each Colony from its Founding to the Present Time.* Simpkin Marshall, London, 1857.

Aspinall, Clara. *Three Years in Melbourne.* L. Booth, London, 1862.

Auhl, Ian and Marfleet, Denis. *Australia's Earliest Mining Era, South Australia 1841-1851. Paintings of S. T. Gill.* Rigby, 1975.

Austin, J.B. *The Mines of South Australia.* Rigby, Adelaide, 1863.

Badham, Herbert E. *A Study of Australian Art.* Currawong Publishing, 1949.

Barrett, Charles (ed.). *Gold in Australia*. Cassell, London, 1951.

Barrett, Charles. *Gold: the Romance of its Discovery in Australia*. United Press, 1944.

Barnard, Loretta. *Samuel Gill, Artist of the Goldfields. Australia Explained*, October 14, 2020.

Blake, L.J. *Gold Escort*. The Hawthorn Press, 1971.

Blake, Les. A Stroll Around Melbourne in the 1860s, *Victorian Historical Magazine*, issue 214, vol. 55, no. 1, March, 1984.

Blainey, Geoffrey. *The Rush that Never Ended: a History of Australian Mining*. Melbourne University Press, 1963.

Bowden, Keith Macrae. *Samuel Thomas Gill Artist*. Published by author, 1971.

Burdett, Basil. Samuel Thomas Gill. An Artist of the Fifties. *Art in Australia*, 15 April 1933, pp. 40-43.

Campbell, Robert. Early South Australian Artists. Unpublished lecture, undated (State Library of South Australia, Call No. 759.99423C189).

Cannon, Michael. *The Australian Thunderer: the Age after the Gold Rush 1854-59*. Heritage Publications, 1971.

Cannon, Michael. *Old Melbourne Town*. Loch Haven Books, Main Ridge (Vic.), 1991.

Cannon, Michael. *The Victorian Goldfields 1852-53: An Original Album by S. T. Gill*. Currey O'Neil, 1982.

Carter, M.T. *Burra 1845-1851: a Directory of Early Folk*. Shalimar Press, 1996.

Carter, Jennifer M.T. Mr White's Station at Charlton. *NLA News*, Vol. XIV, Number 7, April 2004, pp. 18-21.

Clemente, Caroline. *Australian Watercolours 1802-1926 in the collection of the National Gallery of Victoria*. National Gallery of Victoria, 1991.

Currey, John. Introduction. *The Goldfields Illustrated. The Sketches of S .T. Gill.* Lansdowne Press, 1972.

Davidson, Graeme, Hirst, John and Macintyre, Stuart. *The Oxford Companion to Australian History.* Oxford University Press, 1998.

Davison, Graeme. *The Rise and Fall of Marvellous Melbourne.* Revised edition, Melbourne University Press, Carlton, 2002.

Doyle, Helen. *Thematic History Report: A History of the City of Melbourne's Urban Environment.* Context, 2011.

Dutton, Geoffrey. *Paintings of S. T. Gill.* Rigby, Adelaide, 1962.

Dutton, Geoffrey. *S. T. Gill's Australia.* Mead & Beckett Publishing, 1981.

Elliott, Brian. *Marcus Clarke.* Oxford University Press, 1969.

Flannery, Tim (ed.). *The Birth of Melbourne.* Text Publishing, Melbourne, 2002.

Flannery, Tim. *The Explorers.* Text Publishing, Melbourne, 1998.

Flett, James. *The History of Gold Discoveries in Victoria.* Hawthorn Press, 1970.

Freeman, John. *Lights and Shadows of Melbourne Life.* London, 1888.

Gill, S.T. & Chevalier, N. *Victoria Illustrated 1857 & 1862. Introduction and Notes by W.H. Newham.* Lansdowne Press, 1971.

Gowlland, Ralph W, *Drake of the Peaks: A short history of surveyor-explorer John Charles Drake (1806-1844) in Van Diemen's Land, Victoria and South Australia*, R. Gowlland, 1976.

Grandison, R. *Art and Enterprise: images in the Barossa Valley in the Mid 1840s.* Unpublished research paper, 1991, State Library of South Australia Call No. 994.2302G753b.

Greig, A.W. Samuel Thomas Gill, the Artist of the Gold-Fields. *The Victorian Historical Magazine,* vol. 3, March 1914, No. 3, pp.133-144.

Griffith, Charles. *The Present State and Prospects of Port Phillip District of New South Wales.* William Curry and Company, Dublin, 1845.

Grishin, Sasha. *Australian Art: A History.* The Miegunyah Press, 2013.

Grishin, Sasha. Colonial Life and the Art of S. T. Gill. *Australian Public Affairs*, 2015 (95), pp. 109-111.

Grishin, Sasha. *Dr. Doyle's Sketches in Australia: A Collection of Prints from the Original Watercolour Drawings in the Mitchell Library.* Mitchell Library Press and Centaur Press, 1993.

Grishin, Sasha. S. T. Gill: Defining A Landscape. *Voices,* Vol. 11, No. 4, Summer 1992-93, pp. 5-19.

Grishin, Sasha. *S. T. Gill & His Audiences.* National Library of Australia, 2015.

Groom, Barry & Wickman, Warren. *Sydney, the 1850s: The Lost Collections, Eyewitness Accounts and Early Photographs of Sydney.* Macleay Museum, University of Sydney, 1982.

Hall, Susan (ed.). *Travellers' Art.* National Library of Australia, 2003.

Haynes, Roslyn D. *Seeking the Centre: The Australian Desert in Literature, Art and Film.* Cambridge University Press, 1998.

Healey, John (ed). *SA's Greats: The Men and Women of the North Terrace Plaques.* Historical Society of South Australia, 2013.

Horrocks Memoirs (records of the family of John Ainsworth Horrocks). F. Hockliffe, 1890. Bedford.

Horton, James T. *Six Months in South Australia.* J. Cross, London, 1838

Howitt, William. *Land, Labour and Gold: or Two Years in Victoria*. Volume 1. Longman, Brown, Green and Longmans, London, 1855.

Hughes, Robert. *The Art of Australia*. Penguin Books Ltd., 1966.

Humorous Stories of Henry Lawson. Decorated with Watercolours and Sketches by S. T. Gill. Harper Collins Publishers, 2000.

Jones, Shar and Reymond, Michel. *Monsieur Noufflard's House, Watercolours by S. T. Gill, 1857*. Historic Houses Trust of New South Wales, 1983.

Kelly, William. *Life in Victoria, or, Victoria in 1853 and Victoria in 1858*. Chapman & Hall, London, 1859.

Kerr, Joan. *The Dictionary of Australian Artists: Painters, Sketchers, Photographers and Engravers to 1870*. Oxford University Press, 1992.

Kwan, Elizabeth. *Living in South Australia: a Social History*, Volume 1. South Australian Government Printer, 1987.

Lawson, Elizabeth. S. T. Gill's 'Avengers', the Gill-Clarke-Mason-Atkinson Connection. *La Trobe Journal*, No. 57, Autumn 1996.

Livingston, Kevin, Jordan, Richard and Sweely, Gay, eds. *Becoming Australians: The Movement Towards Federation in Ballarat and the Nation*. Wakefield Press, 2001.

Longmire, Anne. Raciness and Ease? S. T. Gill and the *Arm-Chair. Victorian Historical Journal*, Vol. 80, No. 1, June 2009, pp. 22-44.

McCulloch, Alan. *Artists of the Australian Gold Rush*. Lansdowne Editions, 1977.

McCulloch, Alan. *Encyclopaedia of Australian Art*. Hutchinson of Australia, 1977.

McDonald, John. *Art of Australia, Volume 1*. Pan Macmillan, 2008.

Mitchell, Adrian. *The Profilist: the Notebooks of Ethan Dibble*. Wakefield Press Pty. Ltd., 2015.

Moore, William. *List of Early Australian Artists*. Unpublished list compiled by Moore.

Moore, William. *The Story of Australian Art*. Angus & Robertson, 1980.

Morphett, George, C. *John Ainsworth Horrocks*. Pioneer's Association of South Australia, Adelaide, 1946.

Mount Horrocks Historical Society. *John Ainsworth Horrocks of Penwortham: Explorer and Pioneer*. Burra Community Print, 1968.

Mundy, Geofrey Charles. *Our Antipodes, or, Residence and Rambles in the Australian Colonies: with a Glimpse of the Gold Fields, Volume I*. Richard Bentley, London, 1852.

National Library of Australia. The Travellers' Art. 2003 (online collection from voyages & travels in art exhibition).

Otto, Kristin. *Capital: When Melbourne was the Capital city of Australia*. Text Publishing, Melbourne, 2009.

Payton, Philip. *The Cornish Overseas: A History of Cornwall's Great Emigration*. University of Exeter Press, 2020.

Radford, Ron. *19th-Century Australian Art: M.J.M. Carter Collection*. Art Gallery Board of South Australia, 1993.

Radford, Ron & Hylton, Jane. *Australian Colonial Art: 1800-1900*. Art Gallery Board of South Australia, 1995.

Raftopoulos, Robert. *Famous Australian Art: S. T. Gill's Rural Australia*. Oz Publishing Co., 1987.

Ratcliffe, Julian. *The S. T. Gill Collection, the Burra Regional Art Gallery*. Burra History Group, 2010.

Reynolds, Henry. *The Whispering in Our Hearts*. Allen and Unwin, 1998.

Roe, Jill. *Marvellous Melbourne. The Emergence of an Australian City*. Hicks, Smith & Sons, Sydney, 1974.

Serle, Geoffrey. *The Golden Age: A History of the Colony of Victoria, 1851–1861*. Melbourne University Press, Carlton, 1963.

Sexton, Rae & Sexton, Robert T. Art Criticism in the 1840's. *Kalori*, Vol. 13, No. 3, September, 1975, pp. 8-10.

Shaw, Ian W. *The Other Side of the Mountain*. Woodslane Press Pty Ltd., 2020.

Sherer, John. *The Gold-finder of Australia: How He Went, How He Fared, How He Made His Fortune*. Clarke Beeton, London, 1853.

Smith, Bernard. *Australian Paintings, 1788-1960*. Oxford University Press, 1962.

Smith, Bernard. *Australian Paintings, 1788-2000*. Oxford University Press, 2001.

Smith, Bernard. *Place, Taste and Tradition: A Study of Australian Art Since 1788*. Ure Smith, 1945.

Smith, Ray. *Watercolour - Colour*. RD Press, 1993.

Smith, Terry. *Transformations in Australian Art*. Craftsman House, 2002.

Stephens, John. *The Land of Promise, Being An Authentic and Impartial History of the Rise and Progress of the New British Province of South Australia*. Smith Elder, London 1839.

Sturt, Charles. *Narrative of an Expedition into Central Australia Performed Under the Authority of Her Majesty's Government During the Years 1844, 5 and 6, Together with a Notice of the Province of South Australia in 1847*. Corkwood Press, 2001.

Thomas, Daniel. *Outlines of Australian Art.* The Joseph Brown Collection. Third Edition. Macmillan Australia, 1989.

Thomas, Nicholas & Losche, Diane, eds. *Double Vision: Art Histories and Colonial Histories in the Pacific.* Cambridge University Press, 1999.

Townsend, Joseph Phipps. *Rambles and Observations in New South Wales.* Chapman and Hall, London, 1849.

Turnbull, Lucy Hughes. *Sydney: Biography of a City.* Random House, 1999.

Watts, Tim. *The Golden Country. Australia's Changing Identity.* Text Publishing, 2019.

Williams, Gwenneth, *South Australian Exploration to 1856*, Board of Governors of the Public Library, Museum and Art Gallery of South Australia, 1919.

Williams, Michael. *The Making of the South Australian Landscape: A Study in the Historical Geography of Australia.* Academic Press, 1974.

Willis, Anne-Marie. *Illusions of Identity: The Art of Nation.* Hale & Iremonger, 1993.

Wilson, Edward. *Rambles at the Antipodes: A Series of Sketches of Moreton Bay, New Zealand, the Murray River, South Australia and the Overland Route.* W.H. Smith and Sons, London, 1859.

Index

A

B

C

D

E

F

G

H

I

J

K

L

M

N

O

P

Q

R

S

T

U

V

W

Y

Z

Shawline Publishing Group Pty Ltd
www.shawlinepublishing.com.au

SLP
SHAWLINE
PUBLISHING
GROUP

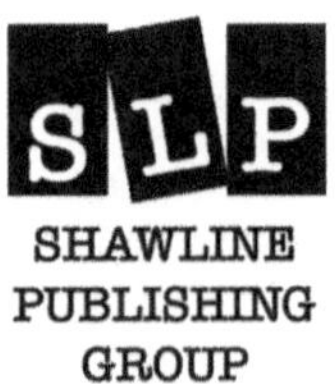

More great Shawline titles can be found by scanning the QR code below.
New titles also available through Books@Home Pty Ltd.
Subscribe today at www.booksathome.com.au or scan the QR code below.

www.ingramcontent.com/pod-product-compliance
Lightning Source LLC
Chambersburg PA
CBHW051456030726
47592CB00006B/1966